Ortho's Plant Selector

Created and designed by
the editorial staff of
ORTHO BOOKS

Project Editor
Cynthia Putnam

Manuscript Editor
Susan Lang

Research Writer
Nancy Patton Wilson-McCune

Designer
Gary Hespenheide

Ortho Books

Publisher
Edward A. Evans

Editorial Director
Christine Jordan

Production Director
Ernie S. Tasaki

Managing Editors
Robert J. Beckstrom
Michael D. Smith
Sally W. Smith

System Manager
Linda M. Bouchard

Product Manager
Richard E. Pile, Jr.

Marketing Administrative Assistant
Daniel Stage

Distribution Specialist
Barbara F. Steadham

Operations Assistant
Georgiann Wright

Technical Consultant
J. A. Crozier, Jr., Ph.D.

Address all inquiries to:
Ortho Books
Chevron Chemical Company
Consumer Products Division
Box 5047
San Ramon, CA 94583

ISBN 0-89721-234-7
Library of Congress Catalog Card Number 90-86162

Chevron Chemical Company
6001 Bollinger Canyon Road, San Ramon, CA 94583

Acknowledgments

Copy Chief
Melinda E. Levine

Editorial Coordinator
Cass Dempsey

Copyeditor
David Sweet

Proofreader
Deborah Bruner

Indexer
Elinor Lindheimer

Editorial Assistants
John Parr
Laurie A. Steele

Associate Editor
Sara Shopkow

Photo Assistant
Mary Sullivan

Layout and Composition by
Nancy Patton Wilson-McCune

Production by
Studio 165

Separations by
Color Tech Corp.

Lithographed in the USA by
Webcrafters, Inc.

Photo Editor
Sarah Bendersky

Photographers
Names of photographers are followed by the page numbers on which their work appears. R=right, C=center, L=left, T=top, B=bottom.

William C. Aplin: 9C, 16, 37, 44, 57, 60, 61, 69, 75
M. Baker: 93, 96
Laurie A. Black: 67
Clyde Childress: 39, 42, 48
Josephine Coatsworth: 18, 56, 71
Saxon Holt: Front cover, 4, 8B, 9B, 59, 82, 83, 89, 92
Susan M. Lammers: 53T
Michael Landis: 1, 7, 14, 20, 21, 25, 41, 43, 47, 52, 58, 86, 87B, back cover TR, back cover BR
Michael McKinley: 6B, 9T, 10, 15, 19, 22, 23, 26, 28, 29, 31, 32, 33, 34, 50, 51, 55, 62, 68, 74, 84, 91, 95, 97, back cover TL
James K. McNair: 30, 94
Jack Napton: 49, 65, 72, 73, 79
Ortho Information Services: 6T, 13, 17, 24, 38, 40, 45, 46, 54, 70, 87T, 90
Pam Peirce: 53B, 66, 88
Tom Tracy: 76, 81, back cover BL

Front Cover
Flowers brighten a garden and bring it to life.

Back Cover
Top left:
The flowers in this border are arranged according to height.

Top right:
Prunus species (flowering cherry) produces a dazzling display of delicate blossoms in spring.

Bottom left:
A water garden creates a feeling of tranquility.

Bottom right:
Pyracantha fortuneana 'Cherri Berri' (firethorn) bears brilliant red fruit through the winter.

Title Page
This geometrical arrangement of flowers includes many that are suitable for cutting and enjoying indoors.

HOW TO USE THIS BOOK

Keep this book handy for finding the perfect plant for a particular spot in the garden or for solving a landscaping problem.

5

Ortho's Plant Selector

FLOWERS

By varying your choice of flowers from year to year, you can alter the look and character of your garden.

11

TREES AND SHRUBS

Spend a little extra time choosing the appropriate trees and shrubs for your garden, since you will live with your choices for many years.

35

VINES AND GROUND COVERS

These practical, often beautiful plants merit widespread use in the garden because of their ability to blanket horizontal and vertical surfaces.

63

SPECIAL GARDENS

Here are a half-dozen theme gardens, each with comprehensive lists of appropriate plants to carry through the motif.

77

How to Use This Book

Keep this book handy for finding the perfect plant for a particular spot in the garden or for solving a landscaping problem.

It is often said that putting the right plant in the right location is the key to successful gardening. But sometimes even an experienced gardener is hard-pressed to think of a suitable plant for a certain spot in the garden. Narrowing the myriad possibilities to the few best choices is often the problem. This is when a good plant list— a catalog of plants that satisfy a specific criterion, such as size, shape, flower color, fragrance, or drought tolerance—comes in handy. It is one of the most useful tools available to gardeners.

Seasoned gardeners know the value of good plant lists. They collect them, save them, and pore over them. They use the lists to spark their imagination and to solve landscaping dilemmas.

Over the years, a great many plant lists have appeared in Ortho garden books. We thought it would be helpful to readers to assemble many of these lists in a separate book. The result—*Ortho's Plant Selector*—is an easy-to-use reference of more than one hundred and fifty plant lists arranged by plant type. Each list consists of flowers, trees, shrubs, vines, or ground covers that all share a common trait, serve a specific function, or flourish under the same growing conditions. The last chapter lists plants appropriate for special, or theme, gardens. In all, there are references to more than one thousand familiar and unfamiliar plants. Keep this book handy and refer to it often: It will make planning a garden easier and more fun.

A curved planting of Pachysandra terminalis *(Japanese spurge) stretches toward* Prunus subhirtella *'Shoegetsu' (flowering cherry tree).*

HOW THIS BOOK IS ORGANIZED

This book was developed as a reference guide to help in the selection of plants. It contains listings of plants that share specific traits or are suitable for different situations. It is not intended to be an encyclopedia and, thus, does not provide any details about a plant, other than the climate zone range and whatever information can be deduced from the title of the list in which the plant is included.

The intention is to provide a wide assortment of lists rather than to present fewer, lengthier lists. Each list is representative: It contains a sampling of the plants that best fit the category and offers plant selections for as many climate zones as possible.

The book uses three levels of organization: plant type, list category, and actual plant list. Often there is a fourth level when a list is subdivided.

The first level of organization is chapters arranged by plant type. The second chapter contains lists of flowers; the third chapter, lists of trees and shrubs; and the fourth chapter, lists of vines and ground covers. The fifth chapter is organized somewhat differently. It contains lists of plants suitable for six special, or theme, gardens: rock, water, Japanese, herb, dry climate, and rose.

The next level of organization is the list category. The lists in the second, third, and fourth chapters are grouped under three categories: appearance, special uses in the garden, and cultivation. *Appearance* refers to aesthetic qualities, such as seasonal color, height, shape, and branching pattern. *Special uses in the garden* refers to specific functions, such as providing fragrance, holding slopes, and trailing over walls or rocks. *Cultivation* refers to growing conditions under which a plant will thrive—for example, wet soil, dry soil, shade, and city pollution. Whether a plant is easy to grow is also considered in this category.

The third level of organization is the actual plant list. Every list relates in some way to the list category. For example, in the second chapter, the plant lists under the category Cultivation consist of the following: Cool-Summer Flowers, Heat-Tolerant Flowers, Flowers for Shady Areas, Flowers That Naturalize, Flowers for Wet Soil, and Drought-Tolerant Flowers.

The fourth level of organization appears when a list is subdivided to provide additional information. For example, the list of Shade Trees on page 42 is divided into three lists: Small (10 to 25 feet high), Medium (25 to 40 feet high), and Large (more than 40 feet high). Mature height is a key consideration in selecting a shade tree, especially since many trees grow too large for today's smaller gardens.

Top: Flanking the lawn are a graceful, curving flower border and a large rock garden. In the flower border, the low edging of snow white Iberis *species (candytuft) contrasts with the tall, colorful spikes of* Antirrhinum majus *(snapdragon). Bottom: Planted for a profusion of early flowers, this garden features a wide variety of spring bulbs as well as spring-blooming trees and shrubs.*

Plant Listings

Within a list, each plant entry consists of the botanical name, a common name, and the climate zone range. The botanical, or Latin, name is listed first and the common name second; in a column to the right of the names the climate zone range appears.

The list is alphabetized by botanical name, since these names are standard. Every plant has a two-part botanical name—the genus and species—that identifies it anywhere in the world. After the species name, there may be another name identifying a variety. A variety may differ from the straight species in size, form, leaf color, or tolerance to environmental extremes such as heat or cold. There are two kinds of varieties: Those occurring in the wild are called natural varieties, and those produced under controlled conditions by plant breeders are called cultivated varieties, or cultivars. In the lists, natural varieties are preceded by the abbreviation *var.*; cultivar names are enclosed in single quotation marks.

Plant encyclopedias and nurseries use botanical names to identify plants, since common names are extremely variable. A plant may be known by different common names in different regions, or several plants may share the same common name. In this book, only one common name—the name most frequently associated with the plant in most areas—is given for each plant. It may differ from the name with which you are familiar.

The climate zone range tells you whether a plant will survive an average winter in your area. The numbers correspond to zones on the Climate Zone Map on page 98. Climate zones are given for all plants except annuals and tender perennials commonly treated as annuals. In these cases, the word *Annual* appears instead. Annuals can be cultivated anywhere, since they die at the end of the growing season. Similarly, climate zones are not given for roses on pages 93 to 97. Roses can be grown in any zone, although many modern roses may need protection in the coldest areas.

The breathtaking blooms of Rhododendron × kosteranum *(mollis hybrid azalea) border a driveway in this rural setting. A group of deciduous azaleas, mollis hybrids are available in flower colors ranging from yellow to vivid red and including white.*

USING THIS BOOK

Ortho's Plant Selector will help you identify plants that meet a certain criterion you have chosen—such as flower color, fragrance, or shade tolerance. Even without a specific criterion to direct your search, you will still find the book useful. The lists themselves may suggest new and interesting ways to use plants. For example, you may not have thought of using prickly plants to direct traffic in the garden until you saw the list entitled Thorny Shrubs for Barriers (page 56). The list entitled Flowers for Dried Arrangements (page 29) may induce you to dedicate a small patch of your flower garden to flowers that can be dried.

Since the book consists only of plant lists, you may need to consult a plant encyclopedia to find out more about a plant. Make sure that the plant is really what you want and that it is suitable for your growing conditions. Although the climate zone range will tell you whether a plant can be expected to survive a winter in

This small pond-side garden features Acer circinatum *(vine maple),* Acer palmatum *'Atropurpureum' (red Japanese maple), and* Pieris japonica *(lily-of-the-valley shrub). Small shrubs and ferns are tucked among the rocks.*

your area, that is just a general indication of the plant's suitability.

There are three reference points that will help you get the most out of *Ortho's Plant Selector:* the Climate Zone Map, the table of contents for each chapter, and the index.

Climate Zone Map

Find your climate zone on the Climate Zone Map (see page 98) adapted from the United States Department of Agriculture (USDA) Plant Hardiness Map of North America. The map was recently updated for the first time since 1965. Most regions are approximately 5° F colder than was indicated on the previous map, and the warmest zones begin farther south than they did before.

The zones are based on average minimum temperatures. Your location may be a zone or two warmer than the map indicates if you live near a large body of water, and it may be a zone or two colder if you live at a high elevation or on a north-facing slope.

Even if a plant is listed as being hardy in your zone, make sure that it is suitable for your growing conditions. Other factors—such as rainfall, summer heat, humidity, wind, and soil conditions—will also influence a plant's ability to adapt to an area. Use the map as a general guide only and not as the final word on plant adaptation.

Table of Contents

Turn to the beginning of each chapter for a review of the plant lists in that chapter. Not only do the tables of contents show you at a glance the substance of each chapter, they also provide a shortcut for finding a particular topic. Use the tables for inspiration when you are short of ideas: A quick review of the topics may suggest interesting ways to use plants or spark your creativity in new directions.

Index

The index, which begins on page 99, will help you locate specific plants as well as list topics. It is also valuable as a handy cross-reference guide to find all the lists in which a particular plant is included. This is important if you are looking for a plant that meets several criteria. Even if you have only one criterion, the index will tell you what other characteristics the plant possesses and what other roles it can play in the garden.

For example, suppose you are looking for a medium-sized shade tree with seasonal interest. Begin by looking up the entry for shade trees in the index and turn to page 42. Katsura tree (*Cercidiphyllum japonicum*) strikes you as a probable choice. Referring back to the index, you find that *Cercidiphyllum* is included in several other lists: Trees With Excellent Fall Color; Trees With an Attractive Winter Silhouette; Small Garden and Patio Trees; and Trees That Are Relatively Pest Free. Your quick examination of the index has yielded the following information about the katsura tree: It is not likely to grow more than 40 feet high, it is generally healthy, it makes a good patio tree, and it provides shade in the summer, colorful foliage in the fall, and a lovely silhouette in the winter. Very swiftly you have found a plant that not only meets your criteria but also has other desirable attributes.

Top: Zinnia elegans (zinnia), Tagetes species (marigold), and other annuals provide a brilliant, long-lasting display of color.
Center: Tropical plants like these are suited to the southernmost climate zones of the United States. It is important to select plants that will flourish in your area.
Bottom: This gnarled old Acer palmatum (Japanese maple) adds beauty and value to the property.

Flowers

*By varying your choice of flowers from year
to year, you can alter the look and character
of your garden.*

When most people think of gardens, they think of flowers. Images of dazzling colors and intricate shapes and memories of sweet scents immediately come to mind. The incredible diversity of flowers available for cultivation nowadays delights gardeners and makes planning a flower garden exciting.

Flowers bring a garden to vibrant life. They are used not only as featured plants but as decorative fillers; there is no better way to brighten dull areas or fill empty spots. Changing the selection of flowers yearly is also an effective, relatively economical way to change the look of your garden.

Annuals and perennials are the workhorses of the garden when it comes to providing color. Although annuals live for a year or less, their flashy blooms fill the garden for months. Perennials live longer, but their blossoms are more fleeting. Most perennials produce bursts of color that last for two to four weeks.

For a truly interesting flower garden, pick a color scheme and mix different sizes and shapes of flowers. Plant for a succession of bloom, so that the garden is colorful throughout the growing season.

Although the flowers listed in this chapter consist almost entirely of annuals, perennials, and bulbs, don't overlook other types of plants when planning a flower display. Trees, shrubs, vines, and ground covers with showy flowers are listed in the third and fourth chapters. Roses are listed separately, beginning on page 93.

Among the flowers planted in this multicolored border are Achillea *species (yarrow),* Gaillardia *species (blanket-flower),* Phlox drummondii *(annual phlox), and* Viola × wittrockiana *(pansy).*

Flowers/Table of Contents

Appearance

Showy Flowers by Season	13
Red and Pink/Spring	13
Red and Pink/Summer	13
Red and Pink/Fall	14
Red and Pink/Winter	15
Blue, Violet, and Purple/Spring	15
Blue, Violet, and Purple/Summer	16
Blue, Violet, and Purple/Fall	17
Blue, Violet, and Purple/Winter	17
Yellow, Orange, and Bronze/Spring	17
Yellow, Orange, and Bronze/Summer	18
Yellow, Orange, and Bronze/Fall	19
Yellow, Orange, and Bronze/Winter	19
Cream and White/Spring	19
Cream and White/Summer	20
Cream and White/Fall	21
Cream and White/Winter	22
Dwarf, Low, Medium, and Tall Flowers	22
Dwarf (up to 8 inches high)	22
Low (8 to 14 inches high)	22
Medium (14 to 30 inches high)	23
Tall (more than 30 inches high)	24
Flowers With a Vertical, Rounded, or Open Form	24
Vertical	24
Rounded	25
Open	25

Special Uses in the Garden

Plants With Attractive Foliage	26
Flowers for Edging	27
Flowers That Drape and Trail	27
Best Flowers for Containers	27
Flowers for Fragrance	28
Flowers for Cutting	28
Flowers for Dried Arrangements	29
Flowers That Attract Birds	30

Cultivation

Cool-Summer Flowers	30
Heat-Tolerant Flowers	31
Flowers for Shady Areas	31
Flowers That Naturalize	32
Flowers for Wet Soil	33
Drought-Tolerant Flowers	33

APPEARANCE

The following lists will help you choose flowers by color, bloom season, height, and form.

SHOWY FLOWERS BY SEASON

Red and Pink/Spring

Antirrhinum majus Snapdragon	Annual
Aquilegia spp. Columbine	3–10
Armeria maritima Sea-pink	2–10
Bergenia cordifolia Bergenia	3–10
Catharanthus roseus Madagascar periwinkle	Annual
Clarkia hybrids Godetia	Annual
Consolida ambigua Rocket-larkspur	Annual
Cyclamen spp. Cyclamen	5–10
Dianthus spp. Carnation, pink	3–10
Dicentra spectabilis Bleedingheart	2–8
Digitalis purpurea Foxglove	4–10
Filipendula rubra Queen-of-the-prairie	3–10
Geranium sanguineum Bloodred cranesbill	3–9
Hemerocallis spp. Daylily	3–10
Heuchera sanguinea Coralbells	3–10

Paeonia hybrid
(herbaceous peony)

Hyacinthus orientalis Hyacinth	4–9
Iberis umbellata Globe candytuft	Annual
Impatiens spp. Impatiens	Annual
Kniphofia uvaria Red-hot-poker	6–10
Lathyrus odoratus Sweet pea	Annual
Lobelia cardinalis Cardinal flower	2–8
Lobularia maritima Sweet alyssum	Annual
Lupinus 'Russell hybrids' Russell lupines	3–9
Matthiola incana Stock	Annual
Paeonia hybrids Herbaceous peony	5–9
Papaver spp. Poppy	1–10
Pelargonium × *hortorum* Geranium	Annual
Penstemon hartwegii Beardtongue	7–10
Petunia × *hybrida* Petunia	Annual
Phlox subulata Moss-pink	2–9
Primula vulgaris English primrose	3–8
Saponaria ocymoides Rock soapwort	4–10
Tulipa spp. and hybrids Tulip	3–10
Viola × *wittrockiana* Pansy	Annual

Red and Pink/Summer

Alcea rosea Hollyhock	3–10
Antirrhinum majus Snapdragon	Annual
Aquilegia spp. Columbine	3–10
Armeria maritima Sea-pink	2–10
Aster spp. Hardy aster	3–9
Astilbe spp. False-spirea	4–8
Begonia × *semperflorens-cultorum* Wax begonia	Annual
Callistephus chinensis China aster	Annual
Catharanthus roseus Madagascar periwinkle	Annual
Celosia cristata Cockscomb	Annual

Clarkia hybrids	
Godetia	Annual
Cleome hasslerana	
Spiderflower	Annual
Consolida ambigua	
Rocket-larkspur	Annual
Cosmos bipinnatus	
Cosmos	Annual
Cuphea ignea	
Cigarflower	Annual
Cyclamen spp.	
Cyclamen	5–10
Dahlia hybrids	
Dahlia	Annual
Dianthus spp.	
Carnation, pink	3–10
Dictamnus albus 'Purpureus'	
Rose gas plant	4–8
Digitalis purpurea	
Foxglove	4–10
Gaillardia spp.	
Blanket-flower	3–10
Geranium sanguineum	
Bloodred cranesbill	3–9
Gerbera jamesonii	
Transvaal daisy	Annual
Gladiolus × *hortulanus*	
Gladiolus	7–10
Helichrysum bracteatum	
Strawflower	Annual
Hemerocallis spp.	
Daylily	3–10
Heuchera sanguinea	
Coralbells	3–10
Hibiscus moscheutos	
Hardy hibiscus	5–10
Iberis umbellata	
Globe candytuft	Annual

Impatiens spp.	
Impatiens	Annual
Ipomoea quamoclit	
Cardinal-climber	Annual
Kniphofia uvaria	
Red-hot-poker	6–10
Lathyrus odoratus	
Sweet pea	Annual
Lavatera hybrids	
Tree mallow	Annual
Liatris spp.	
Gayfeather	3–10
Limonium sinuatum	
Statice	Annual
Linaria maroccana	
Toadflax	Annual
Lobelia cardinalis	
Cardinal flower	2–8
Lobularia maritima	
Sweet alyssum	Annual
Lupinus 'Russell hybrids'	
Russell lupines	3–9
Lythrum salicaria	
Purple loosestrife	3–9
Monarda didyma	
Beebalm	4–10
Nicotiana alata	
Flowering tobacco	Annual
Papaver spp.	
Poppy	1–10
Pelargonium × *hortorum*	
Geranium	Annual
Penstemon hartwegii	
Beardtongue	7–10
Petunia × *hybrida*	
Petunia	Annual
Phlox drummondii	
Annual phlox	Annual
Phlox subulata	
Moss-pink	2–9
Physostegia virginiana	
Obedience	3–9
Portulaca grandiflora	
Rose-moss	Annual
Salvia splendens	
Scarlet sage	Annual
Sedum spectabile	
Stonecrop	3–10
Verbena × *hybrida*	
Garden verbena	Annual
Veronica hybrids	
Speedwell	4–10
Viola × *wittrockiana*	
Pansy	Annual
Zinnia elegans	
Zinnia	Annual

Red and Pink/Fall

Alcea rosea	
Hollyhock	3–10

Pelargonium × *hortorum* 'Salmon Flash' (geranium)

Antirrhinum majus Snapdragon	Annual
Aster spp. Hardy aster	3–9
Begonia × *semperflorens-cultorum* Wax begonia	Annual
Callistephus chinensis China aster	Annual
Catharanthus roseus Madagascar periwinkle	Annual
Celosia cristata Cockscomb	Annual
Cleome hasslerana Spiderflower	Annual
Cosmos bipinnatus Cosmos	Annual
Cuphea ignea Cigarflower	Annual
Cyclamen spp. Cyclamen	5–10
Dahlia hybrids Dahlia	Annual
Dianthus spp. Carnation, pink	3–10
Gaillardia spp. Blanket-flower	3–10
Gerbera jamesonii Transvaal daisy	Annual
Helichrysum bracteatum Strawflower	Annual
Hemerocallis spp. Daylily	3–10
Hibiscus moscheutos Hardy hibiscus	5–10
Impatiens spp. Impatiens	Annual
Liatris spp. Gayfeather	3–10
Lobelia cardinalis Cardinal flower	2–8
Lobularia maritima Sweet alyssum	Annual
Lythrum salicaria Purple loosestrife	3–9
Pelargonium × *hortorum* Geranium	Annual
Petunia × *hybrida* Petunia	Annual
Portulaca grandiflora Rose-moss	Annual
Salvia splendens Scarlet sage	Annual
Sedum spectabile 'Autumn Joy' Stonecrop	3–10
Verbena × *hybrida* Garden verbena	Annual
Zinnia elegans Zinnia	Annual

Helichrysum 'Jewelled Mix' (strawflower)

Red and Pink/Winter

Bergenia cordifolia Bergenia	3–10
Linaria maroccana Toadflax	Annual
Lobularia maritima Sweet alyssum	Annual
Matthiola incana Stock	Annual
Primula vulgaris English primrose	3–8
Viola × *wittrockiana* Pansy	Annual

Blue, Violet, and Purple/Spring

Anemone blanda Greek windflower	5–9
Campanula spp. Bellflower	3–9
Consolida ambigua Rocket-larkspur	Annual
Crocus vernus Giant crocus	3–9
Cynoglossum amabile Chinese forget-me-not	Annual
Delphinium elatum Larkspur	3–9
Digitalis purpurea Foxglove	4–10
Felicia amelloides Blue marguerite	8–10
Hemerocallis hybrids Daylily	3–10
Hyacinthus orientalis Hyacinth	4–9
Iris spp. and hybrids Iris	3–10

Lathyrus odoratus Sweet pea	Annual
Lobelia erinus Edging lobelia	Annual
Lupinus 'Russell hybrids' Russell lupines	3–9
Mertensia virginica Virginia bluebells	3–9
Muscari armeniacum Grape hyacinth	5–9
Myosotis sylvatica Forget-me-not	Annual
Nemophila menziesii Baby-blue-eyes	Annual
Nigella damascena Love-in-a-mist	Annual
Penstemon heterophyllus purdyi Penstemon	6–10
Phlox subulata Moss-pink	2–9
Primula vulgaris English primrose	3–8
Scilla siberica Siberian squill	2–9
Tulipa spp. and hybrids Tulip	3–10
Viola × *wittrockiana* Pansy	Annual

Verbena × *hybrida*
(garden verbena)

Blue, Violet, and Purple/Summer

Agapanthus spp. Lily-of-the-Nile	8–10
Ageratum houstonianum Flossflower	Annual
Anchusa azurea Italian bugloss	4–8
Anchusa capensis Summer forget-me-not	Annual

Aster spp. Hardy aster	3–9
Baptisia australis False-indigo	4–10
Browallia speciosa Bush-violet	Annual
Callistephus chinensis China aster	Annual
Campanula spp. Bellflower	3–9
Centaurea cyanus Bachelor's-button	Annual
Ceratostigma plumbaginoides Blue plumbago	5–10
Consolida ambigua Rocket-larkspur	Annual
Convolvulus tricolor Dwarf morning glory	Annual
Cynoglossum amabile Chinese forget-me-not	Annual
Delphinium elatum Larkspur	3–9
Digitalis purpurea Foxglove	4–10
Echinacea purpurea Purple coneflower	3–9
Echinops exaltatus Globe thistle	3–10
Felicia amelloides Blue marguerite	8–10
Geranium himalayense Lilac cranesbill	3–9
Gomphrena globosa Globe amaranth	Annual
Heliotropium arborescens Heliotrope	Annual
Hemerocallis hybrids Daylily	3–10
Hosta spp. Plantain lily	3–9
Iris spp. and hybrids Iris	3–10
Lathyrus odoratus Sweet pea	Annual
Limonium sinuatum Statice	Annual
Lobelia erinus Edging lobelia	Annual
Lupinus 'Russell hybrids' Russell lupines	3–9
Lythrum salicaria Purple loosestrife	3–9
Mertensia virginica Virginia bluebells	3–9
Myosotis sylvatica Forget-me-not	Annual
Nierembergia hippomanica Cupflower	Annual

Penstemon heterophyllus purdyi Penstemon	6–10
Petunia × hybrida Petunia	Annual
Phlox drummondii Annual phlox	Annual
Phlox subulata Moss-pink	2–9
Platycodon grandiflorus Balloon-flower	3–9
Salvia farinacea Mealycup sage	Annual
Scabiosa caucasica Pincushion-flower	4–10
Stokesia laevis Stokes' aster	5–10
Thalictrum rochebrunianum Lavender mist meadowrue	5–9
Torenia fournieri Wishbone-flower	Annual
Verbena × hybrida Garden verbena	Annual
Veronica hybrids Speedwell	4–10
Viola × wittrockiana Pansy	Annual

Blue, Violet, and Purple/Fall

Ageratum houstonianum Flossflower	Annual
Anchusa azurea Italian bugloss	4–8
Aster spp. Hardy aster	3–9
Browallia speciosa Bush-violet	Annual
Callistephus chinensis China aster	Annual
Campanula spp. Bellflower	3–9
Ceratostigma plumbaginoides Blue plumbago	5–10
Echinops exaltatus Globe thistle	3–10
Gomphrena globosa Globe amaranth	Annual
Hemerocallis hybrids Daylily	3–10
Ipomoea tricolor Morning glory vine	Annual
Iris spp. and hybrids Iris	3–10
Lobelia erinus Edging lobelia	Annual
Lythrum salicaria Purple loosestrife	3–9
Myosotis sylvatica Forget-me-not	Annual
Salvia farinacea Mealycup sage	Annual

Scabiosa caucasica Pincushion-flower	4–10
Stokesia laevis Stokes' aster	5–10
Torenia fournieri Wishbone-flower	Annual
Verbena × hybrida Garden verbena	Annual

Blue, Violet, and Purple/Winter

Lobelia erinus Edging lobelia	Annual
Viola × wittrockiana Pansy	Annual

Yellow, Orange, and Bronze/Spring

Antirrhinum majus Snapdragon	Annual
Aquilegia spp. Columbine	3–10
Aurinia saxatilis Basket-of-gold	3–10
Calendula officinalis Pot marigold	Annual
Cheiranthus cheiri Wallflower	7–10
Clivia miniata Kaffir-lily	9, 10
Coreopsis lanceolata Perennial tickseed	4–10
Dimorphotheca sinuata Cape marigold	Annual
Doronicum cordatum Leopard's-bane	4–9
Euphorbia epithymoides Cushion spurge	4–10

Campanula medium
(Canterbury bells)

Viola × *wittrockiana*
(pansy)

Gazania rigens Gazania	Annual
Hemerocallis hybrids Daylily	3–10
Hyacinthus orientalis Hyacinth	4–9
Iris spp. and hybrids Iris	3–10
Lupinus 'Russell hybrids' Russell lupines	3–9
Lysimachia punctata Yellow loosestrife	5–10
Matthiola incana Stock	Annual
Narcissus spp. and hybrids Daffodil	3–10
Paeonia hybrids Herbaceous peony	5–9
Papaver spp. Poppy	1–10
Petunia × *hybrida* Petunia	Annual
Primula vulgaris English primrose	3–8
Trollius europaeus Globeflower	3–10
Tropaeolum majus Nasturtium	Annual
Tulipa spp. and hybrids Tulip	3–10
Viola × *wittrockiana* Pansy	Annual

Yellow, Orange, and Bronze/Summer

Achillea filipendulina Fernleaf yarrow	3–10

Anthemis tinctoria Golden marguerite	3–10
Antirrhinum majus Snapdragon	Annual
Aquilegia spp. Columbine	3–10
Asclepias tuberosa Butterfly weed	3–10
Aurinia saxatilis Basket-of-gold	3–10
Calendula officinalis Pot marigold	Annual
Celosia cristata Cockscomb	Annual
Cheiranthus cheiri Wallflower	7–10
Chrysanthemum hybrids Hardy chrysanthemum	5–10
Coreopsis lanceolata Perennial tickseed	4–10
Cosmos sulphureus Cosmos	Annual
Dahlia hybrids Dahlia	Annual
Dyssodia tenuiloba Dahlberg daisy	Annual
Gaillardia spp. Blanket-flower	3–10
Gazania rigens Gazania	Annual
Gerbera jamesonii Transvaal daisy	Annual
Geum spp. Avens	6–10
Gladiolus × *hortulanus* Gladiolus	7–10
Gomphrena globosa Globe amaranth	Annual
Helenium autumnale Sneezeweed	3–8
Helianthus spp. Sunflower	3–10
Helichrysum bracteatum Strawflower	Annual
Hemerocallis hybrids Daylily	3–10
Iris spp. and hybrids Iris	3–10
Ligularia dentata Bigleaf ligularia	4–10
Limonium bonduellii Algerian sea-lavender	Annual
Linaria maroccana Toadflax	Annual
Lupinus 'Russell hybrids' Russell lupines	3–9
Lysimachia punctata Yellow loosestrife	5–10
Mimulus × *hybridus* Monkeyflower	Annual

Nemesia strumosa Pouch nemesia	Annual
Papaver spp. Poppy	1–10
Petunia × *hybrida* Petunia	Annual
Rudbeckia spp. Black-eyed-susan	3–10
Sanvitalia procumbens Creeping zinnia	Annual
Solidago hybrids Goldenrod	3–10
Tagetes spp. Marigold	Annual
Thunbergia alata Black-eyed-susan vine	Annual
Tithonia rotundifolia Mexican sunflower	Annual
Trollius europaeus Globeflower	3–10
Tropaeolum majus Nasturtium	Annual
Verbena × *hybrida* Garden verbena	Annual
Viola × *wittrockiana* Pansy	Annual
Zinnia elegans Zinnia	Annual

Yellow, Orange, and Bronze/Fall

Antirrhinum majus Snapdragon	Annual
Celosia cristata Cockscomb	Annual
Chrysanthemum hybrids Hardy chrysanthemum	5–10
Coreopsis lanceolata Perennial tickseed	4–10
Cosmos sulphureus Cosmos	Annual
Dahlia hybrids Dahlia	Annual
Dyssodia tenuiloba Dahlberg daisy	Annual
Gaillardia spp. Blanket-flower	3–10
Gerbera jamesonii Transvaal daisy	Annual
Gomphrena globosa Globe amaranth	Annual
Helenium autumnale Sneezeweed	3–8
Helianthus spp. Sunflower	3–10
Helichrysum bracteatum Strawflower	Annual
Hemerocallis hybrids Daylily	3–10
Iris spp. and hybrids Iris	3–10

Ligularia dentata Bigleaf ligularia	4–10
Petunia × *hybrida* Petunia	Annual
Rudbeckia spp. Black-eyed-susan	3–10
Sanvitalia procumbens Creeping zinnia	Annual
Solidago hybrids Goldenrod	3–10
Tagetes spp. Marigold	Annual
Verbena × *hybrida* Garden verbena	Annual
Zinnia elegans Zinnia	Annual

Yellow, Orange, and Bronze/Winter

Calendula officinalis Pot marigold	Annual
Dyssodia tenuiloba Dahlberg daisy	Annual
Gazania rigens Gazania	Annual
Linaria maroccana Toadflax	Annual
Matthiola incana Stock	Annual
Nemesia strumosa Pouch nemesia	Annual
Viola × *wittrockiana* Pansy	Annual

Dyssodia tenuiloba
(Dahlberg daisy)

Cream and White/Spring

Antirrhinum majus Snapdragon	Annual

Dianthus 'Snow Fire'
(pink)

Aquilegia spp. Columbine	3–10
Bergenia ciliata Winter begonia	3–10
Catharanthus roseus Madagascar periwinkle	Annual
Consolida ambigua Rocket-larkspur	Annual
Convallaria majalis Lily-of-the-valley	2–8
Crocus vernus Giant crocus	3–9
Filipendula ulmaria Queen-of-the-meadow	3–10
Freesia × *hybrida* Freesia	9, 10
Hemerocallis hybrids Daylily	3–10
Hyacinthus orientalis Hyacinth	4–9
Iberis spp. Candytuft	4–10
Iris spp. and hybrids Iris	3–10
Lathyrus odoratus Sweet pea	Annual
Lobularia maritima Sweet alyssum	Annual
Lupinus 'Russell hybrids' Russell lupines	3–9
Matthiola incana Stock	Annual
Narcissus spp. and hybrids Daffodil	3–10
Paeonia hybrids Herbaceous peony	5–9

Papaver spp. Poppy	1–10
Pelargonium × *hortorum* Geranium	Annual
Petunia × *hybrida* Petunia	Annual
Primula vulgaris English primrose	3–8
Tulipa spp. and hybrids Tulip	3–10
Viola × *wittrockiana* Pansy	Annual
Zantedeschia aethiopica Calla lily	8–10

Cream and White/Summer

Achillea ptarmica Sneezewort	3–10
Antirrhinum majus Snapdragon	Annual
Aquilegia spp. Columbine	3–10
Aruncus dioicus Goatsbeard	4–9
Aster spp. Hardy aster	3–9
Astilbe spp. False-spirea	4–8
Begonia × *semperflorens-cultorum* Wax begonia	Annual
Callistephus chinensis China aster	Annual
Catharanthus roseus Madagascar periwinkle	Annual
Cerastium tomentosum Snow-in-summer	3–10
Chrysanthemum hybrids Hardy chrysanthemum	5–10
Cimicifuga racemosa Bugbane	3–9
Cleome hasslerana Spiderflower	Annual
Consolida ambigua Rocket-larkspur	Annual
Cosmos bipinnatus Cosmos	Annual
Dahlia hybrids Dahlia	Annual
Dianthus caryophyllus Carnation	8, 9
Dictamnus albus Gas plant	4–8
Euphorbia marginata Snow-on-the-mountain	Annual
Gerbera jamesonii Transvaal daisy	Annual
Gladiolus × *hortulanus* Gladiolus	7–10

Gypsophila spp.
Baby's breath   3-8

Helichrysum bracteatum
Strawflower   Annual

Hemerocallis hybrids
Daylily   3-10

Hibiscus moscheutos
Hardy hibiscus   5-10

Iberis spp.
Candytuft   4-10

Impatiens spp.
Impatiens   Annual

Ipomoea alba
Moonflower vine   Annual

Iris spp. and hybrids
Iris   3-10

Lathyrus odoratus
Sweet pea   Annual

Lavatera hybrids
Tree mallow   Annual

Lobularia maritima
Sweet alyssum   Annual

Lupinus 'Russell hybrids'
Russell lupines   3-9

Nicotiana alata
Flowering tobacco   Annual

Papaver spp.
Poppy   1-10

Pelargonium × *hortorum*
Geranium   Annual

Petunia × *hybrida*
Petunia   Annual

Phlox drummondii
Annual phlox   Annual

Physostegia virginiana
Obedience   3-9

Stokesia laevis
Stokes' aster   5-10

Verbena × *hybrida*
Garden verbena   Annual

Veronica hybrids
Speedwell   4-10

Viola × *wittrockiana*
Pansy   Annual

Zinnia elegans
Zinnia   Annual

Zantedeschia aethiopica
Calla lily   8-10

Cream and White/Fall

Antirrhinum majus
Snapdragon   Annual

Aruncus dioicus
Goatsbeard   4-9

Aster spp.
Hardy aster   3-9

Begonia × *semperflorens-cultorum*
Wax begonia   Annual

Callistephus chinensis
China aster   Annual

Catharanthus roseus
Madagascar periwinkle   Annual

Chrysanthemum hybrids
Hardy chrysanthemum   5-10

Cimicifuga racemosa
Bugbane   3-9

Cleome hasslerana
Spiderflower   Annual

Cosmos bipinnatus
Cosmos   Annual

Dahlia hybrids
Dahlia   Annual

Dianthus caryophyllus
Carnation   8, 9

Gerbera jamesonii
Transvaal daisy   Annual

Gypsophila paniculata
Perennial baby's breath   3-8

Helichrysum bracteatum
Strawflower   Annual

Hemerocallis hybrids
Daylily   3-10

Hibiscus moscheutos
Hardy hibiscus   5-10

Iris spp. and hybrids
Iris   3-10

Lobularia maritima
Sweet alyssum   Annual

Pelargonium × *hortorum*
Geranium   Annual

Petunia × *hybrida*
Petunia   Annual

Verbena × *hybrida*
Garden verbena   Annual

Zinnia elegans
Zinnia   Annual

Zinnia 'Cherry Ruffle'
(zinnia)

Cream and White/Winter

Bergenia ciliata Winter begonia	3–10
Lobularia maritima Sweet alyssum	Annual
Matthiola incana Stock	Annual
Viola × wittrockiana Pansy	Annual

DWARF, LOW, MEDIUM, AND TALL FLOWERS

Dwarf (up to 8 inches high)

Ageratum houstonianum Flossflower	Annual
Anemone blanda Greek windflower	5–9
Arabis caucasica Wall rockcress	6–10
Campanula poscharskyana Serbian bellflower	3–10
Cerastium tomentosum Snow-in-summer	3–10
Chrysogonum virginianum Goldenstar	5–9
Crocus hybrids Crocus	3–9
Gazania rigens Gazania	Annual
Gypsophila repens Creeping baby's breath	3–8

Astilbe species
(false-spirea)

Iberis sempervirens Evergreen candytuft	4–10
Iris cristata Crested iris	3–8
Lobelia erinus Edging lobelia	Annual
Lobularia maritima Sweet alyssum	Annual
Muscari azureum Grape hyacinth	5–9
Myosotis sylvatica Forget-me-not	Annual
Narcissus bulbocodium Hoop-petticoat daffodil	5–10
Phlox subulata Moss-pink	2–9
Portulaca grandiflora Rose-moss	Annual
Primula vulgaris English primrose	3–8
Sanvitalia procumbens Creeping zinnia	Annual
Scilla siberica Siberian squill	2–9
Tagetes patula 'Janie' Dwarf French marigold	Annual
Tulipa tarda Tulip	4–8
Verbena peruviana Peruvian verbena	9, 10
Viola × wittrockiana Pansy	Annual

Low (8 to 14 inches high)

Anchusa azurea Italian bugloss	4–8
Anemone coronaria Poppy anemone	8–10
Aurinia saxatilis Basket-of-gold	3–10
Begonia × semperflorens-cultorum Wax begonia	Annual
Bergenia spp. Bergenia	3–10
Brachycome iberidifolia Swan river daisy	Annual
Browallia speciosa Bush-violet	Annual
Brunnera macrophylla Siberian bugloss	3–9
Catharanthus roseus Madagascar periwinkle	Annual
Cheiranthus cheiri Wallflower	7–10
Chrysanthemum parthenium Feverfew	6–10
Convolvulus tricolor Dwarf morning glory	Annual
Dianthus barbatus Sweet william	3–9

Dianthus chinensis
China pink   Annual

Dianthus plumarius
Cottage pink   3–9

Dimorphotheca sinuata
Cape marigold   Annual

Eschscholzia californica
California poppy   Annual

Freesia × hybrida
Freesia   9, 10

Galanthus elwesii
Giant snowdrop   2–9

Gerbera jamesonii
Transvaal daisy   Annual

Gomphrena globosa
Globe amaranth   Annual

Helichrysum bracteatum
Strawflower   Annual

Helleborus orientalis
Lenten-rose   3–8

Impatiens wallerana
Busy-lizzie   Annual

Nemesia strumosa
Pouch nemesia   Annual

Nierembergia hippomanica
Cupflower   Annual

Petunia × hybrida
Petunia   Annual

Primula × polyantha
Polyantha primrose   3–8

Pulmonaria saccharata
Bethlehem-sage   3–8

Stokesia laevis
Stokes' aster   5–10

Tagetes patula
French marigold   Annual

Trillium grandiflorum
White wakerobin   3–8

Verbena × hybrida
Garden verbena   Annual

Medium (14 to 30 inches high)

Achillea millefolium
Common yarrow   3–10

Antirrhinum majus
Snapdragon   Annual

Aquilegia spp.
Columbine   3–10

Aster × frikartii
Michaelmas daisy   4–8

Astilbe × arendsii
Astilbe   4–9

Celosia cristata
Cockscomb   Annual

Centaurea cyanus
Bachelor's-button   Annual

Clarkia hybrids
Godetia   Annual

Clivia miniata
Kaffir-lily   9, 10

Cosmos bipinnatus
Cosmos   Annual

Dahlia hybrids
Dahlia   Annual

Dianthus caryophyllus
Carnation   8, 9

Dicentra spectabilis
Bleedingheart   2–8

Euphorbia epithymoides
Cushion spurge   4–10

Gaillardia pulchella
Blanket-flower   Annual

Geranium sanguineum
Bloodred cranesbill   3–9

Geum spp.
Avens   6–10

Heuchera sanguinea
Coralbells   3–10

Iris hybrids
Dutch iris   6–9

Mertensia virginica
Virginia bluebells   3–9

Monarda didyma
Beebalm   4–10

Narcissus hybrids
Daffodil   3–10

Nicotiana alata
Flowering tobacco   Annual

Papaver spp.
Poppy   1–10

Platycodon grandiflorus var. *mariesii*
Dwarf balloon-flower   3–9

Scabiosa caucasica
Pincushion-flower   4–10

Sedum spectabile 'Autumn Joy'
Stonecrop   3–10

Portulaca grandiflora
(rose-moss)

Iris hybrid (iris)

Hibiscus moscheutos 'Southern Belle' Hardy hibiscus	5-10
Lavatera hybrids Tree mallow	Annual
Liatris spicata Spike gayfeather	3-10
Platycodon grandiflorus Balloon-flower	3-9
Rudbeckia hirta Black-eyed-susan	3-10
Thalictrum rochebrunianum Lavender mist meadowrue	5-9
Thermopsis caroliniana False-lupine	4-9

FLOWERS WITH A VERTICAL, ROUNDED, OR OPEN FORM

Vertical

Use these flowers for a spiky, vertical effect in the garden. The tall ones are suitable for the back of a border.

Acanthus mollis Bear's-breech	8-10
Alcea rosea Hollyhock	3-10
Antirrhinum majus Snapdragon	Annual
Astilbe spp. False-spirea	4-8
Celosia cristata Cockscomb	Annual
Cimicifuga racemosa Bugbane	3-9
Consolida ambigua Rocket-larkspur	Annual
Delphinium elatum Larkspur	3-9
Digitalis purpurea Foxglove	4-10
Iris spp. and hybrids Iris	3-10
Liatris spp. Gayfeather	3-10
Lobelia cardinalis Cardinal flower	2-8
Lupinus 'Russell hybrids' Russell lupines	3-9
Matthiola incana Stock	Annual
Moluccella laevis Bells-of-Ireland	Annual
Salvia spp. Sage	4-10
Stachys grandiflora Big betony	4-10
Veronica hybrids Speedwell	4-10

Trollius spp. Globeflower	3-10
Tulipa hybrids Tulip	3-8

Tall (more than 30 inches high)

Achillea filipendulina Fernleaf yarrow	3-10
Alcea rosea Hollyhock	3-10
Aruncus dioicus Goatsbeard	4-9
Asclepias tuberosa Butterfly weed	3-10
Aster novae-angliae New England aster	3-8
Baptisia australis False-indigo	4-10
Cimicifuga racemosa Bugbane	3-9
Coreopsis verticillata Threadleaf tickseed	3-9
Cortaderia selloana Pampas grass	7-10
Delphinium elatum Larkspur	3-9
Digitalis purpurea Foxglove	4-10
Echinacea purpurea Purple coneflower	3-9
Echinops exaltatus Globe thistle	3-10
Filipendula spp. Queen-of-the-prairie	3-10
Gladiolus × *hortulanus* Gladiolus	7-10
Gypsophila paniculata Perennial baby's breath	3-8
Helenium autumnale Sneezeweed	3-8
Helianthus annuus Annual sunflower	Annual
Hemerocallis fulva Tawny daylily	2-10

Rounded

These flowering plants have a rounded, dense, bushy habit with foliage from top to bottom. They look good up front in full view or in the middle of a border.

Anchusa capensis
Summer forget-me-not — Annual

Aruncus dioicus
Goatsbeard — 4–9

Calendula officinalis
Pot marigold — Annual

Callistephus chinensis
China aster — Annual

Catharanthus roseus
Madagascar periwinkle — Annual

Chrysanthemum parthenium
Feverfew — 6–10

Chrysanthemum × superbum
Shasta daisy — 5–10

Clarkia hybrids
Godetia — Annual

Cleome hasslerana
Spiderflower — Annual

Coreopsis verticillata
Threadleaf tickseed — 3–9

Dahlia hybrids
Dahlia — Annual

Dianthus barbatus
Sweet william — 3–9

Eschscholzia californica
California poppy — Annual

Euphorbia epithymoides
Cushion spurge — 4–10

Gaillardia × grandiflora
Blanket-flower — 3–10

Geranium sanguineum
Bloodred cranesbill — 3–9

Gomphrena globosa
Globe amaranth — Annual

Gypsophila paniculata
Perennial baby's breath — 3–8

Helenium autumnale
Sneezeweed — 3–8

Heliotropium arborescens
Heliotrope — Annual

Hemerocallis hybrids
Daylily — 3–10

Hosta spp.
Plantain lily — 3–9

Impatiens wallerana
Busy-lizzie — Annual

Lavatera hybrids
Tree mallow — Annual

Mirabilis jalapa
Four-o'clock — Annual

Paeonia hybrids
Herbaceous peony — 5–9

Pelargonium × hortorum
Geranium — Annual

Rudbeckia hirta
Black-eyed-susan — 3–10

Schizanthus × wisetonensis
Butterfly-flower — Annual

Sedum spectabile
Stonecrop — 3–10

Tagetes spp.
Marigold — Annual

Zinnia elegans
Zinnia — Annual

Open

Because of their rangy habit, these flowers look most attractive when mixed with other plants or when placed behind lower-growing plants in a flower border.

Aquilegia spp.
Columbine — 3–10

Brachycome iberidifolia
Swan river daisy — Annual

Centaurea cyanus
Bachelor's-button — Annual

Cosmos bipinnatus
Cosmos — Annual

Cynoglossum amabile
Chinese forget-me-not — Annual

Echinacea purpurea
Purple coneflower — 3–9

Echinops exaltatus
Globe thistle — 3–10

Helianthus spp.
Sunflower — 3–10

Tagetes 'Yellow Galore' (marigold)

Amaranthus 'Flaming Fountain' (Joseph's-coat)

Lychnis coronaria Rose campion	3–10
Nigella damascena Love-in-a-mist	Annual
Papaver spp. Poppy	1–10
Reseda odorata Mignonette	Annual
Salpiglossis sinuata Painted-tongue	Annual
Scabiosa caucasica Pincushion-flower	4–10
Thalictrum rochebrunianum Lavender mist meadowrue	5–9
Trachymene coerulea Bluelace-flower	Annual

SPECIAL USES IN THE GARDEN

The following lists will help you choose flowers to serve specific functions in the garden.

PLANTS WITH ATTRACTIVE FOLIAGE

Acanthus mollis Bear's-breech	8–10
Alchemilla vulgaris Lady's-mantle	3–8

Amaranthus caudatus Love-lies-bleeding	Annual
Amaranthus tricolor Joseph's-coat	Annual
Amsonia tabernaemontana Bluestar	3–9
Artemisia spp. Artemisia	3–10
Aruncus dioicus Goatsbeard	4–9
Aurinia saxatilis Basket-of-gold	3–10
Baptisia australis False-indigo	4–10
Begonia × *semperflorens-cultorum* Wax begonia	Annual
Bergenia spp. Bergenia	3–10
Brassica olereacea, Acephala group Ornamental cabbage	Annual
Coleus × *hybridus* Coleus	Annual
Coreopsis verticillata Threadleaf tickseed	3–9
Dianthus spp. Carnation, pink	3–10
Helleborus spp. Hellebore	3–10
Heuchera spp. Coralbells	3–10
Hosta spp. Plantain lily	3–9
Iris kaempferi Japanese iris	4–9
Iris sibirica Siberian iris	3–9
Kniphofia uvaria Red-hot-poker	6–10
Kochia scoparia trichophylla 'Childsii' Summer-cypress	Annual
Ligularia dentata Bigleaf ligularia	4–10
Paeonia hybrids Herbaceous peony	5–9
Pelargonium × *hortorum* Geranium	Annual
Polygonatum commutatum Great Solomon's-seal	4–8
Pulmonaria saccharata Bethlehem-sage	3–8
Salvia × *superba* Perennial sage	5–10
Sedum spp. Stonecrop	3–10
Senecio cineraria Dusty-miller	Annual
Stachys byzantina Woolly lamb's-ears	4–10
Thalictrum rochebrunianum Lavender mist meadowrue	5–9

FLOWERS FOR EDGING

Ageratum houstonianum
Flossflower   Annual

Armeria maritima
Sea-pink   2–10

Aurinia saxatilis
Basket-of-gold   3–10

Begonia × *semperflorens-cultorum*
Wax begonia   Annual

Brassica oleracea, Acephala group
Ornamental cabbage   Annual

Browallia speciosa
Bush-violet   Annual

Celosia cristata
Cockscomb   Annual

Chrysanthemum parthenium
Feverfew   6–10

Dianthus chinensis
China pink   Annual

Erigeron karvinskianus
Fleabane   8–10

Geranium spp.
Cranesbill   3–10

Gypsophila repens
Creeping baby's breath   3–8

Heuchera spp.
Coralbells   3–10

Iberis spp.
Candytuft   4–10

Impatiens wallerana
Busy-lizzie   Annual

Linaria maroccana
Toadflax   Annual

Lobelia erinus
Edging lobelia   Annual

Lobularia maritima
Sweet alyssum   Annual

Petunia × *hybrida*
Petunia   Annual

Phlox drummondii
Annual phlox   Annual

Portulaca grandiflora
Rose-moss   Annual

Sedum spp.
Stonecrop   3–10

Senecio cineraria
Dusty-miller   Annual

Stachys byzantina
Woolly lamb's-ears   4–10

Tagetes patula
French marigold   Annual

Torenia fournieri
Wishbone-flower   Annual

Verbena hybrids
Verbena   4–10

Zinnia elegans 'Thumbelina'
Dwarf zinnia   Annual

FLOWERS THAT DRAPE AND TRAIL

These flowers will gracefully spill over edges and borders. In addition to being useful in the garden, they are ideal for both hanging baskets and window boxes.

Browallia speciosa
Bush-violet   Annual

Dianthus barbatus
Sweet william   Annual

Dimorphotheca sinuata
Cape marigold   Annual

Fuchsia × *hybrida*
Common fuchsia   9, 10

Gazania rigens var. *leucolaena*
Trailing gazania   9, 10

Iberis sempervirens
Evergreen candytuft   4–10

Lobelia erinus
Edging lobelia   Annual

Lobularia maritima
Sweet alyssum   Annual

Pelargonium peltatum
Ivy geranium   9, 10

Petunia × *hybrida*
Petunia   Annual

Portulaca grandiflora
Rose-moss   Annual

Sanvitalia procumbens
Creeping zinnia   Annual

Thunbergia alata
Black-eyed-susan vine   Annual

Tropaeolum majus
Nasturtium   Annual

Verbena × *hybrida*
Garden verbena   Annual

Viola tricolor
Johnny-jump-up   4–8

BEST FLOWERS FOR CONTAINERS

Agapanthus africanus
Lily-of-the-Nile   8–10

Antirrhinum majus
Snapdragon   Annual

Begonia × *semperflorens-cultorum*
Wax begonia   Annual

Catharanthus roseus
Madagascar periwinkle   Annual

Celosia cristata
Cockscomb   Annual

Coleus × *hybridus*
Coleus   Annual

Crocus vernus
Giant crocus   3–9

Dahlia hybrids
Dahlia   Annual

Digitalis purpurea
Foxglove   4–10

Impatiens wallerana Busy-lizzie	Annual
Lobularia maritima Sweet alyssum	Annual
Narcissus spp. and hybrids Daffodil	3–10
Pelargonium × *hortorum* Geranium	Annual
Petunia × *hybrida* Petunia	Annual
Salvia farinacea Mealycup sage	Annual
Salvia splendens Scarlet sage	Annual
Sedum spectabile Stonecrop	3–10
Tagetes patula French marigold	Annual
Tropaeolum majus Nasturtium	Annual
Tulipa spp. and hybrids Tulip	3–10
Verbena hybrids Verbena	4–10
Zinnia elegans Zinnia	Annual

FLOWERS FOR FRAGRANCE

Cheiranthus cheiri Wallflower	7–10
Cimicifuga racemosa Bugbane	3–9
Convallaria majalis Lily-of-the-valley	2–8

Dahlia 'Irene Van Der Sweet' (dahlia)

Crinum × *powellii* Crinum-lily	6–10
Dianthus spp. Carnation, pink	3–10
Dictamnus albus Gas plant	4–8
Freesia × *hybrida* Freesia	9, 10
Heliotropium arborescens Heliotrope	Annual
Hosta plantaginea Fragrant hosta	3–9
Hyacinthus orientalis Hyacinth	4–9
Hymenocallis narcissiflora Basketflower	7–10
Iberis amara Rocket candytuft	Annual
Lathyrus odoratus Sweet pea	Annual
Lilium hybrids Lily	4–10
Lobularia maritima Sweet alyssum	Annual
Matthiola incana Stock	Annual
Mirabilis jalapa Four-o'clock	Annual
Narcissus spp. Jonquil	3–10
Nicotiana alata Flowering tobacco	Annual
Paeonia hybrids Herbaceous peony	5–9
Reseda odorata Mignonette	Annual
Tropaeolum majus Nasturtium	Annual

FLOWERS FOR CUTTING

Achillea filipendulina Fernleaf yarrow	3–10
Agapanthus spp. Lily-of-the-Nile	8–10
Anemone coronaria Poppy anemone	8–10
Antirrhinum majus Snapdragon	Annual
Asclepias tuberosa Butterfly weed	3–10
Aster hybrids Aster	3–9
Astilbe × *arendsii* Astilbe	4–9
Calendula officinalis Pot marigold	Annual
Celosia cristata Cockscomb	Annual
Centaurea cyanus Bachelor's-button	Annual

Chrysanthemum × *superbum* Shasta daisy	5–10
Cleome hasslerana Spiderflower	Annual
Consolida ambigua Rocket-larkspur	Annual
Coreopsis lanceolata Perennial tickseed	4–10
Cosmos bipinnatus Cosmos	Annual
Dahlia hybrids Dahlia	Annual
Delphinium elatum Larkspur	3–9
Dianthus spp. Carnation, pink	3–10
Digitalis purpurea Foxglove	4–10
Echinacea purpurea Purple coneflower	3–9
Gaillardia × *grandiflora* Blanket-flower	3–10
Geum spp. Avens	6–10
Gladiolus × *hortulanus* Gladiolus	7–10
Gypsophila spp. Baby's breath	3–8
Hemerocallis hybrids Daylily	3–10
Iris spp. and hybrids Iris	3–10
Liatris spp. Gayfeather	3–10
Lilium hybrids Lily	4–10
Monarda didyma Beebalm	4–10
Narcissus spp. and hybrids Daffodil	3–10
Paeonia hybrids Herbaceous peony	5–9
Physostegia virginiana Obedience	3–9
Rudbeckia hirta Black-eyed-susan	3–10
Salvia farinacea Mealycup sage	Annual
Scabiosa caucasica Pincushion-flower	4–10
Sedum spectabile Stonecrop	3–10
Stokesia laevis Stokes' aster	5–10
Tagetes patula French marigold	Annual
Tulipa spp. and hybrids Tulip	3–10
Zinnia elegans Zinnia	Annual

FLOWERS FOR DRIED ARRANGEMENTS

Achillea filipendulina Fernleaf yarrow	3–10
Armeria maritima Sea-pink	2–10
Celosia cristata Cockscomb	Annual
Cortaderia selloana Pampas grass	7–10
Echinops exaltatus Globe thistle	3–10

Gomphrena globosa Globe amaranth	Annual
Gypsophila spp. Baby's breath	3–8
Helichrysum bracteatum Strawflower	Annual
Hydrangea paniculata 'Grandiflora' Peegee hydrangea	4–9
Lunaria annua Honesty	Annual
Sedum spectabile Stonecrop	3–10
Solidago hybrids Goldenrod	3–10
Stachys byzantina Woolly lamb's-ears	4–10

Echinops exaltatus (globe thistle)

Lupinus 'Russell hybrids' (Russell lupines)

Solidago hybrids	
Goldenrod	3–10
Tagetes spp.	
Marigold	Annual
Zinnia elegans	
Zinnia	Annual

CULTIVATION

The following lists will help you choose flowers that flourish in heat, shade, wet soil, and other special growing conditions.

COOL-SUMMER FLOWERS

Aquilegia spp.	
Columbine	3–10
Astilbe spp.	
False-spirea	4–8
Brachycome iberidifolia	
Swan river daisy	Annual
Cheiranthus cheiri	
Wallflower	7–10
Clarkia hybrids	
Godetia	Annual
Consolida ambigua	
Rocket-larkspur	Annual
Delphinium elatum	
Larkspur	3–9
Helleborus spp.	
Hellebore	3–10
Lathyrus odoratus	
Sweet pea	Annual
Ligularia spp.	
Ligularia	4–10
Lupinus 'Russell hybrids'	
Russell lupines	3–9
Matthiola incana	
Stock	Annual
Mimulus × *hybridus*	
Monkeyflower	Annual
Nemesia strumosa	
Pouch nemesia	Annual
Papaver nudicaule	
Iceland poppy	1–8
Penstemon spp.	
Beardtongue	3–10
Primula spp.	
Primrose	3–9
Salpiglossis sinuata	
Painted-tongue	Annual
Schizanthus × *wisetonensis*	
Butterfly-flower	Annual
Thalictrum rochebrunianum	
Lavender mist meadowrue	5–9
Trachymene coerulea	
Bluelace-flower	Annual
Tropaeolum majus	
Nasturtium	Annual
Viola × *wittrockiana*	
Pansy	Annual

FLOWERS THAT ATTRACT BIRDS

Amaranthus spp.	
Amaranth	Annual
Aquilegia spp.	
Columbine	3–10
Asclepias tuberosa	
Butterfly weed	3–10
Aster spp.	
Hardy aster	3–9
Calendula officinalis	
Pot marigold	Annual
Callistephus chinensis	
China aster	Annual
Centaurea cyanus	
Bachelor's-button	Annual
Chrysanthemum spp.	
Chrysanthemum	2–10
Coreopsis spp.	
Tickseed	3–10
Cosmos spp.	
Cosmos	Annual
Dianthus spp.	
Carnation, pink	3–10
Echinacea purpurea	
Purple coneflower	3–9
Echinops exaltatus	
Globe thistle	3–10
Eschscholzia californica	
California poppy	Annual
Helianthus spp.	
Sunflower	3–10
Limonium spp.	
Statice	3–10
Nigella damascena	
Love-in-a-mist	Annual
Portulaca grandiflora	
Rose-moss	Annual
Rudbeckia spp.	
Black-eyed-susan	3–10
Scabiosa spp.	
Pincushion-flower	4–10
Sedum spectabile	
Stonecrop	3–10

HEAT-TOLERANT FLOWERS

Achillea spp.
Yarrow   3–10

Amsonia tabernaemontana
Bluestar   3–9

Artemisia ssp.
Artemisia   3–10

Aruncus dioicus
Goatsbeard   4–9

Asclepias tuberosa
Butterfly weed   3–10

Baptisia australis
False-indigo   4–10

Begonia × semperflorens-cultorum
Wax begonia   Annual

Brunnera macrophylla
Siberian bugloss   3–9

Catharanthus roseus
Madagascar periwinkle   Annual

Celosia cristata
Cockscomb   Annual

Chrysanthemum spp.
Chrysanthemum   5–10

Cimicifuga racemosa
Bugbane   3–9

Convolvulus tricolor
Dwarf morning glory   Annual

Dahlia hybrids
Dahlia   Annual

Dyssodia tenuiloba
Dahlberg daisy   Annual

Echinacea purpurea
Purple coneflower   3–9

Echinops exaltatus
Globe thistle   3–10

Euphorbia spp.
Spurge   4–10

Filipendula spp.
Queen-of-the-prairie   3–10

Gaillardia × grandiflora
Blanket-flower   3–10

Gomphrena globosa
Globe amaranth   Annual

Helianthus spp.
Sunflower   3–10

Hemerocallis spp.
Daylily   3–10

Hibiscus moscheutos
Hardy hibiscus   5–10

Liatris spp.
Gayfeather   3–10

Lychnis spp.
Campion   3–10

Mirabilis jalapa
Four-o'clock   Annual

Monarda didyma
Beebalm   4–10

Petunia × hybrida
Petunia   Annual

Platycodon grandiflorus
Balloon-flower   3–9

Portulaca grandiflora
Rose-moss   Annual

Rudbeckia hirta
Black-eyed-susan   3–10

Salvia spp.
Sage   4–10

Sanvitalia procumbens
Creeping zinnia   Annual

Scabiosa spp.
Pincushion-flower   4–10

Sedum spp.
Stonecrop   3–10

Senecio cineraria
Dusty-miller   Annual

Solidago hybrids
Goldenrod   3–10

Stachys byzantina
Woolly lamb's-ears   4–10

Stokesia laevis
Stokes' aster   5–10

Tithonia rotundifolia
Mexican sunflower   Annual

Verbena × hybrida
Garden verbena   Annual

Zinnia elegans
Zinnia   Annual

FLOWERS FOR SHADY AREAS

Acanthus mollis
Bear's-breech   8–10

Agapanthus spp.
Lily-of-the-Nile   8–10

Anemone spp.
Anemone   5–10

Aquilegia spp.
Columbine   3–10

Aruncus dioicus
Goatsbeard   4–9

Astilbe spp.
False-spirea   4–8

Mirabilis jalapa
'Jingles Mixed'
(four-o'clock)

Primula species
(primrose)

Begonia × *semperflorens-cultorum* Wax begonia	Annual
Bergenia spp. Bergenia	3–10
Browallia speciosa Bush-violet	Annual
Brunnera macrophylla Siberian bugloss	3–9
Caltha palustris Marshmarigold	4–7
Campanula medium Canterbury bells	3–9
Chrysogonum virginianum Goldenstar	5–9
Cimicifuga racemosa Bugbane	3–9
Clarkia hybrids Godetia	Annual
Clivia miniata Kaffir-lily	9, 10
Convallaria majalis Lily-of-the-valley	2–8
Cyclamen spp. Cyclamen	5–10
Dicentra eximia Bleedingheart	3–10
Digitalis purpurea Foxglove	4–10
Doronicum cordatum Leopard's-bane	4–9
Echinacea purpurea Purple coneflower	3–9
Helleborus spp. Hellebore	3–10
Hemerocallis spp. Daylily	3–10
Hosta spp. Plantain lily	3–9

Impatiens spp. Impatiens	Annual
Ligularia dentata Bigleaf ligularia	4–10
Liriope spp. Lilyturf	6–10
Lobelia cardinalis Cardinal flower	2–8
Mertensia virginica Virginia bluebells	3–9
Mimulus spp. Monkeyflower	7–10
Myosotis sylvatica Forget-me-not	Annual
Nemophila menziesii Baby-blue-eyes	Annual
Nicotiana alata Flowering tobacco	Annual
Nierembergia hippomanica Cupflower	Annual
Polygonatum commutatum Great Solomon's-seal	4–8
Primula spp. Primrose	3–9
Pulmonaria saccharata Bethlehem-sage	3–8
Scilla siberica Siberian squill	2–9
Senecio × *hybridus* Cineraria	Annual
Torenia fournieri Wishbone-flower	Annual
Trillium spp. Trillium	3–10
Trollius europaeus Globeflower	3–10
Viola × *wittrockiana* Pansy	Annual

FLOWERS THAT NATURALIZE

These plants can become permanent residents in your garden, as if they were native. They do not require much maintenance after they become established.

Agapanthus spp. Lily-of-the-Nile	8–10
Anemone blanda Greek windflower	5–9
Armeria maritima Sea-pink	2–10
Asclepias tuberosa Butterfly weed	3–10
Baptisia australis False-indigo	4–10
Centaurea cyanus Bachelor's-button	Annual
Colchicum autumnale Autumn-crocus	5–9
Consolida ambigua Rocket-larkspur	Annual

Coreopsis lanceolata	
Perennial tickseed	4–10
Cosmos bipinnatus	
Cosmos	Annual
Crocus vernus	
Giant crocus	3–9
Dicentra spp.	
Bleedingheart	3–9
Digitalis purpurea	
Foxglove	4–10
Echinacea purpurea	
Purple coneflower	3–9
Eschscholzia californica	
California poppy	Annual
Leucojum spp.	
Snowflake	3–10
Lobularia maritima	
Sweet alyssum	Annual
Lunaria annua	
Honesty	Annual
Moluccella laevis	
Bells-of-Ireland	Annual
Monarda didyma	
Beebalm	4–10
Myosotis sylvatica	
Forget-me-not	Annual
Narcissus spp. and hybrids	
Daffodil	3–10
Papaver rhoeas	
Shirley poppy	Annual
Phlox subulata	
Moss-pink	2–9
Rudbeckia hirta	
Black-eyed-susan	3–10

FLOWERS FOR WET SOIL

Aruncus dioicus	
Goatsbeard	4–9
Aster novae-angliae	
New England aster	3–8
Astilbe spp.	
False-spirea	4–8
Begonia × *semperflorens-cultorum*	
Wax begonia	Annual
Caltha palustris	
Marshmarigold	4–7
Cimicifuga racemosa	
Bugbane	3–9
Cleome hasslerana	
Spiderflower	Annual
Digitalis purpurea	
Foxglove	4–10
Euphorbia marginata	
Snow-on-the-mountain	Annual
Filipendula spp.	
Queen-of-the-prairie	3–10
Hibiscus moscheutos	
Hardy hibiscus	5–10
Hosta sieboldiana	
Plantain lily	3–9

Impatiens wallerana	
Busy-lizzie	Annual
Iris spp. and hybrids	
Iris	3–10
Lobelia cardinalis	
Cardinal flower	2–8
Lysimachia spp.	
Loosestrife	3–10
Lythrum salicaria	
Purple loosestrife	3–9
Mertensia virginica	
Virginia bluebells	3–9
Mimulus × *hybridus*	
Monkeyflower	Annual
Monarda didyma	
Beebalm	4–10
Myosotis sylvatica	
Forget-me-not	Annual
Primula spp.	
Primrose	3–9
Senecio × *hybridus*	
Cineraria	Annual
Torenia fournieri	
Wishbone-flower	Annual
Trollius spp.	
Globeflower	3–10
Tropaeolum majus	
Nasturtium	Annual
Viola × *wittrockiana*	
Pansy	Annual
Zantedeschia aethiopica	
Calla lily	8–10

DROUGHT-TOLERANT FLOWERS

See the list of flowers on page 89 under Dry-Climate Garden.

Monarda didyma
'Granite Pink'
(beebalm)

Trees and Shrubs

Spend a little extra time choosing the appropriate trees and shrubs for your garden, since you will live with your choices for many years.

Trees and shrubs form the framework of a well-designed garden, which is then filled out with flowers and other smaller plants. In addition to defining boundaries and contributing height and depth to the garden, trees and shrubs fulfill many other roles: protection from the sun and wind, traffic control and security, color, and beauty. When placed at the outer edge of a garden, trees and shrubs screen unwanted views, create privacy, and serve as a backdrop for other plants.

The distinction between a tree and a shrub is sometimes blurred. Generally, trees are single-trunked plants that exceed 15 feet at maturity, whereas shrubs tend to be multistemmed plants growing less than 15 feet high. However, some shrubs can be trained to a single trunk, and some small trees can be allowed to become shrublike in their form. Even the rule about height does not always hold true: For example, English laurel (*Prunus laurocerasus*), a plant generally regarded as a shrub, can easily reach 30 feet high.

Because they are typically long-lived, trees and shrubs should be chosen carefully and placed thoughtfully. To help you in the selection process, this chapter lists suitable trees and shrubs for a wide range of situations. Consult the lists on the following pages whether you are looking for a small shade tree, a large pyramidal tree, a shrub that can be sheared into a formal hedge, or a shrub with fragrant flowers.

Trees and shrubs give dimension and definition to a garden. Here, a variety of woody plants with different forms, textures, and scents entices visitors down a meandering path.

Trees and Shrubs/Table of Contents

TREES

Appearance

Broad-Spreading Trees 37
  Small (10 to 25 feet high) 37
  Medium (25 to 40 feet high) 37
  Large (more than 40 feet high) 37
Oval-Upright to Pyramidal Trees 37
  Small (10 to 25 feet high) 37
  Medium (25 to 40 feet high) 38
  Large (more than 40 feet high) 38
Narrow-Upright Trees 38
  Small (10 to 25 feet high) 38
  Medium (25 to 40 feet high) 39
  Large (more than 40 feet high) 39
Trees With Interesting Bark 39
Trees With Excellent Fall Color 39
Trees With an Attractive Winter Silhouette 40
Trees With Showy Fruit 40
Trees With Showy Flowers 41
  Spring 41
  Summer 41
  Fall 41
  Winter 42

Special Uses in the Garden

Shade Trees 42
  Small (10 to 25 feet high) 42
  Medium (25 to 40 feet high) 42
  Large (more than 40 feet high) 42
Small Garden and Patio Trees 43
Fast-Growing Temporary Trees 43
Trees for Screens and Buffers 44
Wall Trees 44
Lawn Trees 44
Trees for Fragrance 45
Trees That Attract Birds 45

Cultivation

Good City Trees 45
Trees for Shady Areas 46
Trees That Are Relatively Pest Free 46
Trees That Can Be Sheared 47

Trees That Tolerate Abuse 47
Trees That Stand Flooding 48
Trees That Tolerate Seacoast Conditions 48
Drought-Tolerant Trees 48

SHRUBS

Appearance

Low, Medium, and Tall Shrubs 49
  Low (up to 3 feet high) 49
  Medium (3 to 6 feet high) 49
  Tall (6 to 15 feet high) 50
Attractive Evergreen Shrubs 50
Shrubs With Colorful Foliage All Season 51
Shrubs With Excellent Fall Color 51
Shrubs With Winter Interest 51
Shrubs With Showy Fruit 52
Shrubs With Showy Flowers 52
  Spring 52
  Summer 53
  Fall 54
  Winter 54

Special Uses in the Garden

Basic Landscape Shrubs 54
Fast-Growing Shrubs for Quick Solutions 55
Shrubs for Informal Hedges 56
Shrubs for Screens 56
Thorny Shrubs for Barriers 56
Shrubs for Fragrance 57
Shrubs That Attract Birds 57

Cultivation

Easy-Maintenance Shrubs 58
Good City Shrubs 58
Shrubs for Shady Areas 59
Shrubs That Are Relatively Pest Free 60
Shrubs That Can Be Trained Into Trees 60
Shrubs That Tolerate Shearing 60
Shrubs That Tolerate Seacoast Conditions 61
Shrubs for Wet Soil 61
Drought-Tolerant Shrubs 61

Trees

APPEARANCE

The following lists will help you choose trees according to mature height, shape, showy flowers, and other aesthetic qualities.

BROAD-SPREADING TREES

Small (10 to 25 feet high)

Chionanthus virginicus
Old-man's-beard   4–9

Cornus kousa
Japanese dogwood   5–9

Elaeagnus angustifolia
Russian olive   2–8

Eriobotrya japonica
Loquat   8–10

Franklinia alatamaha
Franklin tree   5–8

Hamamelis virginiana
Witch hazel   4–9

Ilex cornuta 'Burfordii'
Burford Chinese holly   7–10

Magnolia grandiflora 'St. Mary'
St. Mary magnolia   7–9

Malus floribunda
Japanese flowering crab apple   4–7

Olea europea
Olive   9, 10

Pittosporum tobira
Japanese pittosporum   9, 10

Rhus lancea
African sumac   8–10

Medium (25 to 40 feet high)

Acacia baileyana
Bailey acacia   9, 10

Aesculus glabra
Ohio buckeye   3–7

Albizia julibrissin
Silk tree   7–10

Carpinus caroliniana
American hornbeam   2–9

Cornus florida
Flowering dogwood   5–9

Crataegus viridis 'Winter King'
Green hawthorn   4–9

Halesia carolina
Wild-olive   4–10

Koelreuteria bipinnata
Chinese flame tree   5–9

Magnolia virginiana
Sweet bay magnolia   5–9

Malus baccata
Siberian crab apple   2–9

Large (more than 40 feet high)

Carya illinoinensis
Pecan   6–9

Celtis occidentalis
Common hackberry   2–9

Cinnamomum camphora
Camphor tree   9, 10

Cladrastis lutea
Yellowwood   4–9

Gleditsia triacanthos var. *inermis*
Thornless honeylocust   4–9

Magnolia grandiflora
Southern magnolia   7–9

Phellodendron amurense
Amur cork tree   3–9

Pinus densiflora
Japanese red pine   5–9

Pinus pinea
Italian stone pine   7–10

Quercus rubra
Red oak   4–9

Quercus virginiana
Southern live oak   7–10

Sophora japonica
Japanese pagoda tree   4–10

Zelkova serrata
Sawleaf zelkova   5–9

OVAL-UPRIGHT TO PYRAMIDAL TREES

Small (10 to 25 feet high)

Chamaecyparis pisifera
Sawara cypress   4–8

Carya illinoinensis
(pecan)

Liquidambar styraciflua (sweet gum)

Cotinus coggygria Smoke tree	4–9
Ficus retusa var. *nitida* Indian-laurel	9, 10
Ilex vomitoria Yaupon holly	7–10
Juniperus scopulorum 'Gray Gleam' Gray gleam juniper	3–10
Lagerstroemia indica Crape myrtle	7–10
Laurus nobilis Grecian laurel	9, 10
Malus 'Pink Spires' Pink spires crab apple	5–8
Pinus mugo Swiss mountain pine	2–8
Prunus cerasifera 'Krauter Vesuvius' Purpleleaf plum	9, 10
Stewartia koreana Korean stewartia	5–9
Viburnum lantana Wayfaring tree	3–8

Medium (25 to 40 feet high)

Amelanchier canadensis Shadblow	4–8
Crataegus phaenopyrum Washington thorn	3–9
Diospyros virginiana Common persimmon	5–9
Eucalyptus nicholii Nichol's willowleaf peppermint	8–10
Hymenosporum flavum Sweetshade	9, 10
Juniperus scopulorum Rocky Mountain juniper	3–10
Lagunaria patersonii Primrose tree	9, 10

Magnolia heptapeta Yulan magnolia	6–9
Picea omorika Serbian spruce	4–8
Pyrus calleryana 'Bradford' Bradford pear	4–9
Sorbus alnifolia Korean mountain ash	5–7
Thuja occidentalis American arborvitae	3–8

Large (more than 40 feet high)

Alnus glutinosa Black alder	3–9
Betula nigra River birch	4–9
Cedrus deodara Deodar cedar	7–10
Juniperus virginiana Red cedar	2–9
Larix decidua European larch	2–6
Liquidambar styraciflua Sweet gum	5–9
Liriodendron tulipifera Tulip tree	5–9
Picea abies Norway spruce	2–8
Pinus flexilis Limber pine	4–7
Pseudotsuga menziesii Douglas fir	4–8
Quercus palustris Pin oak	4–9
Taxodium distichum Bald cypress	4–10
Tsuga canadensis Canada hemlock	3–8

NARROW-UPRIGHT TREES

Small (10 to 25 feet high)

Acer platanoides 'Crimson Sentry' Norway maple	4–9
Juniperus chinensis 'Columnaris' Blue column juniper	4–10
Juniperus communis 'Stricta' Irish juniper	3–10
Malus baccata 'Columnaris' Siberian crab apple	2–9
Prunus serrulata 'Amanogawa' Japanese flowering cherry	7–9
Rhamnus frangula 'Columnaris' Tallhedge alder buckthorn	2–8
Sorbus aucuparia 'Fastigiata' European mountain ash	2–7
Taxus × *media* 'Hicksii' Hicks yew	5–7

Medium (25 to 40 feet high)

Acer rubrum 'Bowhall'
Red maple   3–10

Carpinus betulus 'Fastigiata'
European hornbeam   4–9

Pinus sylvestris 'Fastigiata'
Scotch pine   3–8

Podocarpus macrophyllus
Southern-yew   9, 10

Pyrus calleryana 'Chanticleer'
Chanticleer callery pear   4–8

Taxus baccata 'Stricta'
Irish yew   6–8

Thuja occidentalis 'Fastigiata'
American arborvitae   3–8

Trachycarpus fortunei
Windmill palm   8–10

Large (more than 40 feet high)

Acer platanoides 'Columnare'
Norway maple   4–9

✕ *Cupressocyparis leylandii* 'Green Spire'
Green spire cypress   6–10

Cupressus sempervirens 'Stricta'
Italian cypress   7–10

Ginkgo biloba 'Fastigiata'
Maidenhair tree   4–9

Pinus strobus 'Fastigiata'
Fastigiate white pine   4–8

Populus nigra 'Italica'
Lombardy poplar   3–9

Populus tremula 'Erecta'
Upright European aspen   2–8

Quercus robur 'Fastigiata'
English oak   4–9

Tilia americana 'Fastigiata'
Fastigiate American linden   4–8

TREES WITH INTERESTING BARK

Arbutus menziesii
Madrone   7–9

Betula maximowicziana
Monarch birch   6–10

Betula pendula
White birch   2–8

Cladrastis lutea
Yellowwood   4–9

Fagus sylvatica
European beech   4–7

Lagerstroemia indica
Crape myrtle   7–10

Melaleuca spp.
Melaleuca   9, 10

Pinus strobus
Eastern white pine   2–8

Platanus ✕ *acerifolia*
London plane tree   5–9

Prunus spp.
Flowering cherry   2–10

Salix alba var. *vitellina*
Golden willow   2–9

Stewartia koreana
Korean stewartia   5–9

Stewartia pseudocamellia
Japanese stewartia   8, 9

Ulmus parvifolia
Chinese elm   5–9

TREES WITH EXCELLENT FALL COLOR

Acer spp.*
Maple   3–10

Amelanchier canadensis
Shadblow   4–8

Betula spp.*
Birch   2–10

Cercidiphyllum japonicum
Katsura tree   4–9

Cercis canadensis
Eastern redbud   4–9

Cornus spp.*
Dogwood   2–9

Crataegus spp.
Hawthorn   3–9

Diospyros spp.
Persimmon   5–9

Franklinia alatamaha
Franklin tree   5–8

Fraxinus spp.*
Ash   3–9

Ginkgo biloba
Maidenhair tree   4–9

Ginkgo biloba
(maidenhair tree)

Populus tremuloides
(quaking aspen)

Lagerstroemia indica		
Crape myrtle		7–10
Larix kaempferi		
Japanese larch		4–7
Liquidambar styraciflua		
Sweet gum		5–9
Nyssa sylvatica		
Black tupelo		4–9
Oxydendrum arboreum		
Sourwood		4–9
Pistacia chinensis		
Chinese pistachio		6–10
Populus spp.*		
Poplar		2–10
Quercus spp.*		
Oak		4–10
Sapium sebiferum		
Chinese tallow tree		8, 9
Sassafras albidum		
Common sassafras		4–9
Ulmus 'Sapporo Autumn Gold'		
Smooth-leaf elm		4–8
Zelkova serrata		
Sawleaf zelkova		5–9

* Varies with each species.

TREES WITH AN ATTRACTIVE WINTER SILHOUETTE

When leafless, these trees provide a handsome outline against the sky or a background of evergreens. They are winter's visual delights.

Acer spp.	
Maple	3–10

Alnus spp.	
Alder	2–9
Betula spp.	
Birch	2–10
Carpinus betulus	
European hornbeam	4–9
Cercidiphyllum japonicum	
Katsura tree	4–9
Cladrastis lutea	
Yellowwood	4–9
Cornus florida	
Flowering dogwood	5–9
Fagus sylvatica	
European beech	4–7
Ginkgo biloba	
Maidenhair tree	4–9
Gleditsia triacanthos var. *inermis*	
Thornless honeylocust	4–9
Ilex opaca	
American holly	5–9
Lagerstroemia indica	
Crape myrtle	7–10
Liquidambar styraciflua	
Sweet gum	5–9
Liriodendron tulipifera	
Tulip tree	5–9
Malus spp.	
Flowering crab apple	2–9
Metasequoia glyptostroboides	
Dawn redwood	6–8
Nyssa sylvatica	
Black tupelo	4–9
Phellodendron amurense	
Amur cork tree	3–9
Pistacia chinensis	
Chinese pistachio	6–10
Platanus × *acerifolia*	
London plane tree	5–9
Populus spp.	
Poplar	2–10
Salix spp.	
Willow	2–9
Stewartia koreana	
Korean stewartia	5–9
Zelkova serrata	
Sawleaf zelkova	5–9

TREES WITH SHOWY FRUIT

These trees produce an attractive, long-lasting display of colorful fruit or seed capsules.

Amelanchier canadensis	
Shadblow	4–8
Arbutus unedo	
Strawberry tree	8–10
Chionanthus virginicus	
Old-man's-beard	4–9
Crataegus spp.	
Hawthorn	3–9
Diospyros spp.	
Persimmon	5–9

Elaeagnus angustifolia Russian olive	2-8
Ilex spp. Holly	5-10
Koelreuteria paniculata Goldenrain tree	5-9
Malus spp. Flowering crab apple	2-9
Oxydendrum arboreum Sourwood	4-9
Prunus spp. Plum, cherry, cherry-laurel	2-10
Schinus spp. Pepper tree	9, 10
Sorbus spp. Mountain ash	2-7

TREES WITH SHOWY FLOWERS

Spring

Aesculus spp. Horsechestnut	3-10
Catalpa spp. Catalpa	5-10
Cercis spp. Redbud	4-9
Cornus florida Flowering dogwood	5-9
Crataegus spp. Hawthorn	3-9
Halesia carolina Wild-olive	4-10
Jacaranda mimosifolia Jacaranda	10
Laburnum × watereri 'Vossii' Goldenchain tree	5-9
Magnolia spp. Magnolia	4-10
Malus spp. Flowering crab apple	2-9
Prunus spp. Flowering cherry, peach, plum	2-10
Robinia pseudoacacia 'Idahoensis' Black locust	3-9
Sorbus aucuparia European mountain ash	2-7

Summer

Albizia julibrissin Silk tree	7-10
Catalpa spp. Catalpa	5-10
Chionanthus virginicus Old-man's-beard	4-9
Cladrastis lutea Yellowwood	4-9
Cornus kousa Japanese dogwood	5-9

Eucalyptus ficifolia Red-flowering gum	9, 10
Franklinia alatamaha Franklin tree	5-8
Jacaranda mimosifolia Jacaranda	10
Koelreuteria paniculata Goldenrain tree	5-9
Lagerstroemia indica Crape myrtle	7-10
Magnolia grandiflora Southern magnolia	7-9
Melaleuca quinquenervia Cajeput tree	9, 10
Oxydendrum arboreum Sourwood	4-9
Sophora japonica Japanese pagoda tree	4-10
Stewartia pseudocamellia Japanese stewartia	8-9
Styrax japonicus Japanese snowbell	5-9

Fall

Bauhinia blakeana Orchid tree	10
Franklinia alatamaha Franklin tree	5-8
Magnolia grandiflora Southern magnolia	7-9
Melaleuca quinquenervia Cajeput tree	9, 10

Prunus species
(flowering cherry)

Winter

Acacia baileyana
Bailey acacia 9, 10

Bauhinia blakeana
Orchid tree 10

Erythrina spp.
Coral tree 10

Pyrus kawakamii
Evergreen pear 9, 10

Acer saccharum
(sugar maple)

SPECIAL USES IN THE GARDEN

The following lists will help you choose trees to serve specific functions in the garden.

SHADE TREES

Small (10 to 25 feet high)

Acer ginnala
Amur maple 2–8

Acer palmatum
Japanese maple 6–10

Amelanchier laevis
Serviceberry 4–8

Carpinus caroliniana
American hornbeam 2–9

Cercis canadensis
Eastern redbud 4–9

Cercis chinensis
Chinese redbud 6–9

Cornus alternifolia
Pagoda dogwood 5–9

Lagerstroemia indica
Crape myrtle 7–10

Malus spp.
Flowering crab apple 2–9

Prunus cerasifera
Cherry plum 4–8

Vitex agnus-castus
Chaste tree 6–10

Medium (25 to 40 feet high)

Acer campestre
Hedge maple 4–8

Betula populifolia
Gray birch 3–7

Celtis occidentalis
Common hackberry 2–9

Cercidiphyllum japonicum
Katsura tree 4–9

Fraxinus oxycarpa 'Raywood'
Raywood ash 5–9

Koelreuteria paniculata
Goldenrain tree 5–9

Ostrya virginiana
American hop hornbeam 4–9

Oxydendrum arboreum
Sourwood 4–9

Sapium sebiferum
Chinese tallow tree 8, 9

Sophora japonica
Japanese pagoda tree 4–10

Sorbus aucuparia
European mountain ash 2–7

Styrax japonicus
Japanese snowbell 5–9

Syringa reticulata
Japanese tree lilac 3–8

Ulmus 'Sapporo Autumn Gold'
Smooth-leaf elm 4–8

Zelkova serrata
Sawleaf zelkova 5–9

Large (more than 40 feet high)

Acer rubrum
Red maple 3–10

Acer saccharinum
Silver maple 3–8

Acer saccharum
Sugar maple 3–8

Carya illinoinensis
Pecan 6–9

Cladrastis lutea
Yellowwood 4–9

Fagus grandifolia
American beech 3–9

Fraxinus pennsylvanica
Green ash 3–9

Nyssa sylvatica
Black tupelo 4–9

Paulownia tomentosa
Empress tree 7–10

Pistacia chinensis
Chinese pistachio 6–10

Quercus palustris
Pin oak 4–9

Quercus phellos
Willow oak 5–9

Quercus rubra
Red oak 4–9

Tilia cordata
Littleleaf linden 4–8

Tipuana tipu
Tipu tree 9, 10

SMALL GARDEN AND PATIO TREES

These trees provide shade and a seasonal show of flowers, fruit, or foliage. Well-behaved trees, they don't shed excessively and their roots won't pull up patio paving.

Acer palmatum
Japanese maple 6–10

Amelanchier canadensis
Shadblow 4–8

Bauhinia spp.
Orchid tree 10

Cercidiphyllum japonicum
Katsura tree 4–9

Cercis canadensis
Eastern redbud 4–9

Chionanthus virginicus
Old-man's-beard 4–9

Cornus spp.
Dogwood 2–9

Cotinus coggygria
Smoke tree 4–9

Crataegus spp.
Hawthorn 3–9

Eriobotrya japonica
Loquat 8–10

Halesia carolina
Wild-olive 4–10

Koelreuteria paniculata
Goldenrain tree 5–9

Lagerstroemia indica
Crape myrtle 7–10

Leptospermum laevigatum
Australian tea tree 9, 10

Magnolia spp.
Magnolia 4–10

Malus spp.
Flowering crab apple 2–9

Maytenus boaria
Mayten tree 9, 10

Ostrya virginiana
American hop hornbeam 4–9

Oxydendrum arboreum
Sourwood 4–9

Pistacia chinensis
Chinese pistachio 6–10

Prunus spp.
Flowering cherry, peach, plum 2–10

Pyrus calleryana
Callery pear 4–9

Pyrus kawakamii
Evergreen pear 9, 10

Sophora japonica
Japanese pagoda tree 4–10

Stewartia koreana
Korean stewartia 5–9

Styrax japonicus
Japanese snowbell 5–9

Syringa reticulata
Japanese tree lilac 3–8

FAST-GROWING TEMPORARY TREES

These trees will give you a quick landscape. Some are considered weedy, but they can be interplanted with more desirable, slower-growing species and removed as the slower trees reach functional size.

Acacia spp.
Acacia 8–10

Acer saccharinum
Silver maple 3–8

Albizia julibrissin
Silk tree 7–10

Alnus spp.
Alder 2–9

Betula spp.
Birch 2–10

Casuarina cunninghamiana
Beefwood 9, 10

Catalpa spp.
Catalpa 5–10

Eucalyptus spp.
Eucalyptus 7–10

Grevillea robusta
Silk-oak 10

Paulownia tomentosa
Empress tree 7–10

Populus spp.
Poplar 2–10

Robinia pseudoacacia
Black locust 3–9

Salix spp.
Willow 2–9

Sapium sebiferum
Chinese tallow tree 8, 9

Salix species (willow)

Oxydendrum arboreum (sourwood)

Thuja occidentalis	
American arborvitae	3–8
Tsuga canadensis	
Canada hemlock	3–8

WALL TREES

Use a wall tree to soften the side of a building. These trees have well-behaved root systems and habits that allow for close planting to walls.

Acer rubrum	
Red maple	3–10
Agonis flexuosa	
Peppermint tree	9, 10
Betula spp.	
Birch	2–10
Calocedrus decurrens	
Incense cedar	6–9
Carpinus betulus 'Fastigiata'	
European hornbeam	4–9
Chamaecyparis lawsoniana	
Port Orford cedar	6–9
Crataegus phaenopyrum	
Washington thorn	3–9
Cryptomeria japonica	
Japanese cedar	5–9
Eucalyptus spp.	
Eucalyptus	7–10
Ilex opaca	
American holly	5–9
Laurus nobilis	
Grecian laurel	9, 10
Malus spp.	
Flowering crab apple	2–9
Picea glauca	
White spruce	2–8
Podocarpus macrophyllus	
Southern-yew	9, 10
Pyrus kawakamii	
Evergreen pear	9, 10

TREES FOR SCREENS AND BUFFERS

Acer campestre	
Hedge maple	4–8
Cedrus deodara	
Deodar cedar	7–10
Chamaecyparis obtusa	
Hinoki cypress	5–9
Cupressus spp.	
Cypress	6–10
Elaeagnus angustifolia	
Russian olive	2–8
Eucalyptus spp.	
Eucalyptus	7–10
Ilex spp.	
Holly	5–10
Juniperus spp.	
Juniper	2–10
Laurus nobilis	
Grecian laurel	9, 10
Picea spp.	
Spruce	2–8
Pinus spp.	
Pine	2–10
Populus spp.	
Poplar	2–10
Prunus spp.	
Plum, cherry, cherry-laurel	2–10
Sequoia sempervirens	
Coast redwood	7–10

LAWN TREES

These trees are suitable for planting in a lawn, since they are moisture loving and able to compete successfully with lawn grasses.

Acer campestre	
Hedge maple	4–8
Acer ginnala	
Amur maple	2–8
Acer palmatum	
Japanese maple	6–10
Albizia julibrissin	
Silk tree	7–10
Cornus spp.	
Dogwood	2–9
Cotinus coggygria	
Smoke tree	4–9
Crataegus spp.	
Hawthorn	3–9

Fraxinus velutina var. *glabra* 'Modesto' Modesto ash	7–10
Koelreuteria paniculata Goldenrain tree	5–9
Lagerstroemia indica Crape myrtle	7–10
Magnolia × *soulangiana* Saucer magnolia	5–9
Magnolia stellata Star magnolia	5–10
Prunus spp. Flowering cherry, peach, plum	2–10

TREES FOR FRAGRANCE

Acer ginnala Amur maple	2–8
Chionanthus virginicus Old-man's-beard	4–9
Citrus spp. Citrus	9, 10
Cladrastis lutea Yellowwood	4–9
Elaeagnus angustifolia Russian olive	2–8
Halesia carolina Wild-olive	4–10
Hymenosporum flavum Sweetshade	9, 10
Magnolia spp. Magnolia	4–10
Malus spp. Flowering crab apple	2–9
Oxydendrum arboreum Sourwood	4–9
Pittosporum undulatum Victorian box	9, 10
Prunus spp. Flowering cherry, peach, plum	2–10
Robinia pseudoacacia Black locust	3–9
Sophora japonica Japanese pagoda tree	4–10
Styrax japonicus Japanese snowbell	5–9

TREES THAT ATTRACT BIRDS

Amelanchier canadensis Shadblow	4–8
Arbutus menziesii Madrone	7–9
Arbutus unedo Strawberry tree	8–10
Cornus spp. Dogwood	2–9
Crataegus spp. Hawthorn	3–9
Elaeagnus angustifolia Russian olive	2–8

Eriobotrya japonica Loquat	8–10
Ilex spp. Holly	5–10
Juniperus virginiana Red cedar	2–9
Laurus nobilis Grecian laurel	9, 10
Malus spp. Flowering crab apple	2–9
Prunus spp. Plum, cherry, cherry-laurel	2–10
Quercus spp. Oak	4–10
Sorbus spp. Mountain ash	2–7

CULTIVATION

The following lists will help you choose trees that flourish in shade, wet soil, city pollution, and other special growing conditions.

GOOD CITY TREES

These trees tolerate city conditions, such as air pollution, reflected heat, and restricted area for root growth.

Acer spp. Maple	3–10
Aesculus × *carnea* Red horsechestnut	4–8
Carpinus betulus European hornbeam	4–9
Catalpa spp. Catalpa	5–10

Malus floribunda
(flowering crab apple)

Celtis occidentalis Common hackberry	2–9
Chionanthus virginicus Old-man's-beard	4–9
Cotinus coggygria Smoke tree	4–9
Crataegus spp. Hawthorn	3–9
Eucalyptus spp. Eucalyptus	7–10
Fraxinus spp. Ash	3–9
Ginkgo biloba Maidenhair tree	4–9
Koelreuteria paniculata Goldenrain tree	5–9
Laurus nobilis Grecian laurel	9, 10
Malus spp. Flowering crab apple	2–9
Nyssa sylvatica Black tupelo	4–9
Ostrya virginiana American hop hornbeam	4–9
Phellodendron amurense Amur cork tree	3–9
Pinus nigra Austrian pine	4–8

Acer palmatum
(Japanese maple)

Pinus sylvestris Scotch pine	3–8
Pistacia chinensis Chinese pistachio	6–10
Platanus × *acerifolia* London plane tree	5–9
Pyrus calleryana Callery pear	4–9
Robinia pseudoacacia Black locust	3–9
Sophora japonica Japanese pagoda tree	4–10
Tilia cordata Littleleaf linden	4–8
Zelkova serrata Sawleaf zelkova	5–9

TREES FOR SHADY AREAS

Acer circinatum Vine maple	5–9
Acer palmatum Japanese maple	6–10
Aesculus spp. Horsechestnut	3–10
Amelanchier spp. Serviceberry	4–9
Cercis spp. Redbud	4–9
Chamaecyparis spp. False-cypress	4–9
Cornus spp. Dogwood	2–9
Halesia spp. Silverbell	4–8
Hamamelis spp. Witch hazel	4–8
Ilex spp. Holly	5–10
Laurus nobilis Grecian laurel	9, 10
Ligustrum lucidum Glossy privet	8–10
Taxus spp. Yew	5–10
Thuja spp. Arborvitae	3–9
Tsuga canadensis Canada hemlock	3–8

TREES THAT ARE RELATIVELY PEST FREE

Although *pest free* is a relative term, the trees listed here are usually healthy where they are well adapted.

Cedrus spp. Cedar	5–9
Celtis spp. Hackberry	2–9

Cercidiphyllum japonicum Katsura tree	4–9
Chionanthus virginicus Old-man's-beard	4–9
Elaeagnus angustifolia Russian olive	2–8
Ginkgo biloba Maidenhair tree	4–9
Koelreuteria paniculata Goldenrain tree	5–9
Liquidambar styraciflua Sweet gum	5–9
Magnolia spp. Magnolia	4–10
Metasequoia glyptostroboides Dawn redwood	6–8
Nyssa sylvatica Black tupelo	4–9
Olea europea Olive	9, 10
Ostrya virginiana American hop hornbeam	4–9
Phellodendron amurense Amur cork tree	3–9
Pistacia chinensis Chinese pistachio	6–10
Sophora japonica Japanese pagoda tree	4–10
Stewartia spp. Stewartia	4–9
Taxodium distichum Bald cypress	4–10
Zelkova serrata Sawleaf zelkova	5–9

Cercidiphyllum species
(katsura tree)

Platanus × *acerifolia* London plane tree	5–9
Podocarpus macrophyllus Southern-yew	9, 10
Pseudotsuga menziesii Douglas fir	4–8
Thuja spp. Arborvitae	3–9
Tsuga canadensis Canada hemlock	3–8

TREES THAT CAN BE SHEARED

These trees tolerate shearing into tall hedges or other formal shapes. Begin training these plants when they are young.

Cedrus spp. Cedar	5–9
× *Cupressocyparis leylandii* Leyland cypress	6–10
Cupressus spp. Cypress	6–10
Ginkgo biloba Maidenhair tree	4–9
Ilex spp. Holly	5–10
Laurus nobilis Grecian laurel	9, 10
Ligustrum lucidum Glossy privet	8–10
Malus spp. Flowering crab apple	2–9
Olea europea Olive	9, 10
Pittosporum spp. Pittosporum	9, 10

TREES THAT TOLERATE ABUSE

Tolerant of poor growing conditions and neglect, these trees usually succeed when all else fails.

Acacia melanoxylon Blackwood acacia	9, 10
Carya illinoinensis Pecan	6–9
Casuarina cunninghamiana Beefwood	9, 10
Celtis occidentalis Common hackberry	2–9
Elaeagnus angustifolia Russian olive	2–8
Eucalyptus spp. Eucalyptus	7–10
Fraxinus spp. Ash	3–9
Ginkgo biloba Maidenhair tree	4–9
Gleditsia triacanthos var. *inermis* Thornless honeylocust	4–9

Juniperus virginiana Red cedar	2–9
Malus spp. Flowering crab apple	2–9
Melia azedarach Chinaberry	7–10
Melia azedarach 'Umbraculifera' Texas umbrella tree	7–10
Platanus × *acerifolia* London plane tree	5–9
Populus spp. Poplar	2–10
Rhus lancea African sumac	8–10
Robinia pseudoacacia Black locust	3–9
Salix spp. Willow	2–9

TREES THAT STAND FLOODING

Able to survive in standing water for 50 days or longer, these trees are suitable for planting along a shoreline or in low-lying, poorly drained locations.

Acer saccharinum Silver maple	3–8
Betula nigra River birch	4–9
Celtis occidentalis Common hackberry	2–9
Diospyros virginiana Common persimmon	5–9
Fraxinus pennsylvanica Green ash	3–9
Gleditsia triacanthos var. *inermis* Thornless honeylocust	4–9
Liquidambar styraciflua Sweet gum	5–9

Populus nigra 'Italica'
(Lombardy poplar)

Nyssa sylvatica Black tupelo	4–9
Platanus × *acerifolia* London plane tree	5–9
Populus spp. Poplar	2–10
Quercus phellos Willow oak	5–9
Salix spp. Willow	2–9
Taxodium distichum Bald cypress	4–10

TREES THAT TOLERATE SEACOAST CONDITIONS

These trees withstand seacoast conditions including strong winds, salt spray, and sandy soil. Many will lose their natural growth habit and become sculpted by the ocean winds.

Acer platanoides Norway maple	4–9
Acer rubrum Red maple	3–10
Carpinus betulus European hornbeam	4–9
Cupressus macrocarpa Monterey cypress	8–10
Elaeagnus angustifolia Russian olive	2–8
Eucalyptus spp. Eucalyptus	7–10
Hakea laurina Pincushion tree	9, 10
Juniperus virginiana Red cedar	2–9
Leptospermum laevigatum Australian tea tree	9, 10
Nyssa sylvatica Black tupelo	4–9
Picea glauca White spruce	2–8
Pinus canariensis Canary Island pine	8–10
Pinus nigra Austrian pine	4–8
Pinus pinea Italian stone pine	7–10
Platanus × *acerifolia* London plane tree	5–9
Populus nigra 'Italica' Lombardy poplar	3–9
Salix alba var. *vitellina* Golden willow	2–9
Ulmus parvifolia Chinese elm	5–9

DROUGHT-TOLERANT TREES

See the list of trees on page 90 under Dry-Climate Garden.

Shrubs

APPEARANCE

The following lists will help you choose shrubs according to mature height, seasonal bloom, and other aesthetic qualities.

LOW, MEDIUM, AND TALL SHRUBS

Low (up to 3 feet high)

Aucuba japonica 'Nana'
Japanese dwarf aucuba — 6-10

Berberis thunbergii 'Crimson Pygmy'
Crimson pygmy barberry — 5-9

Cotoneaster dammeri
Bearberry cotoneaster — 6-9

Escallonia 'Newport Dwarf'
Escallonia — 8-10

Gardenia jasminoides 'Radicans'
Creeping gardenia — 8-10

Ilex cornuta 'Carissa'
Carissa holly — 7-10

Ilex crenata 'Helleri'
Heller Japanese holly — 5-10

Ilex vomitoria 'Nana'
Dwarf yaupon holly — 7-10

Juniperus horizontalis
Creeping juniper — 3-10

Lantana montevidensis
Trailing lantana — 8-10

Pinus mugo var. *mugo* 'Compacta'
Dwarf mugo pine — 2-8

Pittosporum tobira 'Wheeler's Dwarf'
Wheeler's dwarf tobira — 9, 10

Potentilla fruticosa
Bush cinquefoil — 2-8

Raphiolepis indica 'Ballerina'
Indian-hawthorn — 8-10

Spiraea × *bumalda*
Bumald spirea — 4-10

Thuja occidentalis 'Globosa'
Tom Thumb arborvitae — 3-8

Viburnum davidii
David viburnum — 8-10

Viburnum opulus 'Nanum'
Dwarf cranberrybush — 4-10

Medium (3 to 6 feet high)

Abelia × *grandiflora* 'Edward Goucher'
Goucher abelia — 5-10

Choisya ternata
Mexican orange — 8-10

Clethra alnifolia
Sweet pepperbush — 3-9

Cornus alba 'Sibirica'
Siberian dogwood — 2-8

Cotoneaster apiculatus
Cranberry cotoneaster — 5-10

Daphne odora
Winter daphne — 8-10

Forsythia ovata
Korean forsythia — 4-9

Gardenia jasminoides
Gardenia — 8-10

Hydrangea arborescens 'Grandiflora'
Hills-of-snow hydrangea — 4-9

Ilex × *meserveae*
Blueboy holly — 5-8

Juniperus chinensis 'Armstrongii'
Armstrong juniper — 4-10

Leucothoe fontanesiana
Drooping leucothoe — 4-8

Choisya ternata
(Mexican orange)

Pittosporum tobira 'Variegata' Variegated tobira	9, 10
Plumbago auriculata Cape leadwort	8–10
Rhododendron, P.J.M. hybrids P.J.M. hybrid rhododendrons	4–9
Symphoricarpos orbiculatus Snowberry	3–8
Taxus cuspidata 'Nana' Dwarf Japanese yew	4–8
Viburnum × *carlcephalum* Fragrant snowball	5–9

Tall (6 to 15 feet high)

Aucuba japonica Japanese aucuba	6–10
Camellia japonica Japanese camellia	7–10
Cotoneaster lacteus Red clusterberry	7–10
Forsythia × *intermedia* Border forsythia	5–9
Hibiscus rosa-sinensis Chinese hibiscus	9, 10
Hydrangea paniculata 'Grandiflora' Peegee hydrangea	4–9
Ilex cornuta 'Burfordii' Burford Chinese holly	7–10
Lonicera tatarica Tatarian honeysuckle	3–9
Michelia figo Banana-shrub	8–10
Myrica pensylvanica Bayberry	2–7

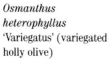

Osmanthus heterophyllus 'Variegatus' (variegated holly olive)

Nerium oleander Oleander	9, 10
Osmanthus heterophyllus 'Gulftide' Gulftide tea olive	7–10
Pieris japonica Lily-of-the-valley shrub	5–9
Pyracantha 'Mohave' Mohave pyracantha	6–10
Rosa rugosa Rugosa rose	2–10
Syringa vulgaris Common lilac	3–8
Viburnum dentatum Arrowwood	3–9
Viburnum plicatum var. *tomentosum* Doublefile viburnum	4–9

ATTRACTIVE EVERGREEN SHRUBS

Abelia × *grandiflora* Glossy abelia	5–10
Arctostaphylos spp. and cvs. Manzanita	2–10
Aucuba japonica Japanese aucuba	6–10
Buxus spp. Boxwood	4–10
Camellia spp. Camellia	7–10
Chamaecyparis spp. False-cypress	4–9
Cotoneaster dammeri Bearberry cotoneaster	6–9
Daphne odora Winter daphne	8–10
Erica spp. Heath	4–9
Escallonia spp. Escallonia	8–10
Euonymus fortunei Wintercreeper	4–10
Ilex spp. Holly	5–10
Juniperus spp. Juniper	2–10
Kalmia latifolia Mountain laurel	4–9
Leucothoe fontanesiana Drooping leucothoe	4–8
Ligustrum spp. Privet	3–10
Mahonia spp. Oregon grape	5–10
Myrtus communis Myrtle	8–10
Nandina domestica Heavenly-bamboo	7–10
Osmanthus spp. Sweet olive	3–10

Photinia spp.	
Photinia	7–10
Pittosporum spp.	
Pittosporum	9, 10
Prunus laurocerasus	
English laurel	7–10
Raphiolepis spp.	
Indian-hawthorn	7–10
Rhododendron spp.	
Rhododendron	2–10
Taxus spp.	
Yew	5–10
Thuja spp.	
Arborvitae	3–9
Viburnum davidii	
David viburnum	8–10
Xylosma congestum	
Shiny xylosma	8–10

SHRUBS WITH COLORFUL FOLIAGE ALL SEASON

Acer palmatum 'Dissectum Atropurpureum'	
Threadleaf Japanese maple	6–10
Aucuba japonica 'Variegata'	
Variegated Japanese aucuba	6–10
Berberis thunbergii 'Crimson Pygmy'	
Crimson pygmy barberry	5–9
Chamaecyparis obtusa 'Nana Aurea'	
Dwarf golden hinoki cypress	5–9
Euonymus fortunei 'Colorata'	
Purpleleaf wintercreeper	4–10
Hydrangea macrophylla 'Tricolor'	
Bigleaf hydrangea	6–10
Juniperus horizontalis 'Wiltonii'	
Blue rug juniper	3–10
Leptospermum scoparium 'Ruby Glow'	
New Zealand tea tree	9, 10
Leucothoe fontanesiana 'Girard's Rainbow'	
Drooping leucothoe	4–8
Photinia × *fraseri*	
Redtip photinia	7–10
Pittosporum tobira 'Variegata'	
Variegated tobira	9, 10
Prunus × *cistena*	
Purpleleaf sand cherry	2–7

SHRUBS WITH EXCELLENT FALL COLOR

Abelia × *grandiflora*	
Glossy abelia	5–10
Berberis thunbergii	
Japanese barberry	4–9
Cotoneaster divaricatus	
Spreading cotoneaster	5–9
Cotoneaster horizontalis	
Rock cotoneaster	5–9
Euonymus alata	
Burning-bush	3–8

Fothergilla major	
Large fothergilla	4–9
Hamamelis spp.	
Witch hazel	4–8
Hydrangea quercifolia	
Oakleaf hydrangea	5–9
Mahonia aquifolium	
Oregon grapeholly	5–9
Nandina domestica	
Heavenly-bamboo	7–10
Rhododendron calendulaceum	
Flame azalea	5–8
Rhus spp.*	
Sumac	3–10
Spiraea × *bumalda*	
Bumald spirea	4–10
Tamarix hispida	
Kashgar tamarisk	5–10
Vaccinium corymbosum	
Highbush blueberry	3–9
Viburnum spp.*	
Viburnum	2–10

* Many species.

Pittosporum tobira
(Japanese pittosporum)

SHRUBS WITH WINTER INTEREST

The branching structure, colorful bark, buds, or fruit of these shrubs add beauty to the winter garden. They are worth braving the cold for a walk through the garden.

Acer palmatum 'Dissectum'	
Cutleaf Japanese maple	6–10
Aronia arbutifolia	
Red chokeberry	5–8

Cornus alba Tatarian dogwood	2-8
Cornus sericea Redosier dogwood	2-8
Corylus avellana 'Contorta' Harry Lauder's walkingstick	5-9
Cytisus × praecox Warminster broom	6-10
Genista spp. Broom	2-10
Hamamelis spp. Witch hazel	4-8
Ilex decidua Possumhaw	6-9
Kerria japonica Japanese rose	5-9
Myrica pensylvanica Bayberry	2-7
Rhus copallina Shining sumac	5-8
Rhus typhina Staghorn sumac	3-9
Rosa hugonis Father Hugo rose	5-10
Rosa virginiana Virginia rose	4-10

SHRUBS WITH SHOWY FRUIT

The ornamental fruit of many shrubs can last for months, whereas the flowers may bloom for only a week or so. Select any of these shrubs for their long-lasting displays of showy fruit.

Arctostaphylos spp. and cvs. Manzanita	2-10
Aronia arbutifolia Red chokeberry	5-8
Berberis darwinii Darwin barberry	8-10

Pyracantha fortuneana 'Cherri Berri' (firethorn)

Berberis thunbergii Japanese barberry	4-9
Carissa spp. Natal-plum	9, 10
Cornus kousa Japanese dogwood	5-9
Cornus mas Cornelian-cherry	4-8
Cotoneaster spp. Cotoneaster	3-10
Elaeagnus pungens Silverberry	7-10
Euonymus alata Burning-bush	3-8
Heteromeles arbutifolia Toyon	8-10
Ilex spp. Holly	5-10
Mahonia spp. Oregon grape	5-10
Nandina domestica Heavenly-bamboo	7-10
Prunus tomentosa Nanking cherry	2-8
Punica granatum Pomegranate	8-10
Pyracantha spp. Firethorn	6-10
Raphiolepis spp. Indian-hawthorn	7-10
Rhus copallina Shining sumac	5-8
Rhus typhina Staghorn sumac	3-9
Symplocos paniculata Sapphireberry	5-8
Vaccinium corymbosum Highbush blueberry	3-9
Viburnum davidii David viburnum	8-10
Viburnum dilatatum Linden viburnum	4-7
Viburnum opulus Cranberrybush	4-10
Viburnum tinus Laurustinus	8-10
Viburnum trilobum American cranberrybush	3-9

SHRUBS WITH SHOWY FLOWERS

Spring

Callistemon citrinus Lemon bottlebrush	8-10
Camellia spp. Camellia	7-10
Ceanothus spp. California wild-lilac	8-10
Chaenomeles speciosa Flowering quince	4-9

Choisya ternata Mexican orange	8–10
Cornus mas Cornelian-cherry	4–8
Daphne odora Winter daphne	8–10
Deutzia gracilis Deutzia	5–8
Erica carnea Spring heath	6–10
Forsythia × intermedia Border forsythia	5–9
Fremontodendron spp. Fremontia	9, 10
Hamamelis × intermedia Witch hazel	5–9
Kalmia latifolia Mountain laurel	4–9
Leptospermum scoparium 'Ruby Glow' New Zealand tea tree	9, 10
Magnolia stellata Star magnolia	5–10
Nerium oleander Oleander	9, 10
Philadelphus coronarius Sweet mock orange	5–8
Pieris japonica Lily-of-the-valley shrub	5–9
Rhododendron spp. Rhododendron, azalea	2–10
Rosa spp. Rose	2–10
Spiraea prunifolia Bridalwreath spirea	5–9
Syringa vulgaris Common lilac	3–8
Viburnum × carlcephalum Fragrant snowball	5–9
Viburnum opulus Cranberrybush	4–10
Viburnum tinus Laurustinus	8–10
Weigela florida Old-fashioned weigela	4–8

Summer

Buddleia davidii Summer-lilac	6–10
Callistemon citrinus Lemon bottlebrush	8–10
Calluna vulgaris Scotch heather	4–9
Cistus × purpureus Rockrose	8–10
Erica vagans Cornish heath	5–9
Fuchsia hybrids Fuchsia	9, 10
Gardenia jasminoides Gardenia	8–10

Hibiscus spp. Hibiscus	5–10
Hydrangea macrophylla Bigleaf hydrangea	6–10
Nerium oleander Oleander	9, 10
Potentilla fruticosa Bush cinquefoil	2–8
Rosa spp. Rose	2–10
Spiraea × bumalda Bumald spirea	4–10
Viburnum × carlcephalum Fragrant snowball	5–9

Rosa 'Chivalry' (hybrid tea rose)

Fuchsia × hybrida 'Annie Rooney' (fuchsia)

Camellia species
(camellia)

Fall

Callistemon citrinus
Lemon bottlebrush   8–10

Camellia spp.
Camellia   7–10

Fuchsia hybrids
Fuchsia   9, 10

Hydrangea macrophylla
Bigleaf hydrangea   6–10

Nerium oleander
Oleander   9, 10

Potentilla fruticosa
Bush cinquefoil   2–8

Rosa spp.
Rose   2–10

Spiraea × bumalda
Bumald spirea   4–10

Viburnum tinus
Laurustinus   8–10

Winter

Callistemon citrinus
Lemon bottlebrush   8–10

Camellia spp.
Camellia   7–10

Chaenomeles speciosa
Flowering quince   4–9

Cornus mas
Cornelian-cherry   4–8

Daphne odora
Winter daphne   8–10

Erica carnea
Spring heath   6–10

Forsythia × intermedia
Border forsythia   5–9

Hamamelis × intermedia
Witch hazel   5–9

Leptospermum scoparium 'Ruby Glow'
New Zealand tea tree   9, 10

Magnolia stellata
Star magnolia   5–10

Viburnum tinus
Laurustinus   8–10

SPECIAL USES IN THE GARDEN

The following lists will help you choose shrubs to serve specific functions in the garden.

BASIC LANDSCAPE SHRUBS

These are among the most popularly planted shrubs across the United States. Attractive and reliable, they are the shrubs that usually come to mind first when you plan a garden.

Abelia × grandiflora
Glossy abelia   5–10

Berberis spp.
Barberry   4–10

Buxus spp.
Boxwood   4–10

Camellia japonica
Japanese camellia   7–10

Chaenomeles speciosa
Flowering quince   4–9

Cotoneaster spp.
Cotoneaster   3–10

Daphne spp.
Daphne   4–10

Escallonia spp.
Escallonia   8–10

Forsythia × intermedia
Border forsythia   5–9

Hydrangea spp.
Hydrangea   4–10

Ilex spp.
Holly   5–10

Juniperus spp.
Juniper   2–10

Ligustrum spp.
Privet   3–10

Lonicera spp.
Honeysuckle   3–10

Mahonia spp.
Oregon grape   5–10

Nandina domestica
Heavenly-bamboo   7–10

Photinia × fraseri
Redtip photinia   7–10

Pieris japonica
Lily-of-the-valley shrub   5–9

Pittosporum spp.
Pittosporum   9, 10

Raphiolepis spp.
Indian-hawthorn — 7–10

Rhododendron spp.
Rhododendron, azalea — 2–10

Rosa spp.
Rose — 2–10

Syringa vulgaris
Common lilac — 3–8

Taxus spp.
Yew — 5–10

Viburnum spp.
Viburnum — 2–10

FAST-GROWING SHRUBS FOR QUICK SOLUTIONS

These shrubs will help fill in your landscape, or cover up ugly features in your yard, in only a few seasons. The solution may be temporary, since the faster a shrub grows, generally the shorter it lives.

Abelia × *grandiflora*
Glossy abelia — 5–10

Berberis spp.
Barberry — 4–10

Callistemon citrinus
Lemon bottlebrush — 8–10

Caragana arborescens
Siberian peashrub — 2–7

Ceanothus spp.
California wild-lilac — 8–10

Choisya ternata
Mexican orange — 8–10

Coprosma spp.
Coprosma — 8–10

Cornus alba
Tatarian dogwood — 2–8

Cornus sericea
Redosier dogwood — 2–8

Cotoneaster dammeri
Bearberry cotoneaster — 6–9

Cotoneaster divaricatus
Spreading cotoneaster — 5–9

Cytisus × *praecox*
Warminster broom — 6–10

Elaeagnus pungens
Silverberry — 7–10

Escallonia spp.
Escallonia — 8–10

Forsythia spp.
Forsythia — 4–9

Hydrangea macrophylla
Bigleaf hydrangea — 6–10

Hypericum calycinum
St. John's wort — 5–10

Kerria japonica
Japanese rose — 5–9

Kolkwitzia amabilis
Beautybush — 6–9

Ligustrum spp.
Privet — 3–10

Escallonia × *exoniensis* 'Frades' (Frades escallonia)

Syringa vulgaris
(common lilac)

Juniperus chinensis 'Armstrongii' Armstrong juniper	4–10
Lavandula spp. Lavender	5–10
Potentilla fruticosa Bush cinquefoil	2–8
Raphiolepis spp. Indian-hawthorn	7–10
Rosa rugosa Rugosa rose	2–10
Sarcococca ruscifolia Sweetbox	5–9
Taxus cuspidata 'Nana' Dwarf Japanese yew	4–8
Viburnum opulus 'Nanum' Dwarf cranberrybush	4–10

SHRUBS FOR SCREENS

Camellia spp. Camellia	7–10
Elaeagnus pungens Silverberry	7–10
Feijoa sellowiana Pineapple guava	8–10
Ilex spp. Holly	5–10
Jasminum mesnyi Primrose jasmine	8, 9
Ligustrum amurense Amur privet	4–8
Osmanthus spp. Sweet olive	3–10
Photinia × *fraseri* Redtip photinia	7–10
Pittosporum spp. Pittosporum	9, 10
Prunus laurocerasus English laurel	7–10
Prunus lusitanica Portugal laurel	7–10
Rhamnus frangula 'Columnaris' Tallhedge alder buckthorn	2–8
Rhus spp. Sumac	3–10
Syringa vulgaris Common lilac	3–8
Viburnum × *burkwoodii* Burkwood viburnum	5–8
Viburnum prunifolium Blackhaw	4–9

Lonicera spp. Honeysuckle	3–10
Nerium oleander Oleander	9, 10
Philadelphus spp. Mock orange	4–8
Prunus laurocerasus English laurel	7–10
Pyracantha spp. Firethorn	6–10
Rhus copallina Shining sumac	5–8
Spiraea spp. Spirea	3–9
Tamarix spp. Tamarisk	2–10
Weigela florida Old-fashioned weigela	4–8

SHRUBS FOR INFORMAL HEDGES

A row of these shrubs makes an attractive, informal hedge less than 5 feet high. Prune only to maintain the natural shape of the shrub.

Abelia × *grandiflora* 'Edward Goucher' Goucher abelia	5–10
Berberis thunbergii 'Atropurpurea' Red barberry	4–9
Euonymus alata Burning-bush	3–8
Ilex crenata Japanese holly	5–10

THORNY SHRUBS FOR BARRIERS

Plant these impenetrable barriers only where you want to keep away people and animals. Don't plant them near public places where they will scratch passersby.

Berberis spp. Barberry	4–10
Carissa spp. Natal-plum	9, 10

Chaenomeles speciosa Flowering quince	4–9	
Elaeagnus pungens Silverberry	7–10	
Ilex cornuta Chinese holly	7–10	
Mahonia spp. Oregon grape	5–10	
Osmanthus heterophyllus Holly olive	7–10	
Pyracantha coccinea Firethorn	6–10	
Ribes speciosum Fuchsia-flowered gooseberry	7–9	
Rosa spp. Rose	2–10	

SHRUBS FOR FRAGRANCE

Buddleia davidii Summer-lilac	6–10
Calycanthus floridus Carolina allspice	4–9
Choisya ternata Mexican orange	8–10
Clethra alnifolia Sweet pepperbush	3–9
Daphne odora Winter daphne	8–10
Gardenia jasminoides Gardenia	8–10
Hamamelis × *intermedia* Witch hazel	5–9
Lavandula spp. Lavender	5–10
Leucothoe fontanesiana Drooping leucothoe	4–8
Lonicera fragrantissima Winter honeysuckle	4–8
Osmanthus fragrans Sweet olive	8–10
Philadelphus coronarius Sweet mock orange	5–8
Pittosporum napaulense Golden-fragrance plant	9, 10
Rosa spp. Rose	2–10
Sarcococca spp. Sweetbox	5–9
Syringa vulgaris Common lilac	3–8
Viburnum × *burkwoodii* Burkwood viburnum	5–8

SHRUBS THAT ATTRACT BIRDS

Berberis spp. Barberry	4–10
Buxus spp. Boxwood	4–10

Cornus alba Tatarian dogwood	2–8
Cornus sericea Redosier dogwood	2–8
Elaeagnus pungens Silverberry	7–10
Euonymus alata Burning-bush	3–8
Euonymus fortunei Wintercreeper	4–10
Hamamelis spp. Witch hazel	4–8
Ilex spp. Holly	5–10
Juniperus spp. Juniper	2–10
Ligustrum spp. Privet	3–10
Lonicera spp. Honeysuckle	3–10

Mahonia spp. Oregon grape	5–10
Myrtus communis Myrtle	8–10
Prunus laurocerasus English laurel	7–10
Pyracantha spp. Firethorn	6–10
Rhus aromatica Fragrant sumac	4–8

Ilex cornuta 'Rotunda' (dwarf Chinese holly)

Rosa spp.	
Rose	2–10
Vaccinium spp.	
Huckleberry	3–9
Viburnum spp.	
Viburnum	2–10

CULTIVATION

The following lists will help you choose shrubs that flourish in shade, wet soil, city pollution, and other special growing conditions.

EASY-MAINTENANCE SHRUBS

Abelia × *grandiflora*	
Glossy abelia	5–10
Aesculus parviflora	
Bottlebrush buckeye	5–9
Aronia arbutifolia	
Red chokeberry	5–8
Berberis spp.	
Barberry	4–10
Calycanthus floridus	
Carolina allspice	4–9
Caragana arborescens	
Siberian peashrub	2–7
Chaenomeles speciosa	
Flowering quince	4–9
Cistus spp.	
Rockrose	8–10
Clethra alnifolia	
Sweet pepperbush	3–9

Thuja occidentalis
(American arborvitae)

Cotoneaster spp.	
Cotoneaster	3–10
Hamamelis spp.	
Witch hazel	4–8
Hypericum spp.	
St. John's wort	5–9
Ilex spp.	
Holly	5–10
Juniperus spp.	
Juniper	2–10
Leptospermum scoparium	
New Zealand tea tree	9, 10
Ligustrum spp.	
Privet	3–10
Myrica pensylvanica	
Bayberry	2–7
Myrtus communis	
Myrtle	8–10
Nandina domestica	
Heavenly-bamboo	7–10
Osmanthus spp.	
Sweet olive	3–10
Pittosporum spp.	
Pittosporum	9, 10
Potentilla fruticosa	
Bush cinquefoil	2–8
Raphiolepis spp.	
Indian-hawthorn	7–10
Spiraea spp.	
Spirea	3–9
Thuja spp.	
Arborvitae	3–9
Xylosma congestum	
Shiny xylosma	8–10

GOOD CITY SHRUBS

These shrubs tolerate the air pollution, restricted sunlight, reduced air circulation, and poor soil typical of urban gardens.

Aesculus parviflora	
Bottlebrush buckeye	5–9
Aronia arbutifolia	
Red chokeberry	5–8
Berberis thunbergii	
Japanese barberry	4–9
Caragana arborescens	
Siberian peashrub	2–7
Chaenomeles speciosa	
Flowering quince	4–9
Cornus alba	
Tatarian dogwood	2–8
Cornus sericea	
Redosier dogwood	2–8
Forsythia spp.	
Forsythia	4–9
Hamamelis virginiana	
Witch hazel	4–9
Hibiscus rosa-sinensis	
Chinese hibiscus	9, 10

Hibiscus syriacus Rose-of-Sharon	5-9
Hydrangea spp. Hydrangea	4-10
Hypericum spp. St. John's wort	5-9
Ilex crenata Japanese holly	5-10
Ilex glabra Inkberry	5-10
Juniperus spp. Juniper	2-10
Kerria japonica Japanese rose	5-9
Ligustrum spp. Privet	3-10
Lonicera spp. Honeysuckle	3-10
Magnolia stellata Star magnolia	5-10
Mahonia aquifolium Oregon grapeholly	5-9
Myrica pensylvanica Bayberry	2-7
Nerium oleander Oleander	9, 10
Philadelphus coronarius Sweet mock orange	5-8
Pittosporum tobira Japanese pittosporum	9, 10
Potentilla fruticosa Bush cinquefoil	2-8
Pyracantha coccinea Firethorn	6-10
Rhus spp. Sumac	3-10
Ribes alpinum Alpine currant	2-7
Rosa rugosa Rugosa rose	2-10
Rosa wichuraiana Memorial rose	5-10
Spiraea × *bumalda* Bumald spirea	4-10
Spiraea × *vanhouttei* Vanhoutte spirea	4-10
Taxus baccata English yew	6-8
Taxus cuspidata Japanese yew	5-8
Vaccinium corymbosum Highbush blueberry	3-9
Viburnum opulus Cranberrybush	4-10

SHRUBS FOR SHADY AREAS

Aucuba japonica Japanese aucuba	6-10
Calycanthus floridus Carolina allspice	4-9

Camellia spp. Camellia	7-10
Coprosma repens Mirror plant	9, 10
Daphne odora Winter daphne	8-10
Fatsia japonica Japanese fatsia	8-10
Fuchsia hybrids Fuchsia	9, 10
Gardenia jasminoides Gardenia	8-10
Gaultheria shallon Salal	6-9
Hydrangea spp. Hydrangea	4-10
Ilex spp. Holly	5-10
Kalmia latifolia Mountain laurel	4-9
Leucothoe fontanesiana Drooping leucothoe	4-8
Pieris japonica Lily-of-the-valley shrub	5-9
Rhododendron spp. Rhododendron, azalea	2-10
Sarcococca spp. Sweetbox	5-9
Ternstroemia gymnanthera Japanese cleyera	7-10

Rhododendron 'Holly Ann' (red-flowering rhododendron) and *R.* 'Honeymoon' (white-flowering rhododendron)

SHRUBS THAT ARE RELATIVELY PEST FREE

Although *pest free* is a relative term, the shrubs listed here are usually healthy where they are well adapted.

Cornus mas Cornelian-cherry	4–8
Cytisus spp. Broom	5–10
Kerria japonica Japanese rose	5–9
Magnolia stellata Star magnolia	5–10
Myrica pensylvanica Bayberry	2–7
Myrtus communis Myrtle	8–10
Podocarpus macrophyllus var. *maki* Shrubby-yew	9, 10
Potentilla fruticosa Bush cinquefoil	2–8
Rhamnus spp. Buckthorn	2–10
Tamarix spp. Tamarisk	2–10
Viburnum sieboldii Siebold viburnum	4–8
Xylosma congestum Shiny xylosma	8–10

Ilex crenata
'Rotundifolia'
(Japanese holly)

SHRUBS THAT CAN BE TRAINED INTO TREES

When the lower branches are removed and upward growth is encouraged, these shrubs will develop into small trees.

Hibiscus syriacus Rose-of-Sharon	5–9
Hydrangea spp. Hydrangea	4–10

Ilex spp. Holly	5–10
Nerium oleander Oleander	9, 10
Osmanthus spp. Sweet olive	3–10
Photinia serrulata Chinese photinia	7–10
Prunus spp. Cherry-laurel	2–10
Syringa reticulata Japanese tree lilac	3–8
Viburnum spp. Viburnum	2–10
Xylosma congestum Shiny xylosma	8–10

SHRUBS THAT TOLERATE SHEARING

Because they accept close clipping, these plants are excellent choices for sheared hedges, topiary, and other formal shapes. The fact that they grow slowly makes them doubly suitable for shearing.

Berberis thunbergii Japanese barberry	4–9
Buxus spp. Boxwood	4–10
Daphne odora Winter daphne	8–10
Gardenia jasminoides Gardenia	8–10
Hebe buxifolia Boxleaf hebe	9, 10
Ilex crenata Japanese holly	5–10
Ilex vomitoria Yaupon holly	7–10
Ligustrum spp. Privet	3–10
Myrtus communis Myrtle	8–10
Paeonia suffruticosa Tree peony	5–9
Photinia × *fraseri* Redtip photinia	7–10
Pittosporum tobira Japanese pittosporum	9, 10
Podocarpus macrophyllus Southern-yew	9, 10
Potentilla fruticosa Bush cinquefoil	2–8
Punica granatum Pomegranate	8–10
Spiraea cantoniensis Bridalwreath spirea	6–9
Spiraea thunbergii Thunberg spirea	4–8
Syzygium paniculatum Australian brush-cherry	9, 10

Teucrium chamaedrys Germander	3–9
Taxus spp. Yew	5–10
Viburnum tinus Laurustinus	8–10
Xylosma congestum Shiny xylosma	8–10

SHRUBS THAT TOLERATE SEACOAST CONDITIONS

These shrubs withstand the strong winds, salt spray, sandy soil, and other conditions found along the seacoast.

Arctostaphylos spp. and cvs. Manzanita	2–10
Callistemon citrinus Lemon bottlebrush	8–10
Ceanothus spp. California wild-lilac	8–10
Cistus spp. Rockrose	8–10
Coprosma spp. Coprosma	8–10
Cotoneaster dammeri Bearberry cotoneaster	6–9
Cotoneaster divaricatus Spreading cotoneaster	5–9
Cotoneaster horizontalis Rock cotoneaster	5–9
Cytisus × *praecox* Warminster broom	6–10
Elaeagnus pungens Silverberry	7–10
Escallonia spp. Escallonia	8–10
Genista spp. Broom	2–10
Hibiscus syriacus Rose-of-Sharon	5–9
Hydrangea macrophylla Bigleaf hydrangea	6–10
Juniperus conferta Shore juniper	5–10
Leptospermum scoparium New Zealand tea tree	9, 10
Lonicera nitida Box honeysuckle	8–10
Myrica pensylvanica Bayberry	2–7
Pittosporum crassifolium Karo	9, 10
Raphiolepis indica Indian-hawthorn	8–10
Rosa rugosa Rugosa rose	2–10
Rosa virginiana Virginia rose	4–10
Rosmarinus officinalis Rosemary	7–10

Ilex glabra (inkberry)

Tamarix spp. Tamarisk	2–10

SHRUBS FOR WET SOIL

Aronia arbutifolia Red chokeberry	5–8
Calycanthus floridus Carolina allspice	4–9
Clethra alnifolia Sweet pepperbush	3–9
Cornus alba Tatarian dogwood	2–8
Cornus sericea Redosier dogwood	2–8
Hamamelis vernalis Vernal witch hazel	5–9
Hypericum densiflorum Dense hypericum	6–10
Ilex glabra Inkberry	5–10
Myrica pensylvanica Bayberry	2–7
Potentilla fruticosa Bush cinquefoil	2–8
Rhododendron viscosum Swamp azalea	4–8
Salix gracilistyla Rosegold pussy willow	5–10
Viburnum opulus Cranberrybush	4–10
Viburnum trilobum American cranberrybush	3–9

DROUGHT-TOLERANT SHRUBS

See the list of shrubs on page 91 under Dry-Climate Garden.

Vines and Ground Covers

These practical, often beautiful plants merit wide-spread use in the garden because of their ability to blanket horizontal and vertical surfaces.

These are the plants that fill out a landscape, carpeting the ground and clambering up fences, walls, and arbors. The ability of vines and ground covers to fill in a surface, either the ground or a vertical structure, makes them among the most practical plants in the garden.

Vines are versatile plants that creep, trail, crawl, and climb, as well as bring color, fragrance, and variety to the garden. They soften the hard edges of a fence or other solid structure and can be used themselves as living walls or screens. Some vines, such as English ivy (*Hedera helix*), can also be used horizontally to cover the ground.

Ground covers include all kinds of plants—low-growing perennials, shrubs, herbs, and sprawling vines—that are valued for their ability to spread rapidly, grow close to the ground, and create a thick carpet. They range in size from a few inches high to approximately 3 feet high. Usually given a supporting role in the garden, ground covers are frequently underrated as beautifiers and landscape problem solvers. In addition to serving as a transition between diverse elements in the garden, ground covers can replace a lawn, hold a hillside, drape over a stone wall, and fill in nooks and crannies.

In this chapter are lists of vines and ground covers that serve many purposes in the garden. Look for plants that fulfill the roles mentioned above as well as for those that beautify a shady area or resist drought.

Asarum europeaum (European wild-ginger) forms an attractive, dense, evergreen mat in moist, shady locations.

Vines and Ground Covers/Table of Contents

VINES

Appearance

Vines With Showy Flowers	65
Spring	65
Summer	65
Fall	66
Winter	66
Foliage Vines	66
Vines With Excellent Fall Color	66

Special Uses in the Garden

Annual Vines for Fast Cover	67
Vines for Arbors and Patio Covers	67
Vines for Fragrance	68
Vines That Attract Birds	68

Cultivation

Vines for Shady Areas	68
Drought-Tolerant Vines	68

GROUND COVERS

Appearance

Low, Medium, and Tall Ground Covers	69
Low (up to 4 inches high)	69
Medium (4 to 12 inches high)	69
Tall (12 to 30 inches high)	69
Ground Covers With Showy Flowers	70
Spring	70
Summer	70
Fall	71
Winter	71
Ground Covers With Excellent Fall Color	71

Special Uses in the Garden

Slope Stabilizers	71
Lawn Alternatives	72
Ground Covers Between Stepping-Stones	73
Ground Covers That Drape, Trail, and Fill	73
Ground Covers for Nooks and Crannies	73
Ground Covers for Fragrance	74
Ground Covers That Attract Birds	74

Cultivation

Easy-Maintenance Ground Covers	74
Ground Covers for Shady Areas	75
Ground Covers for Wet Soil	75
Drought-Tolerant Ground Covers	75

Vines

APPEARANCE

The following lists will help you choose vines according to aesthetic qualities such as seasonal bloom and fall foliage color.

VINES WITH SHOWY FLOWERS

Spring

Allamanda cathartica
Golden trumpetvine   10

Beaumontia grandiflora
Herald's-trumpet   10

Bougainvillea spp.
Bougainvillea   9, 10

Clematis armandii
Evergreen clematis   7–10

Clytostoma callistegioides
Lavender trumpetvine   9, 10

Distictis buccinatoria
Bloodred trumpetvine   9, 10

Gelsemium sempervirens
Carolina jessamine   7–10

Hardenbergia violacea 'Happy Wanderer'
Lilac-vine   9, 10

Hibbertia scandens
Guinea gold vine   9, 10

Jasminum polyanthum
Pink jasmine   8–10

Lonicera japonica 'Halliana'
Hall's honeysuckle   4–10

Macfadyena unguis-cati
Catsclaw   8–10

Mandevilla splendens
Pink allamanda   9, 10

Passiflora caerulea
Blue passionflower   7–10

Passiflora coccinea
Red passionflower   9, 10

Polygonum aubertii
Silver-lace vine   4–8

Rosa hybrids
Climbing rose   4–10

Solanum jasminoides
Potato vine   8–10

Wisteria spp.
Wisteria   4–9

Summer

Allamanda cathartica
Golden trumpetvine   10

Antigonon leptopus
Queen's-wreath   9, 10

Asarina erubescens
Creeping gloxinia   8–10

Beaumontia grandiflora
Herald's-trumpet   10

Bougainvillea spp.
Bougainvillea   9, 10

Campsis radicans
Trumpetcreeper   4–9

Clematis × *jackmanii*
Jackman clematis   3–9

Clytostoma callistegioides
Lavender trumpetvine   9, 10

Distictis buccinatoria
Bloodred trumpetvine   9, 10

Hibbertia scandens
Guinea gold vine   9, 10

Hydrangea anomala petiolaris
Climbing hydrangea   5–9

Jasminum polyanthum
Pink jasmine   8–10

Lonicera japonica 'Halliana'
Hall's honeysuckle   4–10

Lonicera sempervirens
Trumpet honeysuckle   4–9

Mandevilla splendens
Pink allamanda   9, 10

Passiflora caerulea
Blue passionflower   7–10

Passiflora coccinea
Red passionflower   9, 10

Polygonum aubertii
Silver-lace vine   4–8

Rosa hybrids
Climbing rose   4–10

Schizophragma hydrangeoides
Japanese hydrangea vine   5–8

Solanum jasminoides
Potato vine   8–10

Tecomaria capensis
Cape honeysuckle   9, 10

Distictis buccinatoria
(bloodred trumpetvine)

Lonicera sempervirens
(trumpet honeysuckle)

Solanum jasminoides
Potato vine   8–10

Tecomaria capensis
Cape honeysuckle   9, 10

Winter

Gelsemium sempervirens
Carolina jessamine   7–10

Hardenbergia violacea 'Happy Wanderer'
Lilac-vine   9, 10

Pyrostegia venusta
Flame vine   10

Solanum jasminoides
Potato vine   8–10

FOLIAGE VINES

Actinidia arguta
Bower actinidia   4–8

Akebia quinata
Fiveleaf akebia   4–9

Ampelopsis arborea
Pepper vine   7–10

Ampelopsis brevipedunculata
Porcelain ampelopsis   4–9

Aristolochia durior
Dutchman's-pipe   4–9

Ficus pumila
Creeping fig   7–10

Hedera helix
English ivy   5–10

Menispermum canadense
Yellow parilla   5–8

Parthenocissus quinquefolia
Virginia creeper   4–9

Parthenocissus tricuspidata
Boston ivy   5–8

Rhoicissus capensis
Evergreen grape   10

Smilax lanceolata
Jackson brier   7–10

Vitis spp.
Grape   5–10

Fall

Allamanda cathartica
Golden trumpetvine   10

Antigonon leptopus
Queen's-wreath   9, 10

Campsis radicans
Trumpetcreeper   4–9

Clematis × *jackmanii*
Jackman clematis   3–9

Clytostoma callistegioides
Lavender trumpetvine   9, 10

Distictis buccinatoria
Bloodred trumpetvine   9, 10

Hibbertia scandens
Guinea gold vine   9, 10

Hydrangea anomala petiolaris
Climbing hydrangea   5–9

Mandevilla splendens
Pink allamanda   9, 10

Polygonum aubertii
Silver-lace vine   4–8

Pyrostegia venusta
Flame vine   10

VINES WITH EXCELLENT FALL COLOR

Ampelopsis arborea
Pepper vine   7–10

Ampelopsis brevipedunculata
Porcelain ampelopsis   4–9

Celastrus spp.
Bittersweet   3–8

Lonicera sempervirens
Trumpet honeysuckle   4–9

Parthenocissus quinquefolia
Virginia creeper   4–9

Parthenocissus tricuspidata
Boston ivy   5–8

Vitis spp.
Grape   5–10

SPECIAL USES IN THE GARDEN

The following lists will help you choose vines to serve specific functions in the garden.

ANNUAL VINES FOR FAST COVER

Quick and colorful, these vines provide summer shade and a temporary show. They cover in one season and, in most climates, die with the first frost. Although some of these vines are perennial in warm-winter climates, generally they are used as annuals.

Adlumia fungosa
Climbing fumitory

Asarina erubescens
Creeping gloxinia

Cardiospermum halicacabum
Balloon vine

Centrosema virginianum
Butterfly-pea

Clitoria ternatea
Atlantic pea

Cobaea scandens
Cup-and-saucer vine

Cucurbita pepo var. *ovifera*
Yellow-flowered gourd

Dolichos lablab
Hyacinth-bean

Eccremocarpus scaber
Gloryflower

Echinocystis lobata
Wild cucumber

Humulus japonicus
Japanese hop

Ipomoea spp.
Morning glory vine

Lagenaria siceraria
White-flowered gourd

Lathyrus odoratus
Sweet pea

Momordica balsamina
Balsam-apple

Phaseolus coccineus
Scarlet runner bean

Thunbergia alata
Black-eyed-susan vine

Tropaeolum majus
Nasturtium

VINES FOR ARBORS AND PATIO COVERS

These vines are suitable for growing on arbors and other structures. They provide shade and attractive flowers, fruit, or foliage.

Actinidia arguta Bower actinidia	4–8
Akebia quinata Fiveleaf akebia	4–9
Antigonon leptopus Queen's-wreath	9, 10
Aristolochia durior Dutchman's-pipe	4–9
Beaumontia grandiflora Herald's-trumpet	10
Bougainvillea spp.* Bougainvillea	9, 10
*Campsis radicans*** Trumpetcreeper	4–9
Celastrus spp. Bittersweet	3–8
Clematis spp. Clematis	3–10
*Clytostoma callistegioides** Lavender trumpetvine	9, 10
*Distictis buccinatoria*** Bloodred trumpetvine	9, 10
Hardenbergia violacea 'Happy Wanderer' Lilac-vine	9, 10
Hibbertia scandens Guinea gold vine	9, 10
*Hydrangea anomala petiolaris*** Climbing hydrangea	5–9
Jasminum polyanthum Pink jasmine	8–10
Lonicera spp. Honeysuckle	3–10
Polygonum aubertii Silver-lace vine	4–8
Rhoicissus capensis Evergreen grape	10
Rosa hybrids* Climbing rose	4–10
Vitis spp. Grape	5–10
Wisteria spp. Wisteria	4–9

* Must be tied to support.
** Has aerial rootlets or suction disks that may damage the support surface.

Bougainvillea species (bougainvillea)

Wisteria species
(wisteria)

Trachelospermum jasminoides	
Starjasmine	8–10
Wisteria spp.	
Wisteria	4–9

VINES THAT ATTRACT BIRDS

Akebia quinata	
Fiveleaf akebia	4–9
Ampelopsis brevipedunculata	
Porcelain ampelopsis	4–9
Celastrus spp.	
Bittersweet	3–8
Euonymus fortunei	
Wintercreeper	4–10
Hedera helix	
English ivy	5–10
Lonicera spp.	
Honeysuckle	3–10
Parthenocissus quinquefolia	
Virginia creeper	4–9
Parthenocissus tricuspidata	
Boston ivy	5–8
Vitis spp.	
Grape	5–10

CULTIVATION

The following lists will help you choose vines that flourish under special growing conditions.

VINES FOR SHADY AREAS

Aristolochia durior	
Dutchman's-pipe	4–9
Euonymus fortunei	
Wintercreeper	4–10
Ficus pumila	
Creeping fig	7–10
Hedera helix	
English ivy	5–10
Hydrangea anomala petiolaris	
Climbing hydrangea	5–9
Lapageria rosea	
Chilean bellflower	9, 10
Menispermum canadense	
Yellow parilla	5–8
Parthenocissus quinquefolia	
Virginia creeper	4–9
Parthenocissus tricuspidata	
Boston ivy	5–8
Schizophragma hydrangeoides	
Japanese hydrangea vine	5–8
Thunbergia grandiflora	
Blue trumpetvine	10
Trachelospermum jasminoides	
Starjasmine	8–10

VINES FOR FRAGRANCE

Actinidia arguta	
Bower actinidia	4–8
Allamanda cathartica	
Golden trumpetvine	10
Beaumontia grandiflora	
Herald's-trumpet	10
Clematis spp.	
Clematis	3–10
Gelsemium sempervirens	
Carolina jessamine	7–10
Ipomoea alba	
Moonflower vine	Annual
Jasminum spp.	
Jasmine	6–10
Lonicera spp.	
Honeysuckle	3–10
Mandevilla laxa	
Chile jasmine	8–10
Passiflora × *alatocaerulea*	
Passionflower	9, 10
Rosa hybrids	
Climbing rose	4–10

DROUGHT-TOLERANT VINES

See the list of vines on page 92 under Dry-Climate Garden.

Ground Covers

APPEARANCE

The following lists will help you choose ground covers according to height, seasonal bloom, and fall foliage color.

LOW, MEDIUM, AND TALL GROUND COVERS

Low (up to 4 inches high)

Ajuga reptans
Carpet-bugle — 4–10

Arenaria balearica
Corsican sandwort — 3–9

Duchesnea indica
Mock strawberry — 5–10

Euonymus fortunei 'Minima'
Baby wintercreeper — 4–10

Fragaria chiloensis
Beach strawberry — 6–10

Galium odoratum
Sweet woodruff — 4–9

Juniperus horizontalis 'Wiltonii'
Blue rug juniper — 3–10

Laurentia fluviatilis
Bluestar creeper — 9, 10

Lysimachia nummularia
Creeping-charlie — 3–10

Mentha requienii
Corsican mint — 6–10

Phlox subulata
Moss-pink — 2–9

Potentilla tabernaemontani
Spring cinquefoil — 6–10

Sagina subulata
Irish moss — 4–10

Sedum acre
Golden-carpet — 4–10

Soleirolia soleirolii
Babytears — 8–10

Thymus praecox arcticus
Creeping thyme — 3–10

Zoysia tenuifolia
Korean velvetgrass — 6–10

Medium (4 to 12 inches high)

Arctostaphylos uva-ursi
Bearberry — 2–9

Carissa grandiflora 'Green Carpet'
Dwarf natal-plum — 9, 10

Convallaria majalis
Lily-of-the-valley — 2–8

Epimedium grandiflorum
Bishop's-hat — 3–8

Euonymus fortunei var. *radicans*
Wintercreeper — 4–10

Gazania rigens var. *leucolaena*
Trailing gazania — 9, 10

Hedera helix
English ivy — 5–10

Hypericum calycinum
St. John's wort — 5–10

Juniperus conferta 'Blue Pacific'
Blue Pacific juniper — 5–10

Juniperus horizontalis
Creeping juniper — 3–10

Lamium maculatum 'Beacon Silver'
Deadnettle — 4–9

Liriope muscari
Lilyturf — 6–10

Ophiopogon japonicus
Mondograss — 5–10

Pachysandra terminalis
Japanese spurge — 3–10

Pelargonium peltatum
Ivy geranium — 9, 10

Stachys byzantina
Woolly lamb's-ears — 4–10

Vinca minor
Common periwinkle — 5–10

Tall (12 to 30 inches high)

Adiantum pedatum
Maidenhair fern — 3–10

Baccharis pilularis
Dwarf coyotebrush — 7–10

Ceanothus griseus var. *horizontalis*
Carmel creeper — 7–10

Baccharis pilularis
(dwarf coyotebrush)

Drosanthemum floribundum (rosea ice plant)

Cotoneaster dammeri 'Coral Beauty' Bearberry cotoneaster	6–9
Diervilla lonicera Bush honeysuckle	3–8
Gardenia jasminoides 'Radicans' Creeping gardenia	8–10
Hemerocallis spp. Daylily	2–10
Hosta spp. Plantain lily	3–9
Juniperus chinensis 'Parsonii' Parson juniper	4–10
Juniperus chinensis var. *sargentii* Sargent juniper	3–10
Juniperus conferta Shore juniper	5–10
Paxistima canbyi Cliffgreen	3–8
Rhus aromatica 'Gro-low' Fragrant sumac	4–8
Rosmarinus officinalis 'Prostratus' Dwarf rosemary	8–10
Sollya heterophylla Australian bluebell-creeper	9, 10
Trachelospermum jasminoides Starjasmine	8–10
Vinca major Greater periwinkle	7–10

GROUND COVERS WITH SHOWY FLOWERS

Spring

Ajuga reptans Carpet-bugle	4–10
Anemone blanda Greek windflower	5–9
Arabis caucasica Wall rockcress	6–10
Aurinia saxatilis Basket-of-gold	3–10
Carpobrotus spp. Ice plant	9, 10
Ceanothus spp. California wild-lilac	8–10
Convallaria majalis Lily-of-the-valley	2–8
Cytisus × *kewensis* Kew broom	6–10
Delosperma spp. Ice plant	9, 10
Deutzia gracilis 'Nikko' Slender deutzia	5–8
Drosanthemum floribundum Rosea ice plant	9, 10
Erica carnea Spring heath	6–10
Gazania rigens var. *leucolaena* Trailing gazania	9, 10
Gelsemium sempervirens Carolina jessamine	7–10
Iberis sempervirens Evergreen candytuft	4–10
Lampranthus spp. Ice plant	9, 10
Lantana montevidensis Trailing lantana	8–10
Laurentia fluviatilis Bluestar creeper	9, 10
Osteospermum fruticosum Trailing African daisy	9, 10
Phlox subulata Moss-pink	2–9
Potentilla tabernaemontani Spring cinquefoil	6–10
Rosa spinosissima Scotch rose	4–10
Rosmarinus officinalis 'Prostratus' Dwarf rosemary	8–10
Sedum spp. Stonecrop	3–10
Verbena peruviana Peruvian verbena	9, 10

Summer

Achillea tomentosa Woolly yarrow	3–10
Ajuga reptans Carpet-bugle	4–10
Arabis caucasica Wall rockcress	6–10
Carpobrotus spp. Ice plant	9, 10
Cerastium tomentosum Snow-in-summer	3–10
Ceratostigma plumbaginoides Blue plumbago	5–10

Convallaria majalis
Lily-of-the-valley 2–8

Erica vagans
Cornish heath 5–9

Gardenia jasminoides 'Radicans'
Creeping gardenia 8–10

Gazania rigens var. *leucolaena*
Trailing gazania 9, 10

Geranium sanguineum
Bloodred cranesbill 3–8

Hosta spp.
Plantain lily 3–9

Hypericum calycinum
St. John's wort 5–10

Iberis sempervirens
Evergreen candytuft 4–10

Lantana montevidensis
Trailing lantana 8–10

Osteospermum fruticosum
Trailing African daisy 9, 10

Rosa wichuraiana
Memorial rose 5–10

Thymus spp.
Thyme 3–9

Trachelospermum jasminoides
Starjasmine 8–10

Fall

Ceratostigma plumbaginoides
Blue plumbago 5–10

Gazania rigens var. *leucolaena*
Trailing gazania 9, 10

Lantana montevidensis
Trailing lantana 8–10

Osteospermum fruticosum
Trailing African daisy 9, 10

Winter

Gazania rigens var. *leucolaena*
Trailing gazania 9, 10

Gelsemium sempervirens
Carolina jessamine 7–10

Lampranthus spp.
Ice plant 9, 10

Lantana montevidensis
Trailing lantana 8–10

Osteospermum fruticosum
Trailing African daisy 9, 10

Rosmarinus officinalis 'Prostratus'
Dwarf rosemary 8–10

GROUND COVERS WITH EXCELLENT FALL COLOR

Ceratostigma plumbaginoides
Blue plumbago 5–10

Cotoneaster conspicuus var. *decorus*
Wintergreen cotoneaster 7–9

Cotoneaster horizontalis
Rock cotoneaster 5–9

Cotoneaster microphyllus
Small-leaved cotoneaster 6–9

Euonymus fortunei var. *radicans*
Wintercreeper 4–10

Galax urceolata
Wandflower 3–6

Gaultheria procumbens
Creeping wintergreen 4–10

Nandina domestica 'Harbour Dwarf'
Dwarf heavenly-bamboo 7–10

SPECIAL USES IN THE GARDEN

The following lists will help you choose ground covers to serve specific functions in the garden.

SLOPE STABILIZERS

These plants have strong root systems that help prevent soil erosion on slopes and hillsides. Some are vines that sprawl to cover the ground. Many of the plants put down roots wherever the stems touch the ground.

Akebia quinata
Fiveleaf akebia 4–9

Arctostaphylos uva-ursi
Bearberry 2–9

Baccharis pilularis
Dwarf coyotebrush 7–10

Ceanothus griseus var. *horizontalis*
Carmel creeper 7–10

Cistus spp.
Rockrose 8–10

Coprosma × *kirkii*
Coprosma 8–10

Ceratostigma plumbaginoides (blue plumbago)

Coronilla varia
Crown vetch   3–8

Cotoneaster spp.
Cotoneaster   3–10

Gazania rigens var. *leucolaena*
Trailing gazania   9, 10

Hedera helix
English ivy   5–10

Hemerocallis spp.
Daylily   3–10

Juniperus spp.
Juniper   2–10

Lantana montevidensis
Trailing lantana   8–10

Lonicera japonica 'Halliana'
Hall's honeysuckle   4–10

Mahonia repens
Creeping mahonia   5–10

Fragaria chiloensis
(beach strawberry)

Parthenocissus quinquefolia
Virginia creeper   4–9

Phalaris arundinacea var. *picta*
Ribbongrass   5–10

Polygonum cuspidatum var. *compactum*
Fleeceflower   4–10

Pyracantha koidzumii 'Santa Cruz'
Santa Cruz firethorn   6–10

Rosa wichuraiana
Memorial rose   5–10

Rosmarinus officinalis 'Prostratus'
Dwarf rosemary   8–10

Vinca spp.
Periwinkle   5–10

LAWN ALTERNATIVES

These attractive ground covers grow up to 6 inches high and can be used to fill large areas. Some, as noted, can be walked on.

Aegopodium podagraria
Bishop's-weed   3–9

*Ajuga reptans**
Carpet-bugle   4–10

Arctostaphylos uva-ursi
Bearberry   2–9

*Chamaemelum nobile**
Chamomile   7–10

Coronilla varia
Crown vetch   3–8

Dianthus deltoides
Maiden pink   2–10

*Dichondra micrantha**
Dichondra   9, 10

*Duchesnea indica**
Mock strawberry   5–10

Euonymus fortunei
Wintercreeper   4–10

*Fragaria chiloensis**
Beach strawberry   6–10

Gazania rigens var. *leucolaena*
Trailing gazania   9, 10

Hedera helix
English ivy   5–10

Hypericum calycinum
St. John's wort   5–10

Juniperus horizontalis 'Wiltonii'*
Blue rug juniper   3–10

*Laurentia fluviatilis**
Bluestar creeper   9, 10

Liriope spicata
Creeping lilyturf   6–10

Lonicera japonica 'Halliana'
Hall's honeysuckle   4–10

Pachysandra terminalis
Japanese spurge   3–10

*Phyla nodiflora**
Lippia   9, 10

Polygonum capitatum
Pink cloverblossom   6–10

Polygonum cuspidatum var. *compactum*
Fleeceflower   4–10

Potentilla tabernaemontani
Spring cinquefoil   6–10

*Sagina subulata**
Irish moss   4–10

Sedum spp.
Stonecrop   3–10

Trachelospermum jasminoides
Starjasmine   8–10

*Vinca minor**
Common periwinkle   5–10

*Zoysia tenuifolia**
Korean velvetgrass   6–10

* Tolerates foot traffic.

GROUND COVERS BETWEEN STEPPING-STONES

Excellent choices for planting between stepping-stones and around patio paving, these ground covers tolerate foot traffic.

Achillea tomentosa Woolly yarrow	3–10
Arenaria balearica Corsican sandwort	3–9
Chamaemelum nobile Chamomile	7–10
Duchesnea indica Mock strawberry	5–10
Fragaria chiloensis Beach strawberry	6–10
Glechoma hederacea Ground ivy	4–10
Laurentia fluviatilis Bluestar creeper	9, 10
Phyla nodiflora Lippia	9, 10
Sagina subulata Irish moss	4–10
Soleirolia soleirolii Babytears	8–10
Thymus praecox arcticus Creeping thyme	3–10
Vinca minor Common periwinkle	5–10

GROUND COVERS THAT DRAPE, TRAIL, AND FILL

These plants cascade over walls, trail over rocks, and grow to fill in every void. Some need occasional trimming.

Arctostaphylos uva-ursi Bearberry	2–9

Campanula spp. Bellflower	3–9
Cerastium tomentosum Snow-in-summer	3–10
Cotoneaster adpressus Creeping cotoneaster	4–7
Cotoneaster dammeri Bearberry cotoneaster	6–9
Euonymus fortunei Wintercreeper	4–10
Juniperus horizontalis Creeping juniper	3–10
Hedera helix English ivy	5–10
Lysimachia nummularia Creeping-charlie	3–10
Pachysandra terminalis Japanese spurge	3–10
Rosmarinus officinalis 'Prostratus' Dwarf rosemary	8–10
Trachelospermum jasminoides Starjasmine	8–10
Verbena peruviana Peruvian verbena	9, 10
Vinca minor Common periwinkle	5–10

GROUND COVERS FOR NOOKS AND CRANNIES

If you're not sure what to plant in a tight corner or tuck between rocks, try one of these small-scale ground covers.

Arabis caucasica Wall rockcress	6–10
Armeria maritima Sea-pink	2–10
Aurinia saxatilis Basket-of-gold	3–10

Armeria maritima (sea-pink)

Arctostaphylos uva-ursi (bearberry)

Campanula spp. Bellflower	3–9
Chamaemelum nobile Chamomile	7–10
Dianthus 'Tiny Rubies' Pink	3–8
Epimedium grandiflorum Bishop's-hat	3–8
Erodium chamaedryoides Alpine geranium	7–10
Heuchera sanguinea Coralbells	3–10
Iberis sempervirens Evergreen candytuft	4–10
Lamium maculatum 'Beacon Silver' Deadnettle	4–9
Lysimachia nummularia Creeping-charlie	3–10
Mentha requienii Corsican mint	6–10
Sagina subulata Irish moss	4–10
Sedum spp. Stonecrop	3–10
Sempervivum tectorum Hens-and-chickens	4–10
Soleirolia soleirolii Babytears	8–10
Thymus spp. Thyme	3–9

GROUND COVERS FOR FRAGRANCE

Convallaria majalis Lily-of-the-valley	2–8
Galium odoratum Sweet woodruff	4–9
Gardenia jasminoides 'Radicans' Creeping gardenia	8–10
Gelsemium sempervirens Carolina jessamine	7–10
Hosta plantaginea Fragrant hosta	3–9
Mentha requienii Corsican mint	6–10
Pachysandra terminalis Japanese spurge	3–10
Sarcococca spp. Sweetbox	5–9
Trachelospermum jasminoides Starjasmine	8–10
Viola odorata Sweet violet	6–10

GROUND COVERS THAT ATTRACT BIRDS

Arctostaphylos uva-ursi Bearberry	2–9
Ceanothus spp. California wild-lilac	8–10
Cotoneaster dammeri Bearberry cotoneaster	6–9
Duchesnea indica Mock strawberry	5–10
Euonymus fortunei Wintercreeper	4–10
Fragaria chiloensis Beach strawberry	6–10
Juniperus horizontalis Creeping juniper	3–10
Rhus aromatica 'Gro-low' Fragrant sumac	4–8
Rosa spinosissima Scotch rose	4–10
Rosmarinus officinalis 'Prostratus' Dwarf rosemary	8–10

CULTIVATION

The following lists will help you choose ground covers that flourish in shade, wet soil, and other special growing conditions.

EASY-MAINTENANCE GROUND COVERS

Ajuga reptans Carpet-bugle	4–10
Arctostaphylos uva-ursi Bearberry	2–9
Baccharis pilularis Dwarf coyotebrush	7–10
Campanula spp. Bellflower	3–9
Cotoneaster spp. Cotoneaster	3–10
Euonymus fortunei Wintercreeper	4–10

Hedera helix
English ivy   5–10

Hypericum calycinum
St. John's wort   5–10

Iberis sempervirens
Evergreen candytuft   4–10

Juniperus spp.
Juniper   2–10

Liriope spicata
Creeping lilyturf   6–10

Ophiopogon japonicus
Mondograss   5–10

Pachysandra terminalis
Japanese spurge   3–10

Potentilla tabernaemontani
Spring cinquefoil   6–10

Rosmarinus officinalis 'Prostratus'
Dwarf rosemary   8–10

Sedum spp.
Stonecrop   3–10

Trachelospermum jasminoides
Starjasmine   8–10

Vinca minor
Common periwinkle   5–10

GROUND COVERS FOR SHADY AREAS

Adiantum pedatum
Maidenhair fern   3–10

Asarum spp.
Wild-ginger   3–8

Athyrium goeringianum
Japanese painted fern   3–8

Bergenia spp.
Bergenia   3–9

Convallaria majalis
Lily-of-the-valley   2–8

Dryopteris spp.
Wood fern   3–8

Epimedium grandiflorum
Bishop's-hat   3–8

Galium odoratum
Sweet woodruff   4–9

Gaultheria procumbens
Creeping wintergreen   4–10

Hedera helix
English ivy   5–10

Hosta spp.
Plantain lily   3–9

Oxalis oregana
Redwood sorrel   5–10

Pachysandra terminalis
Japanese spurge   3–10

Sagina subulata
Irish moss   4–10

Sarcococca spp.
Sweetbox   5–9

Soleirolia soleirolii
Babytears   8–10

Vinca minor
Common periwinkle   5–10

Viola odorata
Sweet violet   6–10

GROUND COVERS FOR WET SOIL

Aegopodium podagraria
Bishop's-weed   3–9

Asarum spp.
Wild-ginger   3–8

Chrysogonum virginianum
Goldenstar   5–9

Convallaria majalis
Lily-of-the-valley   2–8

Dichondra micrantha
Dichondra   9, 10

Euonymus fortunei
Wintercreeper   4–10

Galax urceolata
Wandflower   3–6

Galium odoratum
Sweet woodruff   4–9

Hemerocallis hybrids
Daylily   3–10

Hosta spp.
Plantain lily   3–9

Lamium maculatum 'Beacon Silver'
Deadnettle   4–9

Mahonia repens
Creeping mahonia   5–10

Paxistima canbyi
Cliffgreen   3–8

Soleirolia soleirolii
Babytears   8–10

DROUGHT-TOLERANT GROUND COVERS

See the list of ground covers on page 92 under Dry-Climate Garden.

Aegopodium podagraria
(bishop's-weed)

Special Gardens

Here are a half-dozen theme gardens, each with comprehensive lists of appropriate plants to carry through the motif.

Instead of simply choosing plants at random, you may want to select a theme for your garden. In a theme garden, all the plants fit a specific category, share a common trait, or contribute to an ambience or mood. In each case, the plants work together to achieve an overall effect. Choose a theme that appeals to you and is compatible with your surroundings.

On the following pages are lists of plants appropriate for six theme gardens: rock, water, Japanese, herb, dry-climate, and rose. Their beauty and practicality make these among the most popular theme gardens.

The rock garden section contains lists of low-growing plants suitable for recreating a small-scale version of a mountain landscape. For a water garden there are lists of aquatic plants as well as landscape plants for the surrounding area. Appropriate plants from Japan and other parts of the world are listed for a Japanese-style garden. In the herb garden section you will find lists of common culinary herbs plus many ornamental species not usually thought of as herbs. In the dry-climate garden section are listings of drought-tolerant plants that will thrive with little or no irrigation once they are established. The rose garden section lists more than one hundred and thirty roses, including many recent award winners.

Acer palmatum *'Dissectum Atropurpureum' (threadleaf Japanese maple) serves as a colorful focal point in this Japanese garden. Ferns are another typical planting in this kind of garden.*

Special Gardens/Table of Contents

ROCK GARDEN

Trees	79
Shrubs and Subshrubs	79
Perennials and Bulbs	80

WATER GARDEN

Aquatic Plants	81
Landscape Plants	82
Trees	82
Shrubs	82
Ground Covers	82
Perennials	83

JAPANESE GARDEN

Trees	84
Shrubs	84
Vines	85
Ground Covers	85
Perennials	85
Ferns	85
Bamboos and Other Grasses	85
Water and Water's-Edge Plants	85

HERB GARDEN

Culinary Herbs	86
Herbs for Fragrance	86
Flowering Herbs	87
Herbs for Ground Covers	88
Herbs for Low Borders and Edgings	88
Herbs for Hedges	88

DRY-CLIMATE GARDEN

Flowers	89
Trees	90
Palms	91
Shrubs	91
Vines	92
Ground Covers	92

ROSE GARDEN

Appearance

Roses by Color	
Red	93
Pink	93
Lavender to Purple	94
Yellow	94
Orange-Red and Orange to Gold	94
White to Cream	94
Bicolor and Multicolor	95

Special Uses in the Garden

Roses for Screens	95
Roses for Hedges	95
Roses for Ground Covers	95
Especially Fragrant Roses	95
Long-Lasting Cut Roses	96

Cultivation

Easiest Roses	96
Hardiest Modern Roses	97
Most-Disease-Resistant Roses	97

Rock Garden

Originally, rock gardens were designed to be small-scale replicas of mountain landscapes. In a traditional alpine garden, plants from high elevations are grown in a miniature version of their native setting. Many other types of rock gardens are possible. They may feature a variety of low-growing plants from around the world, or they may be restricted to plants native to the area in which the garden is located. In these gardens, the emphasis on faithfully recreating a mountainous terrain is not as great; the rocks can be arranged in any manner that pleases you.

Wherever they originate, plants in a rock garden tend to be small-scale species that hug the ground, form spreading mats, or creep over rocks. Appropriate plants include small shrubs, tiny bulbs, and low-growing perennials. Keep in mind that many popular rock-garden plants require full sun and fast drainage.

TREES

Acer palmatum	
Japanese maple	6-10
Cornus florida	
Flowering dogwood	5-9
Cotinus coggygria	
Smoke tree	4-9
Pinus densiflora 'Umbraculifera'	
Tanyosho pine	5-9
Pinus thunbergiana	
Japanese black pine	4-8

SHRUBS AND SUBSHRUBS

Arctostaphylos uva-ursi	
Bearberry	2-9
Berberis × *stenophylla* 'Corallina Compacta'	
Coral barberry	7-10
Calluna vulgaris	
Scotch heather	4-9
Chamaecyparis obtusa 'Nana Aurea'	
Dwarf golden hinoki cypress	5-9
Chamaecyparis pisifera 'Filifera'	
Thread-branch false-cypress	3-8
Cistus spp.	
Rockrose	8-10
Cotoneaster adpressus	
Creeping cotoneaster	4-7
Cotoneaster dammeri 'Coral Beauty'	
Bearberry cotoneaster	6-9
Cotoneaster microphyllus	
Small-leaved cotoneaster	6-9
Cytisus × *kewensis*	
Kew broom	6-10
Daphne cneorum	
Garland-flower	4-7
Erica carnea	
Spring heath	6-10
Erica vagans	
Cornish heath	5-9
Felicia amelloides	
Blue marguerite	8-10
Gaultheria procumbens	
Creeping wintergreen	4-10
Helianthemum nummularium	
Sunrose	5-10
Hypericum coris	
St. John's wort	6-10

Juniperus chinensis var. *procumbens* 'Nana'	
Japanese garden juniper	5-10
Juniperus horizontalis	
Creeping juniper	3-10
Lavandula spp.	
Lavender	5-10
Paxistima canbyi	
Cliffgreen	3-8
Picea glauca 'Conica'	
Dwarf Alberta spruce	2-8
Pinus mugo var. *mugo* 'Compacta'	
Dwarf mugo pine	2-8
Pinus strobus 'Nana'	
Dwarf eastern white pine	4-8
Rhododendron impeditum	
Cloudland rhododendron	5-8
Rhododendron keiskei	
Keisk rhododendron	6-8
Spiraea × *bumalda*	
Bumald spirea	4-10
Taxus cuspidata 'Nana'	
Dwarf Japanese yew	4-8
Teucrium chamaedrys	
Germander	3-9

Felicia amelloides *(blue marguerite) is an example of a small-scale shrub appropriate for a rock garden.*

PERENNIALS AND BULBS

Achillea tomentosa Woolly yarrow	3–10
Anemone coronaria Poppy anemone	8–10
Anemone × hybrida Japanese anemone	6–9
Aquilegia spp. Columbine	3–9
Arabis caucasica Wall rockcress	6–10
Arenaria balearica Corsican sandwort	3–9
Armeria maritima Sea-pink	2–10
Artemisia schmidtiana Silver mound	4–10
Aubrieta deltoidea Stonecress	5–10
Aurinia saxatilis Basket-of-gold	3–10
Campanula spp. Bellflower	3–9
Cerastium tomentosum Snow-in-summer	3–10
Chamaemelum nobile Chamomile	7–10
Chrysogonum virginianum Goldenstar	5–9
Coreopsis auriculata 'Nana' Dwarf tickseed	5–10
Crocus hybrids Crocus	3–9
Cyclamen spp. Cyclamen	5–10
Dianthus deltoides Maiden pink	2–10
Dianthus plumarius Cottage pink	3–9
Dictamnus albus 'Purpureus' Rose gas plant	4–8
Epimedium grandiflorum Bishop's-hat	3–8
Erodium chamaedryoides Alpine geranium	9, 10
Festuca ovina var. *glauca* Blue fescue	3–10
Freesia × hybrida Freesia	9, 10
Fritillaria meleagris Checkered-lily	4–8
Fuchsia procumbens Trailing fuchsia	8–10
Galanthus spp. Snowdrop	2–9
Gazania rigens Gazania	9, 10
Geranium sanguineum Bloodred cranesbill	3–8
Gypsophila repens Creeping baby's breath	3–8

Heuchera spp. Coralbells	3–10
Iberis sempervirens Evergreen candytuft	4–10
Iris cristata Crested iris	3–8
Iris reticulata Violet-scented iris	5–9
Laurentia fluviatilis Bluestar creeper	9, 10
Leucojum spp. Snowflake	3–10
Liriope muscari Lilyturf	6–10
Mimulus spp. Monkeyflower	7–10
Muscari armeniacum Grape hyacinth	5–9
Narcissus bulbocodium Hoop-petticoat daffodil	5–10
Pelargonium × hortorum Geranium	9, 10
Penstemon heterophyllus purdyi Penstemon	6–10
Phlox subulata Moss-pink	2–9
Phyla nodiflora Lippia	9, 10
Platycodon grandiflorus var. *mariesii* Dwarf balloon-flower	3–9
Potentilla tabernaemontani Spring cinquefoil	6–10
Pratia angulata Pratia	7–10
Primula spp. Primrose	3–9
Sagina subulata Irish moss	4–10
Saponaria ocymoides Rock soapwort	4–10
Satureja montana Winter savory	4–9
Saxifraga spp. Saxifrage	2–10
Scilla siberica Siberian squill	2–9
Sedum spp. Stonecrop	3–10
Sempervivum tectorum Hens-and-chickens	4–10
Solidago hybrids Goldenrod	3–10
Thymus spp. Thyme	3–9
Tulipa tarda Tulip	4–8
Verbena peruviana Peruvian verbena	9, 10
Viola spp. Viola	3–10

Water Garden

Nothing is more magical in the garden than water, whether it takes the form of a simple pool or a waterfall splashing into a pond. The sights and sounds of water—and the cooling effect it brings to the garden—never fail to elicit pleasure and serenity. A garden devoted to water and water plants can intensify those feelings.

The following lists offer suggestions for aquatic plants as well as landscape plants suitable for planting around the water feature. The aquatic plants, all of them adapted to North America, include waterlilies and lotus for the center of the pool and bog plants for the edges. There are also floating plants and submerged plants, whose leaves remain underwater where they release oxygen. Although shade- and moisture-loving plants look most natural around the edge of a pool or pond, they may not be suitable for your water garden. The soil around an artificial pool is no moister than it would be without the pool. Choose the plants that are best adapted to your climate and garden conditions.

AQUATIC PLANTS

Acorus calamus Sweet flag	4–10
Aponogeton distachyus Waterhawthorn	5–10
Butomus umbellatus Flowering-rush	6–10
Cabomba caroliniana Cabomba	6–10
Caltha palustris Marshmarigold	4–7
Canna hybrids Water canna	7–10
Colocasia esculenta Taro	9, 10
Crinum americanum Bog-lily	8–10
Cyperus spp. Papyrus	9, 10
Eichhornia crassipes Water hyacinth	9, 10

Eleocharis dulcis Chinese water chestnut	7–10
Elodea canadensis Waterweed	5–10
Equisetum hyemale Horsetail	3–9
Hydrocleys nymphoides Waterpoppy	8–10
Hydrocotyle vulgaris Water pennywort	8–10
Hymenocallis spp. Spider-lily	8–10
Iris fulva Red iris	5–10
Iris pseudacorus Yellowflag	5–8
Iris versicolor Blueflag	4–10
Ludwigia palustris Creeping waterprimrose	9, 10
Ludwigia uruguayensis Primrose-willow	7–10
Marsilea spp. Waterclover	6–10
Myriophyllum spp. Water milfoil	5–10

Nelumbo spp. and cvs. Lotus	5–9
Nymphaea spp. and cvs. Waterlily	3–10
Nymphoides peltata Floatingheart	6–10
Orontium aquaticum Goldenclub	6–10
Peltandra virginica Arrow arum	5–10
Pistia stratiotes Shellflower	9, 10
Pontederia cordata Pickerelrush	3–10
Sagittaria latifolia Arrowhead	5–10
Saururus cernuus Waterdragon	4–10
Scirpus albescens White bulrush	5–10
Thalia dealbata Thalia	6–10
Typha spp. Cattail	2–10
Vallisneria americana Eelgrass	4–10

A wide variety of succulents and tropical plants flourishes around this waterlily pool.

Equisetum hyemale *(horsetail) provides an upright, spiky accent at the water's edge.*

LANDSCAPE PLANTS

Trees

Acer palmatum Japanese maple	6–10
Amelanchier spp. Serviceberry	4–9
Betula pendula White birch	2–8
Cedrus deodara Deodar cedar	7–10
Cercis canadensis Eastern redbud	4–9
Chionanthus virginicus Old-man's-beard	4–9
Cornus spp. Dogwood	2–9
× *Cupressocyparis leylandii* Leyland cypress	6–10
Franklinia alatamaha Franklin tree	5–8
Metasequoia glyptostroboides Dawn redwood	6–8
Oxydendrum arboreum Sourwood	4–9
Pinus parviflora Japanese white pine	4–8
Pinus thunbergiana Japanese black pine	4–8
Prunus subhirtella 'Pendula' Weeping Higan cherry	5–8
Styrax japonicus Japanese snowbell	5–9
Tsuga canadensis Canada hemlock	3–8

Shrubs

Berberis thunbergii 'Atropurpurea' Red barberry	4–9
Buxus sempervirens Common boxwood	6–10
Chamaecyparis obtusa Hinoki cypress	5–9
Chamaecyparis pisifera 'Filifera' Thread-branch false-cypress	3–8
Clethra alnifolia Sweet pepperbush	3–9
Corylopsis glabrescens Fragrant winter hazel	5–8
Corylus avellana 'Contorta' Harry Lauder's walkingstick	5–9
Cytisus scoparius Scotch broom	5–9
Daphne odora Winter daphne	8–10
Enkianthus campanulatus Redvein enkianthus	5–9
Euonymus alata Burning-bush	3–8
Euonymus fortunei Wintercreeper	4–10
Fothergilla major Large fothergilla	4–9
Hamamelis spp. Witch hazel	4–8
Hypericum prolificum Shrubby St. John's wort	4–9
Ilex crenata 'Helleri' Heller Japanese holly	5–10
Jasminum nudiflorum Winter jasmine	6–10
Juniperus spp. Juniper	2–10
Leucothoe fontanesiana Drooping leucothoe	4–8
Myrica pensylvanica Bayberry	2–7
Nandina domestica 'Harbour Dwarf' Dwarf heavenly-bamboo	7–10
Phyllostachys nigra Black bamboo	7–10
Pieris japonica Lily-of-the-valley shrub	5–9
Pinus strobus 'Nana' Dwarf eastern white pine	4–8
Potentilla fruticosa Bush cinquefoil	2–8
Rhododendron spp. Rhododendron, azalea	2–10
Taxus baccata 'Repandens' Weeping English yew	6–8
Yucca filamentosa Adam's-needle	5–10

Ground Covers

Ajuga reptans Carpet-bugle	4–10
Arctostaphylos uva-ursi Bearberry	2–9
Asarum canadense Snakeroot	3–8

Athyrium spp.
Japanese painted fern 2–8

Bergenia spp.
Bergenia 3–9

Calluna vulgaris
Scotch heather 4–9

Ceratostigma plumbaginoides
Blue plumbago 5–10

Cotoneaster dammeri
Bearberry cotoneaster 6–9

Dryopteris spp.
Wood fern 3–8

Epimedium grandiflorum
Bishop's-hat 3–8

Festuca ovina var. *glauca*
Blue fescue 3–10

Galium odoratum
Sweet woodruff 4–9

Hedera helix
English ivy 5–10

Hosta spp.
Plantain lily 3–9

Juniperus spp.
Juniper 2–10

Liriope muscari
Lilyturf 6–10

Onoclea sensibilis
Sensitive fern 5–8

Osmunda cinnamomea
Cinnamon fern 3–8

Osmunda regalis
Royal fern 3–10

Thymus praecox arcticus
Creeping thyme 3–10

Perennials

Achillea spp.
Yarrow 3–9

Aruncus dioicus
Goatsbeard 4–9

Asclepias tuberosa
Butterfly weed 3–9

Aster spp.
Hardy aster 3–9

Astilbe spp.
False-spirea 4–8

Chrysanthemum spp.
Chrysanthemum 5–10

Coreopsis verticillata
Threadleaf tickseed 3–9

Dicentra spectabilis
Bleedingheart 2–8

Echinacea purpurea
Purple coneflower 3–9

Gaillardia × *grandiflora*
Blanket-flower 3–10

Geranium spp.
Cranesbill 3–10

Hemerocallis spp.
Daylily 3–10

Heuchera sanguinea
Coralbells 3–10

Iberis sempervirens
Evergreen candytuft 4–10

Iris spp.
Iris 3–10

Liatris spicata
Spike gayfeather 3–10

Ligularia dentata
Bigleaf ligularia 4–10

Limonium latifolium
Sea-lavender 3–9

Lythrum salicaria
Purple loosestrife 3–9

Miscanthus sinensis
Japanese silvergrass 5–9

Molina caerulea
Moorgrass 5–8

Ophiopogon japonicus
Mondograss 5–10

Opuntia humifusa
Prickly pear cactus 5–10

Paeonia hybrids
Herbaceous peony 5–9

Pennisetum alopecuroides
Rose fountaingrass 6–9

Polygonatum commutatum
Great Solomon's-seal 4–8

Primula spp.
Primrose 3–9

Rodgersia aesculifolia
Rodgersia 4–9

Rudbeckia hirta
Black-eyed-susan 3–10

Salvia spp.
Sage 4–10

Sedum spp.
Stonecrop 3–10

Tiarella cordifolia
Foamflower 4–8

Tradescantia × *andersoniana*
Spiderwort 4–10

Veronica spp.
Speedwell 3–9

The plantings flanking this stream and waterfall realistically reproduce nature on a small scale.

Japanese Garden

As modern life becomes increasingly chaotic, it is not surprising that the Japanese garden—a peaceful sanctuary for contemplating nature—has strong appeal. Be aware that all aspects of creating a Japanese-style garden, including plant selection, require more deliberation and planning than is necessary for most other garden styles.

When choosing plants for a Japanese-style garden, pay close attention to size, shape, texture, and color. The predominant colors in a Japanese garden are various shades of green; reds, yellows, and other vivid colors are used sparingly as accents and to show the changing of seasons. The plant listings below include many traditional Japanese favorites as well as suitable plants from other parts of the world.

The dramatic blooms of Rhododendron *species (rhododendron) provide a seasonal accent in a Japanese garden.*

TREES

Acer ginnala Amur maple	2–8
Acer palmatum Japanese maple	6–10
Amelanchier canadensis Shadblow	4–8
Chamaecyparis obtusa Hinoki cypress	5–9
Cornus florida Flowering dogwood	5–9
Cryptomeria japonica Japanese cedar	5–9
Diospyros kaki Japanese persimmon	7–9
Ginkgo biloba Maidenhair tree	4–9
Koelreuteria paniculata Goldenrain tree	5–9
Pinus thunbergiana Japanese black pine	4–8
Prunus cerasifera Cherry plum	4–8
Prunus serrulata Japanese flowering cherry	5–9
Tsuga canadensis Canada hemlock	3–8

SHRUBS

Acer palmatum 'Dissectum' Cutleaf Japanese maple	6–10
Aucuba japonica Japanese aucuba	6–10
Buxus microphylla Littleleaf boxwood	6–10
Camellia japonica Japanese camellia	7–10
Cercis chinensis Chinese redbud	6–9
Chaenomeles hybrids Flowering quince	4–9
Daphne cneorum Garland-flower	4–7
Forsythia × intermedia Border forsythia	5–9
Ilex crenata Japanese holly	5–10
Juniperus chinensis 'Armstrongii' Armstrong juniper	4–10
Magnolia stellata Star magnolia	5–10
Mahonia bealei Leatherleaf mahonia	6–10
Nandina domestica Heavenly-bamboo	7–10
Pieris japonica Lily-of-the-valley shrub	5–9
Pinus mugo var. *mugo* 'Compacta' Mugo pine	2–8
Pittosporum tobira Japanese pittosporum	9, 10
Rhododendron, Knap Hill-Exbury hybrids Knap Hill-Exbury hybrid azaleas	6–8
Rhododendron, Kurume hybrids Kurume hybrid azaleas	7–10
Spiraea × bumalda Bumald spirea	4–10
Thuja occidentalis 'Globosa' Tom Thumb arborvitae	3–8
Viburnum davidii David viburnum	8–10

VINES

Clematis armandii
Evergreen clematis   7–10

Hydrangea anomala petiolaris
Climbing hydrangea   5–9

Ipomoea alba
Moonflower vine   9, 10

Parthenocissus tricuspidata
Boston ivy   5–8

Wisteria floribunda
Japanese wisteria   4–9

GROUND COVERS

Abelia × *grandiflora* 'Prostrata'
Prostrate glossy abelia   5–10

Arctostaphylos uva-ursi
Bearberry   2–9

Asarum caudatum
Wild-ginger   4–8

Epimedium grandiflorum
Bishop's-hat   3–8

Galax urceolata
Wandflower   3–6

Iberis sempervirens
Evergreen candytuft   4–10

Juniperus horizontalis 'Wiltonii'
Blue rug juniper   3–10

Mentha requienii
Corsican mint   6–10

Ophiopogon japonicus
Mondograss   5–10

Pachysandra terminalis
Japanese spurge   3–10

Sagina subulata
Irish moss   4–10

Sarcococca hookerana var. *humilis*
Sweetbox   5–9

Soleirolia soleirolii
Babytears   8–10

Thymus praecox arcticus
Creeping thyme   3–10

Zoysia tenuifolia
Korean velvetgrass   6–10

PERENNIALS

Anemone × *hybrida*
Japanese anemone   6–9

Arisaema triphyllum
Jack-in-the-pulpit   4–9

Aster × *frikartii*
Michaelmas daisy   4–8

Astilbe spp.
False-spirea   4–8

Chrysanthemum × *morifolium*
Florist's chrysanthemum   5–9

Galanthus nivalis
Common snowdrop   2–9

Helleborus niger
Christmas-rose   3–8

Hemerocallis fulva
Tawny daylily   2–10

Hosta ventricosa
Blue plantain lily   3–9

Paeonia hybrids
Herbaceous peony   5–9

Platycodon grandiflorus
Balloon-flower   3–9

Trillium erectum
Purple trillium   3–8

FERNS

Adiantum pedatum
Maidenhair fern   3–10

Athyrium filix-femina
Lady fern   3–10

Cyrtomium falcatum
Holly fern   9, 10

Polypodium virginianum
American wall fern   3–8

Polystichum acrostichoides
Christmas fern   3–8

BAMBOOS AND OTHER GRASSES

Arundinaria pygmaea
Pygmy bamboo   7–10

Arundinaria simonii
Simon bamboo   7–10

Bambusa glaucescens 'Fernleaf'
Fernleaf hedge bamboo   8–10

Bambusa glaucescens 'Golden Goddess'
Golden-goddess bamboo   8–10

Pennisetum setaceum
Crimson fountaingrass   8–10

Phyllostachys aureosulcata
Yellow-groove bamboo   5–10

Phyllostachys nigra
Black bamboo   7–10

Sasa veitchii
Kuma bamboograss   8–10

Shibataea kumasaca
Bamboo   8–10

WATER AND WATER'S-EDGE PLANTS

Acorus gramineus
Grassyleaf sweet flag   6–10

Cyperus isocladus
Dwarf papyrus   9, 10

Iris kaempferi
Japanese iris   4–9

Nelumbo nucifera
Sacred lotus   *

Nymphaea spp. and cvs.
Waterlily   3–10

* Hardy anywhere submerged rhizomes will
not freeze.

Herb Garden

Tradition has dictated that herbs be planted in a separate garden, either following a formal pattern or a casual arrangement. Formal herb gardens, which originated in the Middle Ages, often feature geometric planting patterns called parterres. Informal herb gardens rely heavily on rambling herbs. Whichever type of herb garden you plant, be sure to include a place to sit among the plants and enjoy their fragrances and beauty.

Although herbs are often associated only with the kitchen, they actually include any plants whose leaves, flowers, seeds, roots, bark, or other parts are used for flavor, fragrance, medicine, cosmetic, or dye. Many of the herbs grown today as ornamentals, such as hollyhock (*Alcea rosea*) and lily-of-the-valley (*Convallaria majalis*), were originally valued for medicinal and other uses. The following lists suggest herbs that fulfill special functions in the modern garden.

Foeniculum vulgare
(fennel), a popular
culinary herb, grows
3 to 5 feet tall.

Angelica spp.	
Angelica	4–8
Anthriscus cerefolium	
Chervil	Annual
Artemisia dracunculus var. *sativa*	
Tarragon	5–10
Borago officinalis	
Borage	Annual
Carum carvi	
Caraway	Annual
Coriandrum sativum	
Coriander	Annual
Cuminum cyminum	
Cumin	Annual
Cymbopogon citratus	
Lemongrass	10
Foeniculum vulgare	
Fennel	7–9
Laurus nobilis	
Bay	9, 10
Mentha spp.	
Mint	3–10
Ocimum basilicum	
Basil	Annual
Origanum majorana	
Marjoram	Annual
Origanum vulgare	
Oregano	3–9
Petroselinum crispum	
Parsley	3–10
Poterium sanguisorba	
Burnet	3–10
Rosmarinus officinalis	
Rosemary	7–10
Salvia officinalis	
Sage	4–10
Satureja hortensis	
Summer savory	Annual
Tropaeolum majus	
Nasturtium	Annual

CULINARY HERBS

Allium schoenoprasum	
Chives	3–9
Anethum graveolens	
Dill	Annual

HERBS FOR FRAGRANCE

Achillea millefolium	
Common yarrow	3–10
Aloysia triphylla	
Lemon-verbena	8–10

Chamaemelum nobile Chamomile	7–10
Convallaria majalis Lily-of-the-valley	2–8
Galium odoratum Sweet woodruff	4–9
Gardenia jasminoides Gardenia	8–10
Heliotropium arborescens Heliotrope	Annual
Jasminum spp. Jasmine	6–10
Lavandula spp. Lavender	5–10
Melissa officinalis Lemonbalm	4–8
Mentha spp. Mint	3–10
Monarda didyma Beebalm	4–10
Myrica pensylvanica Bayberry	2–7
Myrrhis odorata Sweet cicely	4–10
Osmanthus fragrans Sweet olive	8–10
Pelargonium spp. Scented geranium	9, 10
Rosa spp. Rose	2–10
Rosmarinus officinalis Rosemary	7–10
Salvia spp. Sage	4–10
Thymus spp. Thyme	3–9
Viola odorata Sweet violet	6–10

FLOWERING HERBS

Many herbs should be harvested before they flower, but these can be grown for their flowers. Many of these flowers are suitable for cutting.

Achillea millefolium Common yarrow	3–10
Alcea rosea Hollyhock	3–10
Allium schoenoprasum Chives	3–9
Angelica spp. Angelica	4–8
Aquilegia spp. Columbine	3–9

Calendula officinalis Pot marigold	Annual
Carthamus tinctorius Safflower	Annual
Chamaemelum nobile Chamomile	7–10
Chrysanthemum coronarium Crown daisy	Annual
Colchicum autumnale Autumn-crocus	5–9
Consolida ambigua Rocket-larkspur	Annual
Convallaria majalis Lily-of-the-valley	2–8
Delphinium elatum Larkspur	3–9
Dianthus spp. Carnation, pink	3–10
Digitalis purpurea Foxglove	4–10
Heliotropium arborescens Heliotrope	Annual
Lavandula spp. Lavender	5–10
Rosa spp. Rose	2–10
Rosmarinus officinalis Rosemary	7–10
Solidago odora Sweet goldenrod	3–9
Viola odorata Sweet violet	6–10

The spiky blooms of Lavandula species (lavender) are among the most ornamental and aromatic of all herbs.

HERBS FOR GROUND COVERS

Ajuga reptans
Carpet-bugle   4–10

Chamaemelum nobile
Chamomile   7–10

Convallaria majalis
Lily-of-the-valley   2–8

Galium odoratum
Sweet woodruff   4–9

Gaultheria procumbens
Creeping wintergreen   4–10

Hypericum spp.
St. John's wort   5–9

Mentha spp.
Mint   3–10

Nepeta mussinii
Persian catmint   4–10

Rosmarinus officinalis
Rosemary   7–10

Santolina spp.
Lavender-cotton   6–10

Stachys byzantina
Woolly lamb's-ears   4–10

Rosmarinus officinalis *(rosemary) can be used as an informal hedge, or it can be sheared into a formal hedge.*

Teucrium chamaedrys
Germander   3–9

Thymus praecox arcticus
Creeping thyme   3–10

Trachelospermum jasminoides
Starjasmine   8–10

Viola odorata
Sweet violet   6–10

HERBS FOR LOW BORDERS AND EDGINGS

Allium schoenoprasum
Chives   3–9

Buxus spp.
Boxwood   4–10

Chamaemelum nobile
Chamomile   7–10

Hyssopus officinalis
Hyssop   5–10

Ocimum basilicum
Basil   Annual

Petroselinum crispum
Parsley   3–10

Rosmarinus officinalis 'Prostratus'
Dwarf rosemary   8–10

Salvia officinalis
Sage   4–10

Santolina spp.
Lavender-cotton   6–10

Satureja montana
Winter savory   4–9

Thymus spp.
Thyme   3–9

HERBS FOR HEDGES

Angelica spp.
Angelica   4–8

Buxus spp.
Boxwood   4–10

Chrysanthemum balsamita
Costmary   4–10

Hyssopus officinalis
Hyssop   5–10

Levisticum officinale
Lovage   5–7

Monarda didyma
Beebalm   4–10

Origanum vulgare
Oregano   3–9

Rosa eglanteria
Sweetbrier rose   4–10

Rosmarinus officinalis
Rosemary   7–10

Salvia elegans
Pineapple sage   9, 10

Tanacetum vulgare
Tansy   3–10

Teucrium chamaedrys
Germander   3–9

Dry-Climate Garden

As water becomes an increasingly scarce commodity in many parts of the United States, gardeners are choosing plants on the basis of drought hardiness. Until fairly recently, nursery stock was limited almost exclusively to thirsty plants adapted to rainy climates. Now the choice is expanding rapidly as nurseries respond to the demand for plants that require less water. The good news is that you don't have to give up color and variety to garden in a dry climate; water-conserving plants are available to fulfill every garden function.

All the plants listed below will thrive with little or no irrigation once they are established. Many appear on lists elsewhere in the book; check the index, which begins on page 99, to discover other purposes a water-conserving plant may serve in the garden.

FLOWERS

Achillea filipendulina
Fernleaf yarrow — 3–10

Anthemis tinctoria
Golden marguerite — 3–10

Arctotis hybrids
African daisy — 9, 10

Armeria maritima
Sea-pink — 2–10

Asclepias tuberosa
Butterfly weed — 3–10

Aurinia saxatilis
Basket-of-gold — 3–10

Baptisia australis
False-indigo — 4–10

Calendula officinalis
Pot marigold — Annual

Catharanthus roseus
Madagascar periwinkle — Annual

Centaurea cineraria
Dusty-miller — 5–10

Centaurea cyanus
Bachelor's-button — Annual

Ceratostigma plumbaginoides
Blue plumbago — 5–10

Convolvulus tricolor
Dwarf morning glory — Annual

Coreopsis tinctoria
Calliopsis — Annual

Cosmos bipinnatus
Cosmos — Annual

Dietes vegeta
Fortnight-lily — 8–10

Dimorphotheca sinuata
Cape marigold — Annual

Erigeron karvinskianus
Fleabane — 8–10

Eschscholzia californica
California poppy — Annual

Euphorbia marginata
Snow-on-the-mountain — Annual

Gaillardia × *grandiflora*
Blanket-flower — 3–10

Gomphrena globosa
Globe amaranth — Annual

Helianthemum nummularium
Sunrose — 5–10

Hemerocallis hybrids
Daylily — 3–10

Kniphofia uvaria
Red-hot-poker — 6–10

Liatris spicata
Spike gayfeather — 3–10

Limonium perezii
Sea-lavender — 9, 10

Lobularia maritima
Sweet alyssum — Annual

Lychnis coronaria
Rose campion — 3–10

Mirabilis jalapa
Four-o'clock — Annual

Nierembergia hippomanica var. *violacea*
Dwarf cupflower — 7–10

Penstemon heterophyllus purdyi
Penstemon — 6–10

Portulaca grandiflora
Rose-moss — Annual

Sanvitalia procumbens
Creeping zinnia — Annual

Stachys byzantina
Woolly lamb's-ears — 4–10

Tithonia rotundifolia
Mexican sunflower — Annual

Low-growing Arctostaphylos *species (manzanita) takes the place of a lawn.*

TREES

Acacia spp.
Acacia　　　　　　　　　　　8–10

Acer saccharinum
Silver maple　　　　　　　　3–8

Ailanthus altissima
Tree-of-heaven　　　　　　　4–9

Albizia julibrissin
Silk tree　　　　　　　　　　7–10

Alnus cordata
Italian alder　　　　　　　　5–10

Acacia pendula
(weeping acacia),
which grows to about
25 feet high, makes a
striking addition to a
warm-winter garden.

Arbutus unedo
Strawberry tree　　　　　　8–10

Brachychiton populneus
Bottle tree　　　　　　　　　9, 10

Calocedrus decurrens
Incense cedar　　　　　　　6–9

Casuarina stricta
Beefwood　　　　　　　　　9, 10

Catalpa spp.
Catalpa　　　　　　　　　　5–10

Cedrus spp.
Cedar　　　　　　　　　　　5–9

Celtis spp.
Hackberry　　　　　　　　　2–9

Ceratonia siliqua
Carob　　　　　　　　　　　9, 10

Cercidium spp.
Paloverde　　　　　　　　　8–10

Cupressus spp.
Cypress　　　　　　　　　　6–10

Diospyros kaki
Japanese persimmon　　　　7–9

Elaeagnus angustifolia
Russian olive　　　　　　　2–8

Eriobotrya japonica
Loquat　　　　　　　　　　8–10

Eucalyptus spp.
Eucalyptus　　　　　　　　7–10

Geijera parviflora
Australian willow　　　　　8–10

Ginkgo biloba
Maidenhair tree　　　　　　4–9

Gleditsia triacanthos var. *inermis*
Thornless honeylocust　　　4–9

Grevillea robusta
Silk-oak　　　　　　　　　　10

Hakea laurina
Pincushion tree　　　　　　9, 10

Koelreuteria bipinnata
Chinese flame tree　　　　　5–9

Koelreuteria paniculata
Goldenrain tree　　　　　　5–9

Lagerstroemia indica
Crape myrtle　　　　　　　7–10

Leptospermum laevigatum
Australian tea tree　　　　9, 10

Ligustrum lucidum
Glossy privet　　　　　　　8–10

Liquidambar styraciflua
Sweet gum　　　　　　　　5–9

Maclura pomifera
Osage orange　　　　　　　4–9

Melaleuca spp.
Melaleuca　　　　　　　　9, 10

Melia azedarach
Chinaberry　　　　　　　　7–10

Olea europea
Olive　　　　　　　　　　　9, 10

Parkinsonia aculeata
Mexican paloverde　　　　8–10

Pinus pinea
Italian stone pine　　　　　7–10

Pistacia chinensis
Chinese pistachio　　　　　6–10

Podocarpus macrophyllus
Southern yew　　　　　　　9, 10

Prosopis spp.
Mesquite　　　　　　　　　7–10

Prunus cerasifera 'Atropurpurea'
Purpleleaf plum　　　　　　5–9

Quercus agrifolia
Coast live oak　　　　　　　9

Quercus ilex
Holly oak　　　　　　　　　7–10

Quercus suber
Cork oak　　　　　　　　　8–10

Rhus lancea
African sumac　　　　　　　8–10

Robinia pseudoacacia
Black locust　　　　　　　　3–9

Schinus spp.
Pepper tree　　　　　　　　9, 10

Sophora japonica
Japanese pagoda tree　　　4–10

Ziziphus jujuba
Chinese jujube　　　　　　6–10

PALMS

Arecastrum romanzoffianum
Queen palm   9, 10

Brahea armata
Mexican blue palm   8–10

Brahea edulis
Guadalupe fan palm   8–10

Chamaerops humilis
Mediterranean fan palm   8–10

Phoenix canariensis
Canary Island date palm   10

Trachycarpus fortunei
Windmill palm   8–10

Washingtonia spp.
Fan palm   9, 10

SHRUBS

Acacia longifolia
Sydney golden wattle   8–10

Atriplex spp.
Saltbush   5–8

Berberis spp.
Barberry   4–10

Caesalpinia spp.
Bird-of-paradise   9, 10

Callistemon citrinus
Lemon bottlebrush   8–10

Caragana arborescens 'Nana'
Dwarf Siberian peashrub   2–7

Cassia artemisiodes
Feathery cassia   9, 10

Ceanothus spp.
California wild-lilac   8–10

Cercis occidentalis
Western redbud   7–9

Cercocarpus spp.
Mountain mahogany   6–10

Cistus spp.
Rockrose   8–10

Cotoneaster spp.
Cotoneaster   3–10

Cytisus spp.
Broom   5–10

Dodonaea viscosa
Hopbush   8–10

Elaeagnus pungens
Silverberry   7–10

Fallugia paradoxa
Apache-plume   6–10

Feijoa sellowiana
Pineapple guava   8–10

Forestiera neomexicana
Desert-olive   5–10

Grevillea spp.
Grevillea   8–10

Heteromeles arbutifolia
Toyon   8–10

Juniperus spp.
Juniper   2–10

Lavandula spp.
Lavender   5–10

Leptospermum scoparium 'Ruby Glow'
New Zealand tea tree   9, 10

Lonicera tatarica
Tatarian honeysuckle   3–9

Mahonia spp.
Oregon grape   5–10

Myrtus communis
Myrtle   8–10

Nandina domestica
Heavenly-bamboo   7–10

Nerium oleander
Oleander   9, 10

Opuntia spp.
Prickly pear, cholla   5–10

Osmanthus spp.
Sweet olive   3–10

Philadelphus coronarius
Sweet mock orange   5–8

Pittosporum phillyraeoides
Willow pittosporum   9, 10

Podocarpus macrophyllus var. *maki*
Shrubby-yew   9, 10

Prunus caroliniana
Cherry-laurel   7–10

Prunus lusitanica
Portugal laurel   7–10

Punica granatum 'Nana'
Dwarf pomegranate   8–10

Pyracantha coccinea
Firethorn   6–10

Raphiolepis spp.
Indian-hawthorn   7–10

Rhus typhina
Staghorn sumac   3–9

Salvia spp.
Sage   4–10

The bright red blooms of Callistemon citrinus *(lemon bottlebrush) attract hummingbirds.*

Santolina spp. Lavender-cotton	6-10
Shepherdia argentea Silver buffaloberry	2-6
Syringa vulgaris Common lilac	3-8
Tamarix spp. Tamarisk	2-10
Viburnum prunifolium Blackhaw	4-9
Yucca filamentosa Adam's-needle	5-10
Yucca glauca Soapweed	4-10
Xylosma congestum Shiny xylosma	8-10

VINES

Antigonon leptopus Queen's-wreath	9, 10
Bougainvillea spp. Bougainvillea	9, 10
Clytostoma callistegioides Lavender trumpetvine	9, 10
Distictis buccinatoria Bloodred trumpetvine	9, 10
Gelsemium sempervirens Carolina jessamine	7-10
Lonicera japonica 'Halliana' Hall's honeysuckle	4-10
Macfadyena unguis-cati Catsclaw	8-10
Polygonum aubertii Silver-lace vine	4-8
Rosa banksiae Lady Banks rose	8-10
Solanum jasminoides Potato vine	8-10
Tecomaria capensis Cape honeysuckle	9, 10
Vitis spp. Grape	5-10
Wisteria spp. Wisteria	4-9

Gelsemium sempervirens *(Carolina jessamine) can be grown as a vine or allowed to sprawl as a ground cover.*

GROUND COVERS

Achillea tomentosa Woolly yarrow	3-10
Aegopodium podagraria Bishop's-weed	3-9
Antennaria rosea Pink-pussytoes	4-10
Arctostaphylos uva-ursi Bearberry	2-9
Artemisia schmidtiana Silver mound	4-10
Baccharis pilularis Dwarf coyotebrush	7-10
Carpobrotus spp. Ice plant	9, 10
Cerastium tomentosum Snow-in-summer	3-10
Coprosma × *kirkii* Coprosma	8-10
Coronilla varia Crown vetch	3-8
Cotoneaster dammeri Bearberry cotoneaster	6-9
Cotoneaster horizontalis Rock cotoneaster	5-9
Delosperma spp. Ice plant	9, 10
Drosanthemum floribundum Rosea ice plant	9, 10
Gazania rigens var. *leucolaena* Trailing gazania	9, 10
Helianthemum nummularium Sunrose	5-10
Hypericum calycinum St. John's wort	5-10
Juniperus spp. Juniper	2-10
Lampranthus spp. Ice plant	9, 10
Lantana montevidensis Trailing lantana	8-10
Mahonia repens Creeping mahonia	5-10
Osteospermum fruticosum Trailing African daisy	9, 10
Phalaris arundinacea var. *picta* Ribbongrass	5-10
Phlox subulata Moss-pink	2-9
Phyla nodiflora Lippia	9, 10
Rosmarinus officinalis 'Prostratus' Dwarf rosemary	8-10
Sedum spp. Stonecrop	3-10
Teucrium chamaedrys Germander	3-9
Thymus spp. Thyme	3-9
Verbena peruviana Peruvian verbena	9, 10

Rose Garden

Among the most popularly cultivated plants in the United States, roses are available in an astonishing variety of forms and colors. For centuries they have been enjoyed for their fragrance and beauty. Although roses are often grown among other plants, traditionally they were allocated a site of their own. When roses are collected in a separate garden, they seem even lovelier and more impressive than when intermingled with other plantings. The impact they make and the emotions they stir are also heightened in a separate garden. On the practical side, maintenance is easier when the roses are grouped in one place.

In these lists, botanical names are given for species roses only. For modern roses as well as old garden roses, common names or cultivar names are provided. These are the names under which the roses are sold. The lists don't contain zone information, since roses can be grown in any zone as long as they receive protection in areas beyond their hardiness range. A local nursery or rose society will be able to advise you on the appropriate protection for your area.

Key to Abbreviations

Climbing rose	Cl
Floribunda	F
Grandiflora	Gr
Hybrid tea	HT
Miniature rose	M
Modern shrub rose	MS
Old garden rose	OGR
Polyantha	Pol
Species rose	Sp

APPEARANCE

The following lists will help you choose roses by flower color.

Roses by Color

Red

'Beauty Secret'	M
'Black Jade'	M
'Blaze'	Cl
'Christian Dior'	HT
'Chrysler Imperial'	HT
'Crimson Glory'	HT
'Don Juan'	Cl
'Dortmund'	MS
'Europeana'	F
'Eyepaint'	F
'Ferdinand Pichard'	OGR
'General Jacqueminot'	OGR
'Loving Memory'	HT
'Mister Lincoln'	HT
'Olympiad'	HT
'Papa Meilland'	HT
'Paul's Scarlet Climber'	Cl
'Precious Platinum'	HT
'Red Cascade'	M
Rosa moyesii	Sp
'Scarlet Knight'	Gr
'Showbiz'	F
'Swarthmore'	HT
'Uncle Joe'	HT

Hybrid tea 'Perfume Delight' has a heavy, spicy fragrance.

Pink

'Autumn Damask'	OGR
'Betty Prior'	F
'Bewitched'	HT
'Captain Harry Stebbings'	HT
'Century Two'	HT
'Cherish'	F
'Communis'	OGR
'Confidence'	HT
'Constance Spry'	MS
'Duchesse de Brabant'	OGR
'Duet'	HT
'Elizabeth Taylor'	HT
'First Prize'	HT
'Frau Dagmar Hartopp'	MS
'Honorine de Brabant'	OGR
'Jennifer'	M
'Kathleen'	MS
'Keepsake'	HT
'Königin von Dänemark'	OGR
'Marijke Koopman'	HT

'Meidomonac' ('Bonica '82')	MS
'Minnie Pearl'	M
'New Dawn'	Cl
'Old Blush'	OGR
'Perfume Delight'	HT
'Pink Grootendoorst'	MS
'Pink Parfait'	Gr
'Princesse de Monaco'	HT
'Queen Elizabeth'	Gr
Rosa eglanteria	Sp
'Royal Highness'	HT
'Salet'	OGR
'Sexy Rexy'	F
'Silver Jubilee'	HT
'Simplicity'	F
'Sparrieshoop'	MS
'Sweet Surrender'	HT
'The Fairy'	Pol
'Tiffany'	HT
'Touch of Class'	HT

Lavender to Purple

'Angel Face'	F
'Blue Nile'	HT
'Deep Purple'	F
'Intrigue'	F
'Lavender Lace'	M
'Madame Violet'	HT
'Paradise'	HT
'Plum Crazy'	HT
'Reine des Violettes'	OGR
Rosa rugosa	Sp
'Silverado'	HT
'Wise Portia'	MS

The strongly fragrant grandiflora 'Arizona' can be planted as a hedge.

Yellow

'Frühlingsgold'	OGR
'Golden Showers'	Cl
'Golden Wings'	MS
'Gold Medal'	Gr
'Harison's Yellow'	OGR
'Mermaid'	OGR
'Rise 'n' Shine'	M
Rosa hugonis	Sp
'Sunblest'	HT
'Sunny June'	MS
'Sunsprite'	F
'Sutter's Gold'	HT

Orange-Red and Orange to Gold

'Anabell'	F
'Arizona'	Gr
'Baby Darling'	M
'Cary Grant'	HT
'Dolly Parton'	HT
'First Edition'	F
'Folklore'	HT
'Fragrant Cloud'	HT
'Fred Loads'	Cl
'Jean Kenneally'	M
'Lady Rose'	HT
'Marina'	F
'Prominent'	Gr
'Shreveport'	Gr
'Tropicana'	HT

White to Cream

'Blanc Double de Coubert'	MS
'Félicité et Perpétué'	OGR
'Garden Party'	HT
'Iceberg'	F
'Madame Hardy'	OGR
'Maid of Honour'	HT
'Nevada'	MS
'Pascali'	HT
'Pristine'	HT
Rosa banksiae	Sp
Rosa laevigata	Sp
Rosa spinosissima	Sp
Rosa wichuraiana	Sp
'Snow Bride'	M
'Sombreuil'	OGR
'Stanwell Perpetual'	OGR
'White Lightnin' '	Gr
'White Success'	HT

Bicolor and Multicolor

'Broadway'	HT
'Double Delight'	HT
'Double Perfection'	HT
'Flaming Beauty'	HT
'Granada'	HT
'Love'	Gr
'Magic Carrousel'	M
'Mon Cheri'	HT
'Osiria'	HT
'Peace'	HT
'Rainbow's End'	M
Rosa foetida 'Bicolor'	Sp
'Sonia'	Gr

SPECIAL USES IN THE GARDEN

The following lists will help you choose roses to serve specific functions in the garden.

Roses for Screens

'Blaze'	Cl
'Communis'	OGR
'Constance Spry'	MS
'Don Juan'	Cl
'Dortmund'	MS
'Félicité et Perpétué'	OGR
'Folklore'	HT
'Fred Loads'	Cl
'Frühlingsgold'	OGR
'Golden Showers'	Cl
'Harison's Yellow'	OGR
'Kathleen'	MS
'Mermaid'	OGR
'Nevada'	MS
'New Dawn'	Cl
'Paul's Scarlet Climber'	Cl
Rosa banksiae	Sp
Rosa eglanteria	Sp
Rosa foetida 'Bicolor'	Sp
Rosa hugonis	Sp
Rosa laevigata	Sp
Rosa moyesii	Sp
'Salet'	OGR
'Sombreuil'	OGR
'Sparrieshoop'	MS
'Stanwell Perpetual'	OGR

Roses for Hedges

'Arizona'	Gr
'Blanc Double de Coubert'	MS
'Duet'	HT
'Europeana'	F

Old garden rose 'Harison's Yellow' makes a floriferous screen during late spring.

'Eyepaint'	F
'Frau Dagmar Hartopp'	MS
'Golden Wings'	MS
'Iceberg'	F
'Madame Hardy'	OGR
'Meidomonac' ('Bonica '82')	MS
'Old Blush'	OGR
'Pink Grootendorst'	MS
'Queen Elizabeth'	Gr
Rosa rugosa	Sp
'Sexy Rexy'	F
'Showbiz'	F
'Simplicity'	F
'The Fairy'	Pol

Roses for Ground Covers

'Dortmund'	MS
'Félicité et Perpétué'	OGR
'Ferdinand Picard'	OGR
'New Dawn'	Cl
'Red Cascade'	M
Rosa laevigata	Sp
Rosa spinosissima	Sp
Rosa wichuraiana	Sp

Especially Fragrant Roses

'Angel Face'	F
'Arizona'	Gr
'Autumn Damask'	OGR
'Beauty Secret'	M
'Bewitched'	HT
'Blanc Double de Coubert'	MS
'Captain Harry Stebbings'	HT
'Chrysler Imperial'	HT*

Richly fragrant hybrid tea 'Granada' bears long-lasting blooms.

Communis'	OGR
'Confidence'	HT
'Crimson Glory'	HT*
'Dolly Parton'	HT
'Don Juan'	Cl
'Double Delight'	HT*
'Duchesse de Brabant'	OGR
'Folklore'	HT
'Fragrant Cloud'	HT*
'General Jacqueminot'	OGR
'Granada'	HT*
'Honorine de Brabant'	OGR
'Iceberg'	F
'Intrigue'	F
'Keepsake'	HT
'Königin von Dänemark'	OGR
'Madame Hardy'	OGR
'Papa Meilland'	HT*
'Perfume Delight'	HT
Rosa laevigata	Sp
Rosa rugosa	Sp
'Salet'	OGR
'Sombreuil'	OGR
'Sonia'	Gr
'Sunsprite'	F*
'Sutter's Gold'	HT*
'Sweet Surrender'	HT
'Tiffany'	HT*
'White Lightnin' '	Gr

* Winner of the James Alexander Gamble Rose Fragrance Medal awarded by the American Rose Society.

Long-Lasting Cut Roses

'Anabell'	F
'Arizona'	Gr
'Bewitched'	HT
'Blue Nile'	HT
'Captain Harry Stebbings'	HT
'Cary Grant'	HT
'Century Two'	HT
'Chrysler Imperial'	HT
'Double Delight'	HT
'Double Perfection'	HT
'First Edition'	F
'First Prize'	HT
'Flaming Beauty'	HT
'Folklore'	HT
'Garden Party'	HT
'Love'	Gr
'Madame Violet'	HT
'Maid of Honour'	HT
'Marina'	F
'Mister Lincoln'	HT
'Paradise'	HT
'Pascali'	HT
'Peace'	HT
'Precious Platinum'	HT
'Princesse de Monaco'	HT
'Prominent'	Gr
'Royal Highness'	HT
'Shreveport'	Gr
'Silverado'	HT
'Sonia'	Gr
'Sunblest'	HT
'Tiffany'	HT
'Touch of Class'	HT
'Tropicana'	HT
'Uncle Joe'	HT

CULTIVATION

The following lists will help you choose roses that are particularly easy to grow, hardy, or disease resistant.

Easiest Roses

'Beauty Secret'	M
'Betty Prior'	F
'Bewitched'	HT
'Blaze'	Cl
'Broadway'	HT
'Cherish'	F
'Dortmund'	MS
'Duet'	HT
'Europeana'	F

'First Prize'	HT
'Folklore'	HT
'Fragrant Cloud'	HT
'Garden Party'	HT
'Gold Medal'	Gr
'Harison's Yellow'	OGR
'Iceberg'	F
'Magic Carrousel'	M
'Meidomonac' ('Bonica '82')	MS
'Minnie Pearl'	M
'Mister Lincoln'	HT
'Pristine'	HT
'Queen Elizabeth'	Gr
'Rainbow's End'	M
'Rise 'n' Shine'	M
Rosa eglanteria	Sp
'Snow Bride'	M
'Tropicana'	HT

Hardiest Modern Roses *

'Baby Darling'	M
'Bewitched'	HT
'Black Jade'	M
'Blanc Double de Coubert'	MS
'Broadway'	HT
'Captain Harry Stebbings'	HT
'Christian Dior'	HT
'Crimson Glory'	HT
'Dortmund'	MS
'Europeana'	F
'Eyepaint'	F
'Folklore'	HT
'Frau Dagmar Hartopp'	MS
'Garden Party'	HT
'Golden Wings'	MS
'Gold Medal'	Gr
'Iceberg'	F
'Jean Kenneally'	M
'Jennifer'	M
'Kathleen'	MS
'Loving Memory'	HT
'Madame Violet'	HT
'Maid of Honour'	HT
'Marijke Koopman'	HT
'Meidomonac' ('Bonica '82')	MS
'Nevada'	MS
'Pink Grootendoorst'	MS
'Precious Platinum'	HT
'Sunblest'	HT
'Swarthmore'	HT
'Uncle Joe'	HT

* Most species and old garden roses are extremely hardy.

Most-Disease-Resistant Roses

'Broadway'	HT
'Confidence'	HT
'Dortmund'	MS
'First Prize'	HT
'Folklore'	HT
'Gold Medal'	Gr
'Keepsake'	HT
'Lady Rose'	HT
'Madame Violet'	HT
'Maid of Honour'	HT
'Marijke Koopman'	HT
'Meidomonac' ('Bonica '82')	MS
'Olympiad'	HT
'Osiria'	HT
'Pink Parfait'	Gr
'Precious Platinum'	HT
'Pristine'	HT
'Shreveport'	Gr
'Silver Jubilee'	HT
'Sunblest'	HT
'Uncle Joe'	HT
'White Success'	HT

Although its blooms are unscented, modern shrub rose 'Nevada' makes an attractive flowering screen or background planting.

Climate Zone Map

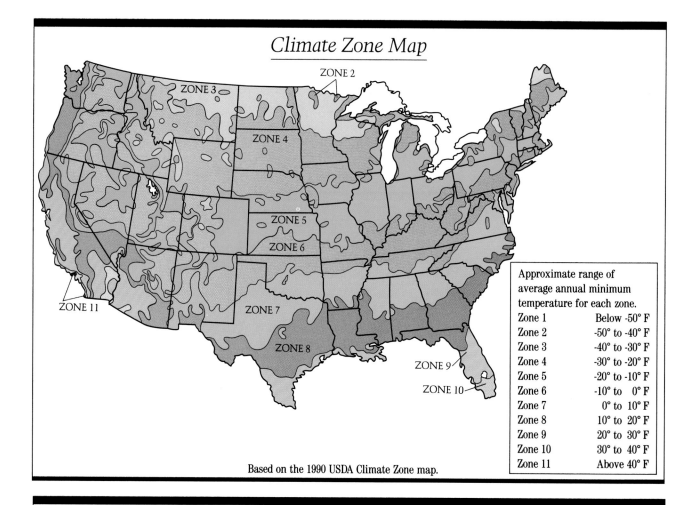

Approximate range of average annual minimum temperature for each zone.

Zone 1	Below -50° F
Zone 2	-50° to -40° F
Zone 3	-40° to -30° F
Zone 4	-30° to -20° F
Zone 5	-20° to -10° F
Zone 6	-10° to 0° F
Zone 7	0° to 10° F
Zone 8	10° to 20° F
Zone 9	20° to 30° F
Zone 10	30° to 40° F
Zone 11	Above 40° F

Based on the 1990 USDA Climate Zone map.

U.S. Measure and Metric Measure Conversion Chart

		Formulas for Exact Measures			Rounded Measures for Quick Reference		
	Symbol	When you know:	Multiply by:	To find:			
Mass (Weight)	oz	ounces	28.35	grams	1 oz		= 30 g
	lb	pounds	0.45	kilograms	4 oz		= 115 g
	g	grams	0.035	ounces	8 oz		= 225 g
	kg	kilograms	2.2	pounds	16 oz	= 1 lb	= 450 g
					32 oz	= 2 lb	= 900 g
					36 oz	= 2¼ lb	= 1000g (1 kg)
Volume	pt	pints	0.47	liters	1 c	= 8 oz	= 250 ml
	qt	quarts	0.95	liters	2 c (1 pt)	= 16 oz	= 500 ml
	gal	gallons	3.785	liters	4 c (1 qt)	= 32 oz	= 1 liter
	ml	milliliters	0.034	fluid ounces	4 qt (1 gal)	= 128 oz	= 3¾ liter
Length	in.	inches	2.54	centimeters	⅜ in.	= 1 cm	
	ft	feet	30.48	centimeters	1 in.	= 2.5 cm	
	yd	yards	0.9144	meters	2 in.	= 5 cm	
	mi	miles	1.609	kilometers	2½ in.	= 6.5 cm	
	km	kilometers	0.621	miles	12 in. (1 ft)	= 30 cm	
	m	meters	1.094	yards	1 yd	= 90 cm	
	cm	centimeters	0.39	inches	100 ft	= 30 m	
					1 mi	= 1.6 km	
Temperature	°F	Fahrenheit	5/9 (after subtracting 32)	Celsius	32°F	= 0°C	
	°C	Celsius	9/5 (then add 32)	Fahrenheit	212°F	= 100°C	
Area	in.²	square inches	6.452	square centimeters	1 in.²	= 6.5 cm²	
	ft²	square feet	929.0	square centimeters	1 ft²	= 930 cm²	
	yd²	square yards	8361.0	square centimeters	1 yd²	= 8360 cm²	
	a.	acres	0.4047	hectares	1 a.	= 4050 m²	

INDEX
Page numbers in italic type indicate references to illustrations.

A

Abelia × grandiflora
  attractive evergreen, 50
  for basic landscaping, 54
  easy maintenance, 58
  'Edward Goucher'
    for informal hedge, 56
    medium-height, 49
  for fall color, 51
  fast growing, 55
  for Japanese garden, 85
Abuse-tolerant trees, 47–48
Acacia spp.
  baileyana
    medium, broad, 37
    showy flowers, 41
    winter flowers, 42
  drought tolerant, 90
  fast growing, 43
  longifolia, drought tolerant, 91
  melanoxylon, abuse tolerant, 47
  pendula, 90
Acanthus mollis
  attractive foliage, 26
  for shady area, 31
  vertical form, 24
Acer spp.
  campestre
    for lawns, 44
    medium height, for shade, 42
    for screen or buffer, 44
  circinatum, for shady area, 46
  for city garden, 45
  for fall color, 39
  ginnala
    for fragrance, 45
    for Japanese garden, 84
    for lawns, 44
    small, for shade, 42
  for lawns, 44
  palmatum, *9, 46*
    for all-year color, 51
    for Japanese garden, 84
    for patio garden, 43
    for rock garden, 79
    for shady area, 46
    small, for shade, 42
    for water garden, 82
    for winter interest, 51
  palmatum 'Atropurpureum', *8*
  palmatum 'Dissectum'
    for Japanese garden, 84
    for winter interest, 51
  palmatum 'Dissectum Atropurpureum', *76–77*
    for all-year color, 51
  platanoides, for seacoast, 48
  platanoides 'Columnare', large, narrow upright, 39
  platanoides 'Crimson Sentry', small, narrow upright, 38
  rubrum
    large, for shade, 42
    for seacoast, 48
    for wall planting, 44
  rubrum 'Bowhall', medium, narrow upright, 39
  saccharinum
    drought tolerant, 90
    fast growing, 43
    flood tolerant, 48
    large, for shade, 42
  saccharum, *42*
    large, for shade, 42
  for winter silhouette, 40
Achillea spp., *10–11*
  filipendulina
    for cutting, 28
    for dried arrangements, 29

Achillea (continued)
  drought tolerant, 89
  tall, 24
  yellow-hued, summer flowers, 18
  heat tolerant, 31
  millefolium
    for herb garden, 86, 87
    medium height, 23
  ptarmica, white-hued, summer flowers, 20
  tomentosa
    drought tolerant, 92
    for rock garden, 80
    showy, summer flowers, 70
    traffic tolerant, 73
  for water garden, 83
Acorus spp.
  for Japanese garden, 85
  for water garden, 81
Actinidia arguta
  for arbor or patio cover, 67
  attractive foliage, 66
  for fragrance, 68
Adam's-needle. *See Yucca filamentosa*
Adiantum pedatum
  for Japanese garden, 85
  for shady area, 75
  tall, 69
Adlumia fungosa, for fast cover, 67
Aegopodium podagraria, *75*
  drought tolerant, 92
  lawn alternative, 72
  for wet soil, 75
Aesculus spp.
  × *carnea*, for city garden, 45
  glabra, medium, broad, 37
  parviflora (shrub)
    for city garden, 58
    easy maintenance, 58
  for shady area, 46
  showy, spring flowers, 41
Agapanthus spp.
  blue-hued, summer flowers, 16
  for containers, 27
  for cutting, 28
  for naturalizing, 32
  for shady area, 31
Ageratum houstonianum
  blue-hued, summer-to-fall flowers, 16, 17
  dwarf, 22
  for edging, 27
Agonis flexuosa, for wall planting, 44
Ailanthus altissima, drought tolerant, 90
Ajuga reptans
  easy maintenance, 74
  for herb garden, 88
  lawn alternative, 72
  low growing, 69
  showy, spring-to-summer flowers, 70
  for water garden, 82
Akebia quinata
  for arbor or patio cover, 67
  for attracting birds, 68
  attractive foliage, 66
  slope stabilizer, 71
Albizia julibrissin
  drought tolerant, 90
  fast growing, 43
  for lawns, 44
  medium, broad, 37
  showy, summer flowers, 41
Alcea rosea
  for herb garden, 87
  red-hued, fall-to-summer flowers, 13, 14
  tall, vertical form, 24
Alchemilla vulgaris, attractive foliage, 26
Alder. *See Alnus* spp.
Allamanda, pink. *See Mandevilla splendens*
Allamanda cathartica
  for fragrance, 68
  showy, spring-to-fall flowers, 65, 66
Allium schoenoprasum, for herb garden, 86, 87, 88

Allspice, Carolina. *See Calycanthus floridus*
Alnus spp.
  cordata, drought tolerant, 90
  fast growing, 43
  glutinosa, large, oval pyramidal, 38
  for winter silhouette, 40
Aloysia triphylla, for herb garden, 86
Amaranthus spp., *26*
  for attracting birds, 30
  attractive foliage, 26
Amelanchier spp.
  canadensis
    for attracting birds, 45
    for fall color, 39
    for Japanese garden, 84
    medium, oval pyramidal, 38
    for patio garden, 43
    showy fruit, 40
  laevis, small, for shade, 42
  for shady area, 46
  for water garden, 82
Ampelopsis spp.
  arborea
    attractive foliage, 66
    for fall color, 66
  brevipedunculata
    for attracting birds, 68
    for fall color, 66
Amsonia tabernaemontana
  attractive foliage, 26
  heat tolerant, 31
Anchusa spp.
  blue-hued, summer flowers, 16
  rounded form, 25
Anemone poppy. *See Anemone coronaria*
Anemone spp.
  blanda
    blue-hued, spring flowers, 15, 70
    dwarf, 22
    for naturalizing, 32
    showy flowers, 70
  coronaria
    for cutting, 28
    low growing, 22
    for rock garden, 80
  × *hybrida*
    for Japanese garden, 85
    for rock garden, 80
  for shady area, 31
Anethum graveolens, for herb garden, 86
Angelica spp., for herb garden, 86, 87, 88
Antennaria rosea, drought tolerant, 92
Anthemis tinctoria
  drought tolerant, 89
  yellow-hued, summer flowers, 18
Anthriscus cerefolium, for herb garden, 86
Antigonon leptopus
  for arbor or patio cover, 67
  drought tolerant, 92
  showy, fall-to-summer flowers, 66
Antirrhinum majus, *6*
  for containers, 27
  for cutting, 28
  medium height, 23
  red-hued flowers, 13, 15
  spring-to-fall flowers, 13, 15, 17, 18, 19, 20, 21
  vertical form, 24
  white-hued flowers, 19, 20, 21
  yellow-hued flowers, 17, 18, 19
Apache-plume. *See Fallugia paradoxa*
Aponogeton distachyus, for water garden, 81
Aquatic plants, 81, 85
Aquilegia spp.
  for attracting birds, 30
  for cool summers, 30
  for herb garden, 87
  medium height, 23
  open form, 25
  red-hued flowers, 13

Aquilegia (continued)
  for rock garden, 80
  for shady area, 31
  spring-to-summer flowers, 13, 17, 18, 20
  white-hued flowers, 20
  yellow-hued flowers, 17, 18
Arabis caucasica
  dwarf, 22
  for nooks and crannies, 73
  for rock garden, 80
  showy, spring-to-summer flowers, 70
Arbors, vines for, 67
Arborvitae. *See Thuja* spp.
Arbutus spp.
  menziesii
    for attracting birds, 45
    for bark interest, 39
  unedo
    for attracting birds, 45
    drought tolerant, 90
    showy fruit, 40
Arctostaphylos spp., *89*
  attractive evergreen, 50
  for seacoast, 61
  showy fruit, 52
  uva-ursi, *74*
    for attracting birds, 74
    for draping or trailing, 73
    drought tolerant, 92
    easy maintenance, 74
    for Japanese garden, 84
    lawn alternative, 72
    medium height, 69
    for rock garden, 79
    slope stabilizer, 71
    for water garden, 82
Arctotis hybrids, drought tolerant, 89
Arecastrum romanzoffianum, drought tolerant, 91
Arenaria balearica
  low growing, 69
  for rock garden, 80
  traffic tolerant, 73
Arisaema triphyllum, for Japanese garden, 85
Aristolochia durior
  for arbor or patio cover, 67
  attractive foliage, 66
  for shady area, 68
Armeria maritima, *73*
  for dried arrangements, 29
  drought tolerant, 89
  for edging, 27
  for naturalizing, 32
  for nooks and crannies, 73
  red-hued, spring-to-summer flowers, 13
  for rock garden, 80
Aronia arbutifolia
  for city garden, 58
  easy maintenance, 58
  showy fruit, 52
  for wet soil, 61
  for winter interest, 51
Arrowhead. *See Sagittaria latifolia*
Arrowwood. *See Viburnum dentatum*
Artemisia spp.
  attractive foliage, 26
  heat tolerant, 31
  for herb garden, 86
  schmidtiana
    drought tolerant, 92
    for rock garden, 80
Arum, arrow. *See Peltandra virginica*
Aruncus dioicus
  attractive foliage, 26
  heat tolerant, 31
  rounded form, 25
  for shady area, 31
  tall, 24
  for water garden, 83
  for wet soil, 33
  white-hued, summer-to-fall flowers, 20, 21
Arundinaria spp., for Japanese garden, 85

Asarina erubescens
for fast cover, 67
showy, summer flowers, 65
Asarum spp., *62–63*
canadense, for water garden, 82
caudatum, for Japanese garden, 85
for shady area, 75
for wet soil, 75
Asclepias tuberosa
for attracting birds, 30
for cutting, 28
drought tolerant, 89
heat tolerant, 31
for naturalizing, 32
tall, 24
for water garden, 83
yellow-hued, summer flowers, 18
Ash. *See Fraxinus* spp.
Aspen. *See Populus* spp.
Aster, China. *See Callistephus chinensis*
Aster, hardy. *See Aster* spp.
Aster, Stokes. *See Stokesia laevis*
Aster spp.
for attracting birds, 30
blue-hued flowers, 16, 17
for cutting, 28
× *frikartii*
for Japanese garden, 85
medium height, 23
novae-angliae
tall, 24
for wet soil, 33
red-hued flowers, 13, 15
summer-to-fall flowers, 13, 15, 16, 17, 20, 21
for water garden, 83
white-hued flowers, 20, 21
Astilbe spp., *22*
× *arendsii*
for cutting, 28
medium height, 23
for cool summers, 30
for Japanese garden, 85
red-hued flowers, 13
for shady area, 31
summer flowers, 13, 20
vertical form, 24
for water garden, 83
for wet soil, 33
white-hued flowers, 20
Athyrium spp.
filix-femina, for Japanese garden, 85
goeringianum, for shady area, 75
for water garden, 83
Atriplex spp., drought tolerant, 91
Aubrieta deltoidea, for rock garden, 80
Aucuba japonica
attractive evergreen, 50
for Japanese garden, 84
'Nana', low growing, 49
for shady area, 59
tall, 50
'Variegata', for all-year color, 51
Aurinia saxatilis
attractive foliage, 26
drought tolerant, 89
for edging, 27
low growing, 22
for nooks and crannies, 73
for rock garden, 80
showy flowers, 70
yellow-hued, spring-to-summer flowers, 17, 18, 70
Autumn-crocus. *See Colchicum autumnale*
Avens. *See Geum* spp.
Azalea. *See Rhododendron* spp.

B

Baby-blue-eyes. *See Nemophila menziesii*
Baby's breath. *See Gypsophila* spp.
Babytears. *See Soleirolia soleirolii*

Baccharis pilularis, 69
drought tolerant, 92
easy maintenance, 74
slope stabilizer, 71
tall, 69
Bachelor's-button. *See Centaurea cyanus*
Bald cypress. *See Taxodium distichum*
Balloon-flower. *See Platycodon* spp.
Balloon vine. *See Cardiospermum halicacabum*
Balsam-apple. *See Momordica balsamina*
Bamboo. *See Arundinaria* spp.; *Bambusa glaucescens*; *Phyllostachys* spp.; *Shibataea kumasaca*
Bamboograss, kuma. *See Sasa veitchii*
Bambusa glaucescens, for Japanese garden, 85
Banana-shrub. *See Michelia figo*
Baptisia australis
attractive foliage, 26
blue-hued, summer flowers, 16
drought tolerant, 89
heat tolerant, 31
for naturalizing, 32
tall, 24
Barberry. *See Berberis* spp.
Bark interest, trees with, 39
Barrier shrubs, 56–57
Barrier trees, 44
Basil. *See Ocimum basilicum*
Basketflower. *See Hymenocallis narcissiflora*
Basket-of-gold. *See Aurinia saxatilis*
Bauhinia spp.
for patio garden, 43
showy, fall-to-winter flowers, 41, 42
Bay. *See Laurus nobilis*
Bayberry. *See Myrica pensylvanica*
Bearberry. *See Arctostaphylos uva-ursi*
Beardtongue. *See Penstemon hartwegii*
Bear's-breech. *See Acanthus mollis*
Beaumontia grandiflora
for arbor or patio cover, 67
for fragrance, 68
showy, spring-to-summer flowers, 65
Beautybush. *See Kolkwitzia amabilis*
Beebalm. *See Monarda didyma*
Beech. *See Fagus* spp.
Beefwood. *See Casuarina cunninghamiana*
Begonia × *semperflorens-cultorum*
attractive foliage, 26
for containers, 27
for edging, 27
heat tolerant, 31
low growing, 22
red-hued flowers, 13, 15
for shady area, 32
summer-to-fall flowers, 13, 15, 20, 21
for wet soil, 33
white-hued flowers, 20, 21
Bellflower. *See Campanula* spp.
Bellflower, Chilean. *See Lapageria rosea*
Bellflower, Serbian. *See Campanula poscharskyana*
Bells-of-Ireland. *See Moluccella laevis*
Berberis spp.
for attracting birds, 57
for basic landscaping, 54
darwinii, showy fruit, 52
drought tolerant, 91
easy maintenance, 58
fast growing, 55
× *stenophylla* 'Corallina Compacta', for rock garden, 79
for thorny barrier, 56
thunbergii
for city garden, 58
for fall color, 51
for shearing, 60
showy fruit, 52

Berberis (continued)
thunbergii 'Atropurpurea'
for informal hedge, 56
for water garden, 82
thunbergii 'Crimson Pygmy'
for all-year color, 51
low growing, 49
Bergenia spp.
attractive foliage, 26
ciliata, white-hued, winter-to-spring flowers, 20, 22
cordifolia, red-hued, winter-to-spring flowers, 13, 15
low growing, 22
for shady area, 32, 75
for water garden, 83
Bethlehem-sage. *See Pulmonaria saccharata*
Betony, big. *See Stachys grandiflora*
Betula spp.
for fall color, 39
fast growing, 43
maximowicziana, for bark interest, 39
nigra
flood tolerant, 48
large, oval pyramidal, 38
pendula
for bark interest, 39
for water garden, 82
populifolia, medium, for shade, 42
for wall planting, 44
for winter silhouette, 40
Bird-of-paradise. *See Caesalpinia* spp.
Birds, plants for attracting
flowers, 30
ground covers, 74
shrubs, 57
trees, 45
vines, 68
Bishop's-hat. *See Epimedium grandiflorum*
Bishop's-weed. *See Aegopodium podagraria*
Bittersweet. *See Celastrus* spp.
Black-eyed-susan. *See Rudbeckia* spp.
Black-eyed-susan vine. *See Thunbergia alata*
Blackhaw. *See Viburnum prunifolium*
Black locust. *See Robinia pseudoacacia*
Blanket-flower. *See Gaillardia* spp.
Bleedingheart. *See Dicentra spectabilis*
Bluebell, Virginia. *See Mertensia virginica*
Bluebell-creeper, Australian. *See Sollya heterophylla*
Blueberry, highbush. *See Vaccinium corymbosum*
Blueflag. *See Iris versicolor*
Blue flowers, 15–17
Bluestar. *See Amsonia tabernaemontana*
Bluestar creeper. *See Laurentia fluviatilis*
Borago officinalis, for herb garden, 86
Borders, 6, 7, *10–11*
Botanical names, described, 7
Bottlebrush, lemon. *See Callistemon citrinus*
Bottle tree. *See Brachychiton populneus*
Bougainvillea spp., *67*
for arbor or patio cover, 67
drought tolerant, 92
showy, spring-to-summer flowers, 65
Box, Victorian. *See Pittosporum undulatum*
Boxwood. *See Buxus* spp.
Brachychiton populneus, drought tolerant, 90
Brachycome iberidifolia
for cool summers, 30
low growing, 22
open form, 25
Brahea spp., drought tolerant, 91

Brassica oleracea, Acephala group
attractive foliage, 26
for edging, 27
Broad-spreading trees, 37
Bronze-colored flowers, 17–19
Broom. *See Cytisus* spp.; *Genista* spp.
Browallia speciosa
blue-hued, summer-to-fall flowers, 16, 17
draping or trailing, 27
for edging, 27
low growing, 22
for shady area, 32
Brunnera macrophylla
heat tolerant, 31
low growing, 22
for shady area, 32
Buckeye. *See Aesculus* spp.
Buckthorn. *See Rhamnus* spp.
Buddleia davidii
for fragrance, 57
showy, summer flowers, 53
Buffaloberry, silver. *See Shepherdia argentea*
Buffers, trees for, 44
Bugbane. *See Cimicifuga racemosa*
Bugloss, Italian. *See Anchusa* spp.
Bugloss, Siberian. *See Brunnera macrophylla*
Bulrush, white. *See Scirpus albescens*
Burnet. *See Poterium sanguisorba*
Burning-bush. *See Euonymus alata*
Bush-cherry, Australian. *See Syzygium paniculatum*
Bush-violet. *See Browallia speciosa*
Busy-lizzie. *See Impatiens wallerana*
Butomus umbellatus, for water garden, 81
Butterfly-flower. *See Schizanthus* × *wisetonensis*
Butterfly-pea. *See Centrosema virginianum*
Butterfly weed. *See Asclepias tuberosa*
Buxus spp.
for attracting birds, 57
attractive evergreen, 50
for basic landscaping, 54
for herb garden, 88
microphylla, for Japanese garden, 84
sempervirens, for water garden, 82
for shearing, 60

C

Cabbage, ornamental. *See Brassica olereacea*
Cabomba caroliniana, for water garden, 81
Caesalpinia spp., drought tolerant, 91
Cajeput tree. *See Melaleuca quinquenervia*
Calendula officinalis
for attracting birds, 30
for cutting, 28
drought tolerant, 89
for herb garden, 87
rounded form, 25
yellow-hued, winter-to-summer flowers, 17, 18, 19
California poppy. *See Eschscholzia californica*
Calliopsis. *See Coreopsis tinctoria*
Callistemon citrinus, *91*
drought tolerant, 91
fast growing, 55
for seacoast, 61
showy, all-year flowers, 52, 53, 54
Callistephus chinensis
for attracting birds, 30
blue-hued flowers, 16, 17
red-hued flowers, 13, 15
rounded form, 25
summer-to-fall flowers, 13, 15, 16, 17, 20, 21
white-hued flowers, 20, 21

Calluna vulgaris
　for rock garden, 79
　showy, summer flowers, 53
　for water garden, 83
Calocedrus decurrens
　drought tolerant, 90
　for wall planting, 44
Caltha palustris
　for shady area, 32
　for water garden, 81
　for wet soil, 33
Calycanthus floridus
　easy maintenance, 58
　for fragrance, 57
　for shady area, 59
　for wet soil, 61
Camellia spp., *54*
　attractive evergreen, 50
　japonica
　　for basic landscaping, 54
　　for Japanese garden, 84
　　tall, 50
　for screen, 56
　for shady area, 59
　showy, fall-to-spring flowers, 52, 54
Campanula spp.
　blue-hued, spring-to-fall flowers, 15, 16, 17
　for draping or trailing, 73
　easy maintenance, 74
　medium, 17
　for shady area, 32
　for nooks and crannies, 74
　poscharskyana, dwarf, 22
　for rock garden, 80
Camphor tree. *See Cinnamomum camphora*
Campsis radicans
　for arbor or patio cover, 67
　showy, summer-to-fall flowers, 65, 66
Candytuft. *See Iberis* spp.
Canna hybrids, for water garden, 81
Cape honeysuckle. *See Tecomaria capensis*
Cape leadwort. *See Plumbago auriculata*
Cape marigold. *See Dimorphotheca sinuata*
Caragana arborescens
　for city garden, 58
　easy maintenance, 58
　fast growing, 55
　'Nana', drought tolerant, 91
Caraway. *See Carum carvi*
Cardinal-climber. *See Ipomoea quamoclit*
Cardinal flower. *See Lobelia cardinalis*
Cardiospermum halicacabum, for fast cover, 67
Carissa spp.
　grandiflora 'Green Carpet', medium ground cover, 69
　showy fruit, 52
　for thorny barrier, 56
Carmel creeper. *See Ceanothus griseus* var. *horizontalis*
Carnation. *See Dianthus* spp.
Carob. *See Ceratonia siliqua*
Carpet-bugle. *See Ajuga reptans*
Carpinus spp.
　betulus
　　for city garden, 45
　　for seacoast, 48
　　for winter silhouette, 40
　betulus 'Fastigiata'
　　medium, narrow upright, 39
　　for wall planting, 44
　caroliniana
　　broad, 37
　　for shade, 42
　　small-to-medium, 42
Carpobrotus spp.
　drought tolerant, 92
　showy, spring-to-summer flowers, 70

Carthamus tinctorius, for herb garden, 87
Carum carvi, for herb garden, 86
Carya illinoinensis, 37
　abuse tolerant, 47
　broad, 37
　large, 37, 42
　for shade, 42
Cassia artemisiodes, drought tolerant, 91
Casuarina spp.
　cunninghamiana
　　abuse tolerant, 47
　　fast growing, 43
　stricta, drought tolerant, 90
Catalpa spp.
　for city garden, 45
　drought tolerant, 90
　fast growing, 43
　showy, spring-to-summer flowers, 41
Catharanthus roseus
　for containers, 27
　drought tolerant, 89
　heat tolerant, 31
　low growing, 22
　red-hued flowers, 13, 15
　rounded form, 25
　spring-to-fall flowers, 13, 15, 20, 21
　white-hued flowers, 20, 21
Catmint, Persian. *See Nepeta mussinii*
Catsclaw. *See Macfadyena unguis-cati*
Cattail. *See Typha* spp.
Ceanothus spp.
　for attracting birds, 74
　drought tolerant, 91
　fast growing, 55
　griseus var. *horizontalis*
　　slope stabilizer, 71
　　tall, 69
　for seacoast, 61
　showy, spring flowers, 52, 70
Cedar. *See Cedrus* spp.
Cedar, Japanese. *See Cryptomeria japonica*
Cedar, Port Orford. *See Chamaecyparis lawsoniana*
Cedar, red. *See Juniperus virginiana*
Cedrus spp.
　deodara
　　large, oval pyramidal, 38
　　for screen or buffer, 44
　　for water garden, 82
　drought tolerant, 90
　pest free, 46
　for shearing, 47
Celastrus spp.
　for arbor or patio cover, 67
　for attracting birds, 68
　for fall color, 66
Celosia cristata
　for containers, 27
　for cutting, 28
　for dried arrangements, 29
　for edging, 27
　heat tolerant, 31
　medium height, 23
　red-hued flowers, 13, 15
　summer-to-fall flowers, 13, 15, 18, 19
　vertical form, 24
　yellow-hued flowers, 18, 19
Celtis spp.
　abuse tolerant, 47
　drought tolerant, 90
　occidentalis
　　broad, 37
　　for city garden, 46
　　flood tolerant, 48
　　medium-to-large, 37, 42
　　for shade, 42
　pest free, 46
Centaurea spp.
　cineraria, drought tolerant, 89

Centaurea (*continued*)
　cyanus
　　for attracting birds, 30
　　blue-hued, summer flowers, 16
　　for cutting, 28
　　drought tolerant, 89
　　medium height, 23
　　for naturalizing, 32
　　open form, 25
Centrosema virginianum, for fast cover, 67
Cerastium tomentosum
　for draping or trailing, 73
　drought tolerant, 92
　dwarf, 22
　for rock garden, 80
　showy flowers, 70
　spring-to-summer flowers, 20, 70
　white-hued flowers, 20
Ceratonia siliqua, drought tolerant, 90
Ceratostigma plumbaginoides, 71
　blue-hued flowers, 16, 17
　drought tolerant, 89
　for fall color, 71
　summer-to-fall flowers, 16, 17, 70, 71
　showy flowers, 70, 71
　for water garden, 83
Cercidiphyllum japonicum, 47
　for fall color, 39
　medium height, for shade, 42
　for patio garden, 43
　pest free, 47
　for winter silhouette, 40
Cercidium spp., drought tolerant, 90
Cercis spp.
　canadensis
　　for fall color, 39
　　for patio garden, 43
　　small, for shade, 42
　　for water garden, 82
　chinensis
　　for Japanese garden, 84
　　small, for shade, 42
　occidentalis, drought tolerant, 91
　for shady area, 46
　showy, spring flowers, 41
Cercocarpus spp., drought tolerant, 91
Chaenomeles speciosa
　for basic landscaping, 54
　for city garden, 58
　easy maintenance, 58
　for Japanese garden, 84
　showy, winter-to-spring flowers, 52, 54
　for thorny barrier, 57
Chamaecyparis spp.
　attractive evergreen, 50
　lawsoniana, for wall planting, 44
　obtusa
　　for Japanese garden, 84
　　for screen or buffer, 44
　　for water garden, 82
　obtusa 'Nana Aurea'
　　for all-year color, 51
　　for rock garden, 79
　pisifera
　　'Filifera', for water garden, 82
　　small, oval pyramidal, 37
　for shady area, 46
Chamaemelum nobile
　for herb garden, 87, 88
　lawn alternative, 72
　for nooks and crannies, 74
　for rock garden, 80
　traffic tolerant, 73
Chamaerops humilis, drought tolerant, 91
Chamomile. *See Chamaemelum nobile*
Chaste tree. *See Vitex agnus-castus*
Cheiranthus cheiri
　for cool summers, 30
　for fragrance, 28
　low growing, 22
　yellow-hued, spring-to-summer flowers, 17, 18

Cherry, flowering. *See Prunus* spp.
Cherry plum. *See Prunus cerasifera*
Chervil. *See Anthriscus cerefolium*
Chestnut, Chinese water. *See Eleocharis dulcis*
Chinaberry. *See Melia azedarach*
Chionanthus virginicus
　for city garden, 46
　for fragrance, 45
　for patio garden, 43
　pest free, 47
　showy flowers, 41
　showy fruit, 40
　small, broad, 37
　summer flowering, 41
　for water garden, 82
Chives. *See Allium schoenoprasum*
Choisya ternata, 49
　fast growing, 55
　for fragrance, 57
　medium height, 49
　showy, spring flowers, 53
Cholla. *See Opuntia* spp.
Christmas fern. *See Polystichum acrostichoides*
Christmas-rose. *See Helleborus niger*
Chrysanthemum spp.
　for attracting birds, 30
　balsamita, for herb garden, 88
　coronarium, for herb garden, 87
　heat tolerant, 31
　hybrids
　　summer-to-fall flowers, 18, 19, 20, 21
　　white-hued flowers, 20, 21
　　yellow-hued flowers, 18, 19
　× *morifolium*, for Japanese garden, 85
　parthenium
　　for edging, 27
　　low growing, 22
　　rounded form, 25
　× *superbum*
　　for cutting, 29
　　rounded form, 25
　for water garden, 83
Chrysogonum virginianum
　dwarf, 22
　for rock garden, 80
　for shady area, 32
　for wet soil, 75
Cigarflower. *See Cuphea ignea*
Cimicifuga racemosa
　for fragrance, 28
　heat tolerant, 31
　for shady area, 32
　tall, vertical form, 24
　for wet soil, 33
　white-hued, summer-to-fall flowers, 20, 21
Cineraria. *See Senecio* × *hybridus*
Cinnamomum camphora, large, broad, 37
Cinquefoil. *See Potentilla* spp.
Cistus spp.
　drought tolerant, 91
　easy maintenance, 58
　× *purpureus*, showy, summer flowers, 53
　for rock garden, 79
　for seacoast, 61
　slope stabilizer, 71
Citrus spp., for fragrance, 45
City gardens
　shrubs for, 58–59
　trees for, 45–46
Cladrastis lutea
　for bark interest, 39
　broad, 37
　for fragrance, 45
　large, 37, 42
　for shade, 42

Cladrastis lutea (*continued*)
  showy, summer flowers, 41
  for winter silhouette, 40
Clarkia hybrids
  for cool summers, 30
  medium height, 23
  red-hued, spring-to-summer flowers, 13, 14
  rounded form, 25
  for shady area, 32
Clematis spp.
  armandii
    for Japanese garden, 85
    showy, spring flowers, 65
    for fragrance, 68
  × *jackmanii*, showy, summer-to-fall flowers, 65, 66
Cleome hasslerana
  for cutting, 29
  red-hued flowers, 14, 15
  rounded form, 25
  summer-to-fall flowers, 14, 15, 20, 21
  for wet soil, 33
  white-hued flowers, 20, 21
Clethra alnifolia
  easy maintenance, 58
  for fragrance, 57
  medium height, 49
  for water garden, 82
  for wet soil, 61
Cleyera, Japanese. *See Ternstroemia gymnanthera*
Cliffgreen. *See Paxistima canbyi*
Climate zones, 8–9
Clitoria ternatea, for fast cover, 67
Clivia miniata
  medium height, 23
  for shady area, 32
  yellow-hued, spring flowers, 17
Cloudland rhododendron. *See Rhododendron impeditum*
Cloverblossom, pink. *See Polygonum capitatum*
Clusterberry, red. *See Cotoneaster lacteus*
Clytostoma callistegioides
  for arbor or patio cover, 67
  drought tolerant, 92
  showy, spring-to-fall flowers, 65, 66
Cobaea scandens, for fast cover, 67
Cockscomb. *See Celosia cristata*
Colchicum autumnale
  for herb garden, 87
  for naturalizing, 32
Coleus × *hybridus*
  attractive foliage, 26
  for containers, 27
Colocasia esculenta, for water garden, 81
Color. *See Fall color; specific colors*
Columbine. *See Aquilegia* spp.
Coneflower, purple. *See Echinacea purpurea*
Consolida ambigua
  blue-hued flowers, 15, 16
  for cool summers, 30
  for cutting, 29
  for herb garden, 87
  for naturalizing, 32
  red-hued flowers, 13, 14
  spring-to-summer flowers, 13, 14, 15, 16, 20
  vertical form, 24
  white-hued flowers, 20
Containers, flowers for, 27–28
Convallaria majalis
  for fragrance, 28, 74
  for herb garden, 87, 88
  medium ground cover, 69
  for shady area, 32, 75
  showy-flowered ground cover, 70, 71
  spring-to-summer flowers, 20, 70
  for wet soil, 75
  white-hued flowers, 20

Convolvulus tricolor
  blue-hued, summer flowers, 16
  drought tolerant, 89
  heat tolerant, 31
  low growing, 22
Cool summers, flowers for, 30
Coprosma spp.
  fast growing, 55
  × *kirkii*
    drought tolerant, 92
    slope stabilizer, 71
  repens, for shady area, 59
  for seacoast, 61
Coralbells. *See Heuchera sanguinea*
Coral tree. *See Erythrina* spp.
Coreopsis spp.
  for attracting birds, 30
  auriculata 'Nana', for rock garden, 80
  lanceolata
    for cutting, 29
    for naturalizing, 33
    yellow-hued, spring-to-fall flowers, 17, 18, 19
  tinctoria, drought tolerant, 89
  verticillata
    attractive foliage, 26
    rounded form, 25
    tall, 24
    for water garden, 83
Coriandrum sativum, for herb garden, 86
Cork tree, Amur. *See Phellodendron amurense*
Cornelian-cherry. *See Cornus mas*
Cornus spp.
  alba
    for attracting birds, 57
    for city garden, 58
    fast growing, 55
    'Sibirica', medium, 49
    for wet soil, 61
    for winter interest, 52
  alternifolia, small, for shade, 42
    for attracting birds, 45
    for fall color, 39
  florida
    for Japanese garden, 84
    medium, broad, 37
    for rock garden, 79
    showy, spring flowers, 41
    for winter silhouette, 40
  kousa
    showy, summer flowers, 41
    showy fruit, 52
    small, broad, 37
    for lawns, 44
  mas
    pest free, 60
    showy, winter-to-spring flowers, 53, 54
    showy fruit, 52
    for patio garden, 43
  sericea
    for attracting birds, 57
    for city garden, 58
    fast growing, 55
    for wet soil, 61
    for winter interest, 52
  for shady area, 46
  for water garden, 82
Coronilla varia
  drought tolerant, 92
  lawn alternative, 72
  slope stabilizer, 71
Cortaderia selloana
  for dried arrangements, 29
  tall, 24
Corylopsis glabrescens, for water garden, 82
Corylus avellana 'Contorta'
  for water garden, 82
  for winter interest, 52
Cosmos spp.
  for attracting birds, 30
  bipinnatus
    for cutting, 29

Cosmos (*continued*)
  drought tolerant, 89
  medium height, 23
  for naturalizing, 33
  open form, 25
  red-hued flowers, 14, 15
  summer-to-fall flowers, 14, 15, 20, 21
  white-hued flowers, 20, 21
  sulphureus, yellow-hued, summer-to-fall flowers, 18, 19
Costmary. *See Chrysanthemum balsamita*
Cotinus coggygria
  for city garden, 46
  for lawns, 44
  for patio garden, 43
  for rock garden, 79
  small, oval pyramidal, 38
Cotoneaster spp.
  adpressus
    for draping or trailing, 73
    for rock garden, 79
  apiculatus, medium, 49
  for basic landscaping, 54
  conspicuus var. *decorus*, for fall color, 71
  dammeri
    for attracting birds, 74
    attractive evergreen, 50
    for draping or trailing, 73
    drought tolerant, 92
    fast growing, 55
    low growing, 49
    for seacoast, 61
    for water garden, 83
  dammeri 'Coral Beauty'
    for rock garden, 79
    tall, 70
  divaricatus
    for fall color, 51
    fast growing, 55
    for seacoast, 61
  drought tolerant, 91
  easy maintenance, 58, 74
  horizontalis
    drought tolerant, 92
    for fall color, 51, 71
    for seacoast, 61
  lacteus, tall, 50
  microphyllus
    for fall color, 71
    for rock garden, 79
  showy fruit, 52
  slope stabilizer, 72
Coyotebrush, dwarf. *See Baccharis pilularis*
Crab apple. *See Malus* spp.
Cranberrybush. *See Viburnum opulus*
Cranberrybush, American. *See Viburnum trilobum*
Cranesbill. *See Geranium* spp.
Crape myrtle. *See Lagerstroemia indica*
Crataegus spp.
  for attracting birds, 45
  for city garden, 46
  for fall color, 39
  for lawns, 44
  for patio garden, 43
  phaenopyrum
    medium, oval pyramidal, 38
    for wall planting, 44
  showy, spring flowers, 41
  showy fruit, 40
  viridis 'Winter King', medium, broad, 37
Cream or white flowers, 19–22
  roses, 94
Creeping-charlie. *See Lysimachia nummularia*
Crinum spp.
  americanum, for water garden, 81
  × *powellii*, for fragrance, 28
Crocus spp.
  hybrids

Crocus (*continued*)
  dwarf, 22
  for rock garden, 80
  vernus
    blue-hued flowers, 15
    for containers, 27
    for naturalizing, 33
    spring flowers, 15, 20
    white-hued flowers, 20
Crown vetch. *See Coronilla varia*
Cryptomeria japonica
  for Japanese garden, 84
  for wall planting, 44
Cucumber, wild. *See Echinocystis lobata*
Cucurbita pepo var. *ovifera*, for fast cover, 67
Culinary herbs, 86
Cultivars, defined, 7
Cuminum cyminum, for herb garden, 86
Cup-and-saucer vine. *See Cobaea scandens*
Cupflower. *See Nierembergia hippomanica*
Cuphea ignea, red-hued, fall-to-summer flowers, 14, 15
× *Cupressocyparis leylandii*
  'Green Spire', large, narrow upright, 39
  for shearing, 47
  for water garden, 82
Cupressus spp.
  drought tolerant, 90
  macrocarpa, for seacoast, 48
  for screen or buffer, 44
  sempervirens 'Stricta', large, narrow upright, 39
  for shearing, 47
Currant, alpine. *See Ribes alpinum*
Cutting gardens, plants for
  flowers, 28–29
  herbs, 87
  roses, 96
Cyclamen spp.
  red-hued, spring-to-fall flowers, 13, 14, 15
  for rock garden, 80
  for shady area, 32
Cymbopogon citratus, for herb garden, 86
Cynoglossum amabile
  blue-hued, spring-to-summer flowers, 15, 16
  open form, 25
Cyperus spp.
  for Japanese garden, 85
  for water garden, 81
Cypress. *See Chamaecyparis* spp.; × *Cupressocyparis leylandii*; *Cupressus* spp.
Cyrtomium falcatum, for Japanese garden, 85
Cytisus spp.
  drought tolerant, 91
  × *kewensis*
    for rock garden, 79
    showy, spring flowers, 70
  pest free, 60
  × *praecox*
    fast growing, 55
    for seacoast, 61
    for winter interest, 52
  scoparius, for water garden, 82

D
Daffodil. *See Narcissus* spp.
Dahlia hybrids, *28*
  for containers, 27
  for cutting, 29
  heat tolerant, 31
  medium height, 23
  red-hued flowers, 14, 15
  rounded form, 25

summer-to-fall flowers, 14, 15, 18, 19, 20, 21
white-hued flowers, 20, 21
yellow-hued flowers, 18, 19
Daisy, African. *See Arctotis* hybrids
Daisy, crown. *See Chrysanthemum coronarium*
Daisy, Michaelmas. *See Aster × frikartii*
Daisy, Shasta. *See Chrysanthemum × superbum*
Daisy, Swan river. *See Brachycome iberidifolia*
Daisy, trailing African. *See Osteospermum fruticosum*
Daisy, Transvaal. *See Gerbera jamesonii*
Daphne spp.
  for basic landscaping, 54
  cneorum
    for Japanese garden, 84
    for rock garden, 79
  odora
    attractive evergreen, 50
    for fragrance, 57
    medium height, 49
    for shady area, 59
    for shearing, 60
    showy, winter-to-spring flowers, 53, 54
    for water garden, 82
Dawn redwood. *See Metasequoia glyptostroboides*
Daylily. *See Hemerocallis* spp.
Deadnettle. *See Lamium maculatum* 'Beacon Silver'
Delosperma spp.
  drought tolerant, 92
  showy, spring flowers, 70
Delphinium elatum
  blue-hued, spring-to-summer flowers, 15, 16
  for cool summers, 30
  for cutting, 29
  for herb garden, 87
  tall, vertical form, 24
Desert-olive. *See Forestiera neomexicana*
Deutzia gracilis, showy, spring flowers, 53
  'Nikko' (ground cover), 70
Dianthus spp., *20*
  for attracting birds, 30
  attractive foliage, 26
  barbatus
    draping or trailing, 27
    low growing, 22
    rounded form, 25
  caryophyllus
    medium height, 23
    white-hued, summer-to-fall flowers, 20, 21
  chinensis
    for edging, 27
    low growing, 23
    for cutting, 29
  deltoides
    lawn alternative, 72
    for rock garden, 80
    for fragrance, 28
    for herb garden, 87
  plumarius
    low growing, 23
    for rock garden, 80
    red-hued, summer-to-fall flowers, 13, 14, 15
    'Tiny Rubies', for nooks and crannies, 74
Dicentra spp.
  eximia, for shady area, 32
    for naturalizing, 33
  spectabilis
    medium height, 23
    red-hued, spring flowers, 13
    for water garden, 83

Dichondra micrantha
  lawn alternative, 72
  for wet soil, 75
Dictamnus albus
  for fragrance, 28
  'Purpureus'
    red-hued, summer flowers, 14
    for rock garden, 80
    white-hued, summer flowers, 20
Diervilla lonicera, tall, 70
Dietes vegeta, drought tolerant, 89
Digitalis purpurea
  blue-hued flowers, 15, 16
  for containers, 27
  for cutting, 29
  for herb garden, 87
  for naturalizing, 33
  red-hued flowers, 13, 14
  for shady area, 32
  spring-to-summer flowers, 13, 14, 15, 16
  tall, vertical form, 24
  for wet soil, 33
Dill. *See Anethum graveolens*
Dimorphotheca sinuata
  draping or trailing, 27
  drought tolerant, 89
  low growing, 23
  yellow-hued, spring flowers, 17
Diospyros spp.
  for fall color, 39
  kaki
    drought tolerant, 90
    for Japanese garden, 84
    showy fruit, 40
  virginiana
    flood tolerant, 48
    medium, oval pyramidal, 38
Distictis buccinatoria, *65*
  for arbor or patio cover, 67
  drought tolerant, 92
  showy, spring-to-fall flowers, 65, 66
Dodonaea viscosa, drought tolerant, 91
Dogwood. *See Cornus* spp.
Dolichos lablab, for fast cover, 67
Doronicum cordatum
  for shady area, 32
  yellow-hued, spring flowers, 17
Drainage problems. *See* Wet soil
Draping or trailing plants
  flowers, 27
  ground covers, 73
  vines, 63–64, 65–68
Dried arrangements, flowers for, 29
Drosanthemum floribundum, *70*
  drought tolerant, 92
  showy, spring flowers, 70
Dry-climate gardens, 89–92
Dryopteris spp.
  for shady area, 75
  for water garden, 83
Duchesnea indica
  for attracting birds, 74
  lawn alternative, 72
  low growing, 69
Dusty-miller. *See Centaurea cineraria*
Dutchman's-pipe. *See Aristolochia durior*
Dwarf flowers, 22
Dyssodia tenuiloba, *19*
  heat tolerant, 31
  yellow-hued, summer-to-winter flowers, 18, 19

E

Easy-to-maintain plants. *See* Low-maintenance plants
Eccremocarpus scaber, for fast cover, 67
Echinacea purpurea
  for attracting birds, 30
  blue-hued, summer flowers, 16
  for cutting, 29
  heat tolerant, 31
  for naturalizing, 33
  open form, 25

Echinacea purpurea (*continued*)
  for shady area, 32
  for water garden, 83
Echinocystis lobata, for fast cover, 67
Echinops exaltatus, *29*
  for attracting birds, 30
  blue-hued, summer-to-fall flowers, 16, 17
  for dried arrangements, 29
  heat tolerant, 31
  open form, 25
  tall, 24
Edging
  flowers for, 27
  herbs for, 88
Eelgrass. *See Vallisneria americana*
Eichhornia crassipes, for water garden, 81
Elaeagnus spp.
  angustifolia
    abuse tolerant, 47
    for attracting birds, 45
    drought tolerant, 90
    for fragrance, 45
    pest free, 47
    for screen or buffer, 44
    for seacoast, 48
    showy fruit, 41
    small, broad, 37
  pungens
    for attracting birds, 57
    drought tolerant, 91
    fast growing, 55
    for screen, 56
    for seacoast, 61
    showy fruit, 52
    for thorny barrier, 57
Eleocharis dulcis, for water garden, 81
Elm. *See Ulmus* spp.
Elodea canadensis, for water garden, 81
Empress tree. *See Paulownia tomentosa*
Enkianthus campanulatus, for water garden, 82
Epimedium grandiflorum
  for Japanese garden, 85
  medium height, 69
  for nooks and crannies, 74
  for rock garden, 80
  for shady area, 75
  for water garden, 83
Equisetum hyemale, for water garden, 81, *82*
Erica spp.
  attractive evergreen, 50
  carnea
    for rock garden, 79
    showy, winter-to-spring flowers, 53, 54, 70
  vagans
    for rock garden, 79
    showy, summer flowers, 53, 71
Erigeron karvinskianus
  drought tolerant, 89
  for edging, 27
Eriobotrya japonica
  for attracting birds, 45
  drought tolerant, 90
  for patio garden, 43
  small, broad, 37
Erodium chamaedryoides
  for nooks and crannies, 74
  for rock garden, 80
Erythrina spp., showy, winter flowers, 41, 42
Escallonia spp., *55*
  attractive evergreen, 50
  for basic landscaping, 54
  fast growing, 55
  'Newport Dwarf', low growing, 49
  for seacoast, 61
Eschscholzia californica
  for attracting birds, 30
  drought tolerant, 89
  low growing, 23

Eschscholzia californica (*continued*)
  for naturalizing, 33
  rounded form, 25
Eucalyptus spp.
  abuse tolerant, 47
  for city garden, 46
  drought tolerant, 90
  fast growing, 43
  ficifolia, showy, summer flowers, 41
  nicholii, medium, oval pyramidal, 38
  for seacoast, 48
  for wall planting, 44
Euonymus spp.
  alata
    for attracting birds, 57
    for fall color, 51
    for informal hedge, 56
    showy fruit, 52
    for water garden, 82
  fortunei
    for attracting birds, 57, 68, 74
    attractive evergreen, 50
    'Colorata', for all-year color, 51
    for draping or trailing, 73
    easy maintenance, 74
    lawn alternative, 72
    'Minima', low growing, 69
    for shady area, 68
    for water garden, 82
    for wet soil, 75
  fortunei var. *radicans*
    for fall color, 71
    medium height, 69
Euphorbia spp.
  epithymoides
    medium height, 23
    rounded form, 25
    yellow-hued, spring flowers, 17
    heat tolerant, 31
  marginata
    drought tolerant, 89
    for wet soil, 33
    white-hued, summer flowers, 20
Evergreen shrubs, attractive, 50–51

F

Fagus spp.
  grandifolia, large, for shade, 42
  sylvatica
    for bark interest, 39
    for winter silhouette, 40
Fall color, plants for
  ground covers, 71
  shrubs, 51
  trees, 39–40
  vines, 66
Fall-flowering plants
  flowers
    blue-hued, 17
    red-hued, 14–15
    white-hued, 21
    yellow-hued, 19
  ground covers, 71
  shrubs, 54
  trees, 41
  vines, 66
Fallugia paradoxa, drought tolerant, 91
False-cypress. *See Chamaecyparis* spp.
False-indigo. *See Baptisia australis*
False-lupine. *See Thermopsis caroliniana*
False-spirea. *See Astilbe* spp.
Fast-growing plants
  shrubs, 56–57
  trees, 43
  vines, 67
Fatsia japonica, for shady area, 59
Feijoa sellowiana
  drought tolerant, 91
  for screen, 56
Felicia amelloides, *79*
  blue-hued, spring-to-summer flowers, 15, 16
  for rock garden, 79
Fennel. *See Foeniculum vulgare*

Fern, American wall. *See Polypodium virginianum*
Fern, Christmas. *See Polystichum acrostichoides*
Fern, cinnamon. *See Osmunda* spp.
Fern, holly. *See Cyrtomium falcatum*
Fern, Japanese painted. *See Athyrium* spp.
Fern, lady. *See Athyrium filix-femina*
Fern, maidenhair. *See Adiantum pedatum*
Fern, royal. *See Osmunda* spp.
Fern, sensitive. *See Onoclea sensibilis*
Fern, wood. *See Dryopteris* spp.
Ferns, for Japanese gardens, 85
Fescue, blue. *See Festuca ovina* var. *glauca*
Festuca ovina var. *glauca*
  for rock garden, 80
  for water garden, 83
Feverfew. *See Chrysanthemum parthenium*
Ficus spp.
  pumila
    attractive foliage, 66
    for shady area, 68
  retusa var. *nitida*, small, oval pyramidal, 38
Filipendula spp.
  heat tolerant, 31
  rubra, red-hued, spring flowers, 13
  tall, 24
  ulmaria, white-hued, spring flowers, 20
  for wet soil, 33
Fir, Douglas. *See Pseudotsuga menziesii*
Firethorn. *See Pyracantha* spp.
Flame tree, Chinese. *See Koelreuteria bipinnata*
Flame vine. *See Pyrostegia venusta*
Fleabane. *See Erigeron karvinskianus*
Fleeceflower. *See Polygonum cuspidatum* var. *compactum*
Floatingheart. *See Nymphoides peltata*
Flood-tolerant trees, 48
Flossflower. *See Ageratum houstonianum*
Flowering plants, showy
  See also specific flowers
  herbs, 88
  ground covers, 70–71
  shrubs, 52–54
  trees, 41–42
  vines, 65–66
Flowering-rush. *See Butomus umbellatus*
Foamflower. *See Tiarella cordifolia*
Foeniculum vulgare, 86
  for herb garden, 86
Foliage, attractive
  flowers with, 26
  shrubs with, 50–51
  vines with, 66
Forestiera neomexicana, drought tolerant, 91
Forget-me-not. *See Myosotis sylvatica*
Forget-me-not, summer. *See Anchusa* spp.
Forget-me-not, Chinese. *See Cynoglossum amabile*
Forsythia spp.
  for city garden, 58
  fast growing, 55
  × *intermedia*
    for basic landscaping, 54
    for Japanese garden, 84
    showy, winter-to-spring flowers, 53, 54
    tall, 50
  ovata, medium, 49
Fothergilla major
  for fall color, 51
  for water garden, 82

Fountaingrass. *See Pennisetum* spp.
Four-o'clock. *See Mirabilis jalapa*
Foxglove. *See Digitalis purpurea*
Fragaria chiloensis, 72
  for attracting birds, 74
  lawn alternative, 72
  low growing, 69
  traffic tolerant, 73
Fragrance, plants for
  flowers, 28
  ground covers, 74
  herbs, 86–87
  roses, 95–96
  shrubs, 57
  trees, 45
  vines, 68
Franklinia alatamaha
  for fall color, 39
  showy, summer-to-fall flowers, 41
  small, broad, 37
  for water garden, 82
Fraxinus spp.
  abuse tolerant, 47
  for city garden, 46
  for fall color, 39
  oxycarpa 'Raywood', medium, for shade, 42
  pennsylvanica
    flood tolerant, 48
    large, for shade, 42
  velutina var. *glabra* 'Modesto', for lawns, 45
Freesia × *hybrida*
  for fragrance, 28
  low growing, 23
  for rock garden, 80
  white-hued, spring flowers, 20
Fremontodendron spp., showy, spring flowers, 53
Fritillaria meleagris, for rock garden, 80
Fruit, showy
  shrubs with, 52
  trees with, 40–41
Fuchsia-flowered gooseberry. *See Ribes speciosum*
Fuchsia spp.
  × *hybrida*, trailing, 27, *53*
  hybrids
    for shady area, 59
    showy, summer-to-fall flowers, 53, 54
  procumbens, for rock garden, 80
Fumitory, climbing. *See Adlumia fungosa*

G
Gaillardia spp., 10–11
  × *grandiflora*
    for cutting, 29
    drought tolerant, 89
    heat tolerant, 31
    rounded form, 25
    for water garden, 83
  pulchella, medium height, 23
  red-hued flowers, 14
  summer-to-fall flowers, 14, 15, 18, 19
  yellow-hued flowers, 18, 19
Galanthus spp.
  elwesii, low growing, 23
  nivalis, for Japanese garden, 85
  for rock garden, 80
Galax urceolata
  for fall color, 71
  for Japanese garden, 85
  for wet soil, 75
Galium odoratum
  for fragrance, 74
  for herb garden, 87, 88
  low growing, 69
  for shady area, 75
  for water garden, 83
  for wet soil, 75

Gardenia jasminoides
  for fragrance, 57
  for herb garden, 87
  medium height, 49
  'Radicans'
    for fragrance, 74
    low-growing shrub, 49
    showy, summer flowers, 71
    tall ground cover, 70
  for shady area, 59
  for shearing, 60
  showy, summer flowers, 53
Garland-flower. *See Daphne cneorum*
Gas plant. *See Dictamnus albus*
Gaultheria spp.
  procumbens
    for fall color, 71
    for herb garden, 88
    for rock garden, 79
    for shady area, 75
  shallon, for shady area, 59
Gayfeather. *See Liatris* spp.
Gazania rigens
  dwarf, 22
  for rock garden, 80
  var. *leucolaena*
    draping or trailing, 27
    drought tolerant, 92
    lawn alternative, 72
    medium height, 69
    showy, all-year flowers, 70, 71
    slope stabilizer, 72
  yellow-hued, winter-to-summer flowers, 18, 19
Geijera parviflora, drought tolerant, 90
Gelsemium sempervirens, *92*
  drought tolerant, 90
  for fragrance, 68, 74
  showy, winter-to-spring flowers, 65, 66, 70, 71
Genista spp.
  for seacoast, 61
  for winter interest, 52
Geranium. *See Pelargonium* spp.
Geranium, alpine. *See Erodium chamaedryoides*
Geranium spp.
  for edging, 27
  himalayense, blue-hued, summer flowers, 16
  sanguineum
    medium height, 23
    red-hued flowers, 13, 14
    for rock garden, 80
    rounded form, 25
    showy-flowered ground cover, 71
    spring-to-summer flowers, 13, 14, 71
  for water garden, 83
Gerbera jamesonii
  low growing, 23
  red-hued flowers, 14, 15
  summer-to-fall flowers, 14, 15, 18, 19, 20, 21
  white-hued flowers, 20, 21
  yellow-hued flowers, 18, 19
Germander. *See Teucrium chamaedrys*
Geum spp.
  for cutting, 29
  medium height, 23
  yellow-hued, summer flowers, 18
Ginger, wild. *See Asarum* spp.
Gingko biloba, *39*
  abuse tolerant, 47
  for city garden, 46
  drought tolerant, 90
  for fall color, 39
  'Fastigiata', large, narrow-upright, 39
  for Japanese garden, 84
  pest free, 47
  for shearing, 47
  for winter silhouette, 40
Gladiolus × *hortulanus*
  for cutting, 29
  red-hued flowers, 14
  summer flowers, 14, 18, 20

Gladiolus × *hortulanus* (*continued*)
  tall, 24
  white-hued flowers, 20
  yellow-hued flowers, 18
Glechoma hederacea, traffic tolerant, 73
Gleditsia triacanthos var. *inermis*
  abuse tolerant, 47
  drought tolerant, 90
  flood tolerant, 48
  large, broad, 37
  for winter silhouette, 40
Globe amaranth. *See Gomphrena globosa*
Globe candytuft. *See Iberis umbellata*
Globeflower. *See Trollius* spp.
Globe thistle. *See Echinops exaltatus*
Gloryflower. *See Eccremocarpus scaber*
Gloxinia, creeping. *See Asarina erubescens*
Goatsbeard. *See Aruncus dioicus*
Godetia. *See Clarkia* hybrids
Golden-carpet. *See Sedum acre*
Goldenchain tree. *See Laburnum* × *wateri* 'Vossii'
Goldenclub. *See Orontium aquaticum*
Golden-fragrance plant. *See Pittosporum napaulense*
Goldenrain tree. *See Koelreuteria paniculata*
Goldenrod. *See Solidago* hybrids
Goldenstar. *See Chrysogonum virginianum*
Gomphrena globosa
  blue-hued flowers, 16, 17
  for dried arrangements, 29
  drought tolerant, 89
  heat tolerant, 31
  low growing, 23
  rounded form, 25
  summer-to-fall flowers, 16, 17, 18, 19
  yellow-hued flowers, 18, 19
Gooseberry, fuchsia-flowered. *See Ribes speciosum*
Gourd, white-flowered. *See Lagenaria siceraria*
Gourd, yellow-flowered. *See Cucurbita pepo* var. *ovifera*
Grape. *See Vitis* spp.
Grape, evergreen. *See Rhoicissus capensis*
Grape hyacinth. *See Muscari armeniacum*
Grasses, for Japanese gardens, 85
Grevillea spp.
  drought tolerant, 90, 91
  robusta, fast growing, 43
Guinea gold vine. *See Hibbertia scandens*
Gum, red-flowering. *See Eucalyptus ficifolia*
Gypsophila spp.
  for cutting, 29
  for dried arrangements, 29
  paniculata
    rounded form, 25
    tall, 24
    white-hued, fall flowers, 21
  repens
    dwarf, 22
    for edging, 27
    for rock garden, 80
    white-hued, summer flowers, 21

H
Hackberry. *See Celtis* spp.
Hackberry, common. *See Celtis occidentalis*
Hakea laurina
  drought tolerant, 90
  for seacoast, 48

Halesia spp.
  carolina
    broad, 37
    for fragrance, 45
    medium height, 37
    for patio garden, 43
    showy, spring flowers, 41
  for shady area, 46
Hamamelis spp.
  for attracting birds, 57
  easy maintenance, 58
  for fall color, 51
  × *intermedia*
    for fragrance, 57
    showy, winter-to-spring flowers, 53, 54
  for shady area, 46
  vernalis, for wet soil, 61
  virginiana
    for city garden, 58
    small, broad, 37
  for water garden, 82
  for winter interest, 52
Hanging baskets, flowers for, 27
Hardenbergia violacea 'Happy Wanderer'
  for arbor or patio cover, 67
  showy, winter-to-spring flowers, 65, 66
Harry Lauder's walkingstick. *See Corylus avellana* 'Contorta'
Hawthorn. *See Crataegus* spp.
Heath. *See Erica* spp.
Heather, Scotch. *See Calluna vulgaris*
Heat-tolerant flowers, 31
Heavenly-bamboo. *See Nandina domestica*
Hebe buxifolia, for shearing, 60
Hedera helix
  for attracting birds, 68
  attractive foliage, 66
  for draping or trailing, 73
  easy maintenance, 75
  lawn alternative, 72
  medium height, 69
  for shady area, 68, 75
  slope stabilizer, 72
  for water garden, 83
Hedges
  herbs for, 88
  roses for, 95
  shrubs for, 56
Helenium autumnale
  rounded form, 25
  tall, 24
  yellow-hued, summer-to-fall flowers, 18, 19
Helianthemum nummularium
  drought tolerant, 89, 92
  for rock garden, 79
Helianthus spp.
  annuus, tall, 24
  for attracting birds, 30
  heat tolerant, 31
  open form, 25
  yellow-hued, summer-to-fall flowers, 18, 19
Helichrysum bracteatum, *15*
  for dried arrangements, 29
  low growing, 23
  red-hued flowers, 14, 15
  summer-to-fall flowers, 14, 15, 18, 19, 21
  white-hued flowers, 21
  yellow-hued flowers, 18, 19
Heliotropium arborescens
  blue-hued, summer flowers, 16
  for fragrance, 28
  for herb garden, 87
  rounded form, 25
Helleborus spp.
  attractive foliage, 26
  for cool summers, 30
  niger, for Japanese garden, 85
  orientalis, low growing, 23
  for shady area, 32

Hemerocallis spp.
  fulva
    for Japanese garden, 85
    tall, 24
  heat tolerant, 31
  hybrids
    blue-hued flowers, 15, 16, 17
    for cutting, 29
    drought tolerant, 89
    rounded form, 25
    spring-to-fall flowers, 15, 16, 17, 18, 19, 20, 21
    white-hued flowers, 20, 21
    yellow-hued flowers, 18, 19
  red-hued, spring-to-fall flowers, 13, 14, 15
  for shady area, 32
  slope stabilizer, 72
  tall ground cover, 70
  for water garden, 83
  for wet soil, 75
Hemlock, Canada. *See Tsuga canadensis*
Hens-and-chickens. *See Sempervivum tectorum*
Herald's-trumpet. *See Beaumontia grandiflora*
Herb gardens, 86–88
Heteromeles arbutifolia
  drought tolerant, 91
  showy fruit, 52
Heuchera spp.
  attractive foliage, 26
  for edging, 27
  for rock garden, 80
  sanguinea
    medium height, 23
    for nooks and crannies, 74
    red-hued, spring-to-summer flowers, 13, 14
  for water garden, 83
Hibbertia scandens
  for arbor or patio cover, 67
  showy, spring-to-fall flowers, 65, 66
Hibiscus spp.
  moscheutos
    heat tolerant, 31
    red-hued flowers, 14, 15
    'Southern Belle', tall, 24
    summer-to-fall flowers, 14, 15, 21
    for wet soil, 33
    white-hued flowers, 21
  rosa-sinensis
    for city garden, 58
    tall, 50
  showy, summer flowers, 53
  syriacus
    for city garden, 59
    for seacoast, 61
    for training as tree, 60
Holly. *See Ilex* spp.
Hollyhock. *See Alcea rosea*
Holly oak. *See Quercus ilex*
Holly olive. *See Osmanthus heterophyllus*
Honesty. *See Lunaria annua*
Honeylocust, thornless. *See Gleditsia triacanthos* var. *inermis*
Honeysuckle. *See Lonicera* spp.
Honeysuckle, bush. *See Diervilla lonicera*
Hop, Japanese. *See Humulus japonicus*
Hopbush. *See Dodonaea viscosa*
Hop hornbeam, American. *See Ostrya virginiana*
Hornbeam. *See Carpinus* spp.
Horsechestnut. *See Aesculus* spp.
Horsetail. *See Equisetum hyemale*
Hosta spp.
  attractive foliage, 26
  blue-hued, summer flowers, 16, 71
  plantaginea, for fragrance, 28, 74
  rounded form, 25
  for shady area, 32, 75

Hosta (*continued*)
  showy-flowered ground cover, 71
  sieboldiana, for wet soil, 33
  tall ground cover, 70
  ventricosa, for Japanese garden, 85
  for water garden, 83
  for wet soil, 75
Hot summers, flowers for, 31
Humulus japonicus, for fast cover, 67
Hyacinth-bean. See Dolichos lablab
Hyacinthus orientalis
  blue-hued flowers, 15
  for fragrance, 28
  red-hued flowers, 13
  spring flowers, 13, 15, 18, 20
  white-hued flowers, 20
  yellow-hued flowers, 18
Hydrangea spp.
  anomala petiolaris
    for arbor or patio cover, 67
    for Japanese garden, 85
    for shady area, 68
    showy, summer-to-fall flowers, 65, 66
  arborescens 'Grandiflora', medium, 49
  for basic landscaping, 54
  for city garden, 59
  macrophylla
    fast growing, 55
    for seacoast, 61
    showy, summer-to-fall flowers, 53, 54
  macrophylla 'Tricolor', for all-year color, 51
  paniculata 'Grandiflora'
    for dried arrangements, 29
    tall, 50
  quercifolia, for fall color, 51
  for shady area, 59
  for training as tree, 60
Hydrangea vine, Japanese. *See Schizophragma hydrangeoides*
Hydrocleys nymphoides, for water garden, 81
Hydrocotyle vulgaris, for water garden, 81
Hymenocallis spp.
  narcissiflora, for fragrance, 28
  for water garden, 81
Hymenosporum flavum
  for fragrance, 45
  medium, oval pyramidal, 38
Hypericum spp.
  calycinum
    drought tolerant, 92
    easy maintenance, 75
    fast growing, 55
    lawn alternative, 72
    medium height, 69
    showy, summer flowers, 71
  for city garden, 59
  coris, for rock garden, 79
  densiflorum, for wet soil, 61
  easy maintenance, 58
  for herb garden, 88
  prolificum, for water garden, 82
Hyssopus officinalis, for herb garden, 88

I

Iberis spp., *6*
  amara, for fragrance, 28
  for edging, 27
  sempervirens
    draping or trailing, 27
    dwarf, 22
    easy maintenance, 75
    for Japanese garden, 85
    for nooks and crannies, 74
    for rock garden, 80
    showy flowers, 70, 71
    for water garden, 83
  spring-to-summer flowers, 13, 14, 20, 21, 70, 71
  umbellata, red-hued flowers, 13, 14
  white-hued flowers, 20, 21

Ice plant. *See Carpobrotus* spp.; *Delosperma* spp.; *Lampranthus* spp.
Ice plant, rosea. *See Drosanthemum floribundum*
Ilex spp.
  for attracting birds, 45, 57
  attractive evergreen, 50
  for basic landscaping, 54
  cornuta, *57*
    'Carissa', low growing, 49
    for thorny barrier, 57
  cornuta 'Burfordii'
    small, broad tree, 37
    tall shrub, 50
  crenata, *60*
    for city garden, 59
    for informal hedge, 56
    for Japanese garden, 84
    for shearing, 60
  crenata 'Helleri'
    low growing, 49
    for water garden, 82
  decidua, for winter interest, 52
  easy maintenance, 58
  glabra, *61*
    for city garden, 59
    for wet soil, 61
  × *meserveae*, medium height, 49
  opaca
    for wall planting, 44
    for winter silhouette, 40
    for screen or buffer, 44, 56
    for shady area, 46, 59
    for shearing, 47
    showy fruit, 41, 52
    for training as tree, 60
  vomitoria
    'Nana', low growing, 49
    small, oval-pyramidal tree, 38
    for shearing, 60
Impatiens spp.
  red-hued flowers, 13, 14, 15
  for shady area, 32
  spring-to-fall flowers, 13, 14, 15, 21
  wallerana
    for containers, 28
    for edging, 27
    low growing, 23
    rounded form, 25
    for wet soil, 33
    white-hued flowers, 21
Incense cedar. *See Calocedrus decurrens*
Indian-hawthorn. *See Raphiolepis* spp.
Inkberry. *See Ilex glabra*
Ipomoea spp.
  alba
    for fragrance, 68
    for Japanese garden, 84
    white-hued, summer flowers, 21
  for fast temporary cover, 67
  quamoclit, red-hued, summer flowers, 14
  tricolor, blue-hued, fall flowers, 17
Irish moss. *See Sagina subulata*
Iris spp.
  cristata
    dwarf, 22
    for rock garden, 80
  fulva, for water garden, 81
  and hybrids, *24*
    blue-hued flowers, 15, 16, 17
    for cutting, 29
    medium height, 23
    spring-to-fall flowers, 15, 16, 17, 18, 19, 20, 21
    vertical form, 24
    for wet soil, 33
    white-hued flowers, 20, 21
    yellow-hued flowers, 18, 19
  kaempferi
    attractive foliage, 26
    for Japanese garden, 85

Iris (continued)
  pseudacorus, for water garden, 81
  reticulata, for rock garden, 80
  siberica, attractive foliage, 26
  versicolor, for water garden, 81
  for water garden, 83
Ivy, Boston. *See Parthenocissus
  tricuspidata*
Ivy, English. *See Hedera helix*
Ivy, ground. *See Glechoma hederacea*
Ivy geranium. *See Pelargonium
  peltatum*

J
Jacaranda mimosifolia, showy, spring-
  to-summer flowers, 41
Jack-in-the-pulpit. *See Arisaema
  triphyllum*
Jackson brier. *See Smilax lanceolata*
Japanese garden, *76–77*, 84–85
Jasmine, Chile. *See Mandevilla laxa*
Jasminum spp.
  for fragrance, 68
  for herb garden, 87
  mesnyi, for screen, 56
  nudiflorum, for water garden, 82
  polyanthum
    for arbor or patio cover, 67
    showy, spring-to-summer flowers, 65
Jessamine, Carolina. *See Gelsemium
  sempervirens*
Johnny-jump-up. *See Viola tricolor*
Joseph's-coat. *See Amaranthus* spp.
Jujube, Chinese. *See Ziziphus jujuba*
Juniperus spp.
  for attracting birds, 57
  attractive evergreen, 50
  for basic landscaping, 54
  chinensis 'Armstrongii'
    for informal hedge, 56
    for Japanese garden, 84
    medium height, 49
  chinensis 'Columnaris', small, narrow
    upright, 38
  chinensis 'Parsonii', tall ground
    cover, 70
  chinensis var. *procumbens* 'Nana', for
    rock garden, 79
  chinensis var. *sargentii*, tall ground
    cover, 70
  for city garden, 59
  communis 'Stricta', small, narrow
    upright, 38
  conferta
    'Blue Pacific', medium, 69
    for seacoast, 61
    tall ground cover, 70
  drought tolerant, 91, 92
  easy maintenance, 58, 75
  horizontalis
    for attracting birds, 74
    for draping or trailing, 73
    low-growing shrub, 49
    medium ground cover, 69
    for rock garden, 79
  horizontalis 'Wiltonii'
    for all-year color, 51
    for Japanese garden, 85
    lawn alternative, 72
    low growing, 69
  scopulorum, medium, oval pyra-
    midal, 38
  scopulorum 'Gray Gleam', small, oval
    pyramidal, 38
    for screen or buffer, 44
    slope stabilizer, 72
  virginiana
    abuse tolerant, 48
    for attracting birds, 45
    large, oval pyramidal, 38
    for seacoast, 48
    for water garden, 82, 83

K
Kalmia latifolia
  attractive evergreen, 50
  for shady area, 59
  showy, spring flowers, 53
Karo. *See Pittosporum crassifolium*
Katsura tree. *See Cercidiphyllum
  japonicum*
Kerria japonica
  for city garden, 59
  fast growing, 55
  pest free, 60
  for winter interest, 52
Kniphofia uvaria
  attractive foliage, 26
  drought tolerant, 89
  red-hued flowers, spring-to-summer,
    13, 14
Kochia scoparia trichophylla 'Childsii',
  attractive foliage, 26
Koelreuteria spp.
  bipinnata, small, broad, 37
  paniculata
    for city garden, 46
    drought tolerant, 90
    for Japanese garden, 84
    for lawns, 45
    medium height, 42
    for patio garden, 43
    pest free, 47
    for shade, 42
    showy, summer flowers, 41
    showy fruit, 41
Kolkwitzia amabilis, fast growing, 55

L
Laburnum × *wateri* 'Vossii', showy,
  spring flowers, 41
Lady's mantle. *See Alchemilla vulgaris*
Lagenaria siceraria, for fast cover, 67
Lagerstroemia indica
  for bark interest, 39
  drought tolerant, 90
  for fall color, 40
  for lawns, 45
  oval pyramidal, 38
  for patio garden, 43
  for shade, 42
  showy, summer flowers, 41
  small, 38, 42
  for winter silhouette, 40
Lagunaria patersonii, medium, oval
  pyramidal, 38
Lamb's-ears, woolly. *See Stachys
  byzantina*
Lamium maculatum 'Beacon Silver'
  medium height, 69
  for nooks and crannies, 74
  for wet soil, 75
Lampranthus spp.
  drought tolerant, 92
  showy, winter-to-spring flowers, 70, 71
Landscaping
  basic shrubs for, 54–55
  theme gardens, 77–97
Lantana montevidensis
  drought tolerant, 92
  low growing, 49
  showy, all-year flowers, 70, 71
  slope stabilizer, 72
Lapageria rosea, for shady area, 68
Larch. *See Larix* spp.
Large trees. *See* Tall trees
Larix spp.
  decidua, large, oval pyramidal, 38
  kaempferi, for fall color, 40
Larkspur. *See Delphinium elatum*
Lathyrus odoratus
  blue-hued flowers, 16
  for cool summers, 30
  for fast temporary cover, 67
  for fragrance, 28
  red-hued flowers, 13, 14
  spring-to-summer flowers, 13, 14, 16,
    20, 21

Lathyrus odoratus (continued)
  white-hued flowers, 20, 21
Laurel, cherry-. *See Prunus* spp.
Laurel, Grecian. *See Laurus nobilis*
Laurel, Indian-. *See Ficus retusa* var.
  nitida
Laurel, mountain. *See Kalmia latifolia*
Laurel, Portugal. *See Prunus lusitanica*
Laurentia fluviatilis
  lawn alternative, 72
  low growing, 69
  for rock garden, 80
  showy, spring flowers, 70
  traffic tolerant, 73
Laurus nobilis
  for attracting birds, 45
  for city garden, 46
  for herb garden, 86
  for screen or buffer, 44
  for shady area, 46
  for shearing, 47
  small, oval pyramidal, 38
  for wall planting, 44
Laurustinus. *See Viburnum tinus*
Lavandula spp., *87*
  drought tolerant, 91
  for fragrance, 57
  for herb garden, 87
  for informal hedge, 56
  for rock garden, 79
Lavatera hybrids
  red-hued flowers, 14
  rounded form, 25
  summer flowers, 14, 21
  tall, 24
  white-hued flowers, 21
Lavender. *See Lavandula* spp.
Lavender-cotton. *See Santolina* spp.
Lawn alternatives, 72
Lawn trees, 44–45
Lemonbalm. *See Melissa officinalis*
Lemongrass. *See Cymbopogon citratus*
Lemon-verbena. *See Aloysia triphylla*
Lenten-rose. *See Helleborus orientalis*
Leopard's-bane. *See Doronicum
  cordatum*
Leptospermum spp.
  laevigatum
    drought tolerant, 90
    for patio garden, 43
    for seacoast, 48
  scoparium
    easy maintenance, 58
    for seacoast, 61
  scoparium 'Ruby Glow'
    for all-year color, 51
    drought tolerant, 91
    showy, winter-to-spring flowers,
      53, 54
Leucojum spp.
  for naturalizing, 33
  for rock garden, 80
Leucothoe fontanesiana
  attractive evergreen, 50
  for fragrance, 57
  'Girard's Rainbow', for all-year
    color, 51
  medium height, 49
  for shady area, 59
  for water garden, 82
Levisticum officinale, for herb
  garden, 88
Liatris spp.
  for cutting, 29
  heat tolerant, 31
  red-hued, summer-to-fall flowers, 14, 15
  spicata
    drought tolerant, 89
    tall, 24
    for water garden, 83
    vertical form, 24

Ligularia spp.
  for cool summers, 30
  dentata
    attractive foliage, 26
    for water garden, 83
    yellow-hued, summer-to-fall flowers,
      18, 19
  for shady area, 32
Ligustrum spp.
  amurense, for screen, 56
  for attracting birds, 57
  attractive evergreen, 50
  for basic landscaping, 54
  for city garden, 59
  easy maintenance, 58
  fast growing, 55
  lucidum
    drought tolerant, 90
    for shady area, 46
    for shearing, 47, 60
Lilac, common. *See Syringa vulgaris*
Lilac, Japanese tree. *See Syringa
  reticulata*
Lilac, summer-. *See Buddleia davidii*
Lilac, wild. *See Ceanothus* spp.
Lilac-vine. *See Hardenbergia violacea*
  'Happy Wanderer'
Lilium hybrids
  for cutting, 29
  for fragrance, 28
Lily. *See Lilium* hybrids
Lily, bog-. *See Crinum americanum*
Lily, calla. *See Zantedeschia aethiopica*
Lily, checkered-. *See Fritillaria
  meleagris*
Lily, crinum-. *See Crinum* × *powellii*
Lily, fortnight-. *See Dietes vegeta*
Lily, Kaffir-. *See Clivia miniata*
Lily, plantain. *See Hosta* spp.
Lily, spider-. *See Hymenocallis* spp.
Lily-of-the-Nile. *See Agapanthus* spp.
Lily-of-the-valley. *See Convallaria
  majalis*
Lily-of-the-valley shrub. *See Pieris
  japonica*
Lilyturf. *See Liriope* spp.
Limonium spp.
  for attracting birds, 30
  bonduellii, yellow-hued, summer
    flowers, 18
  latifolium, for water garden, 83
  perezii, drought tolerant, 89
  sinuatum
    blue-hued flowers, 16
    red-hued flowers, 14
    summer flowers, 14, 16
Linaria maroccana
  for edging, 27
  red-hued flowers, 14, 15
  summer or winter flowers, 14, 15, 18, 19
  yellow-hued flowers, 18, 19
Linden. *See Tilia* spp.
Linden viburnum. *See Viburnum
  dilatatum*
Lippia. *See Phyla nodiflora*
Liquidambar styraciflua, *38*
  drought tolerant, 90
  for fall color, 40
  flood tolerant, 48
  large, oval pyramidal, 38
  pest free, 47
  for winter silhouette, 40
Liriodendron tulipifera
  large, oval pyramidal, 38
  for winter silhouette, 40
Liriope spp.
  muscari
    medium height, 69
    for rock garden, 80
    for water garden, 83
  for shady area, 32
  spicata
    easy maintenance, 75
    lawn alternative, 72

Live oak. *See Quercus agrifolia; Q. virginiana*
Lobelia spp.
  cardinalis
    red-hued, spring-to-fall flowers, 13, 14, 15
    for shady area, 32
    vertical form, 24
    for wet soil, 33
  erinus
    blue-hued, all-year flowers, 16, 17
    draping or trailing, 27
    dwarf, 22
    edging, 27
Lobularia maritima
  all-year flowers, 13, 14, 15, 20, 21, 22
  for containers, 28
  draping or trailing, 27
  drought tolerant, 89
  dwarf, 22
  for edging, 27
  for fragrance, 28
  for naturalizing, 33
  red-hued flowers, 13, 14, 15
  white-hued flowers, 20, 21, 22
London plane tree. See Platanus × acerifolia
Lonicera spp.
  for arbor or patio cover, 67
  for attracting birds, 57, 68
  for basic landscaping, 54
  for city garden, 59
  fast growing, 56
  for fragrance, 68
  fragrantissima, for fragrance, 57
  japonica 'Halliana'
    drought tolerant, 92
    lawn alternative, 72
    showy, spring-to-summer flowers, 65
    slope stabilizer, 72
  nitida, for seacoast, 61
  sempervirens, 66
    for fall color, 66
    showy, summer flowers, 65
  tatarica
    drought tolerant, 91
    tall, 50
Loosestrife, purple. *See Lythrum salicaria*
Loosestrife, yellow. *See Lysimachia punctata*
Loquat. *See Eriobotrya japonica*
Lotus. *See Nelumbo* spp.
Lovage. *See Levisticum officinale*
Love-in-a-mist. *See Nigella damascena*
Love-lies-bleeding. *See Amaranthus* spp.
Low-growing plants
  flowers, 22-23
  ground covers, 69
  shrubs, 49
  trees. *See* Small trees
Low-maintenance plants
  flowers, 32-33
  ground covers, 74-75
  roses, 96-97
  shrubs, 58
  trees, 47-48
Ludwigia spp., for water garden, 81
Lunaria annua
  for dried arrangements, 29
  for naturalizing, 33
Lupinus 'Russell hybrids', *30*
  blue-hued flowers, 16
  for cool summers, 30
  red-hued flowers, 13, 14
  spring-to-summer flowers, 13, 14, 16, 18, 20, 21
  vertical form, 24
  white-hued flowers, 20, 21
  yellow-hued flowers, 18
Lychnis spp.
  coronaria
    drought tolerant, 89
    open form, 26

Lychnis (*continued*)
  heat tolerant, 31
Lysimachia spp.
  nummularia
    for draping or trailing, 73
    low growing, 69
    for nooks and crannies, 74
  punctata, yellow-hued, spring-to-summer flowers, 18
  for wet soil, 33
Lythrum salicaria
  blue-hued flowers, 16, 17
  red-hued flowers, 14, 15
  summer-to-fall flowers, 14, 15, 16, 17
  for water garden, 83
  for wet soil, 33

M
Macfadyena unguis-cati
  drought tolerant, 92
  showy, spring flowers, 65
Maclura pomifera, drought tolerant, 90
Madrone. *See Arbutus menziesii*
Magnolia spp.
  for fragrance, 45
  grandiflora
    large, broad, 37
    'St. Mary', small, broad, 37
    showy, summer-to-fall flowers, 41
  heptapeta, medium, oval pyramidal, 38
  for patio garden, 43
  pest free, 47
  showy, spring flowers, 41
  × *soulangiana*, for lawns, 45
  stellata
    for city garden, 59
    for Japanese garden, 84
    for lawns, 45
    pest free, 60
    showy, winter-to-spring flowers, 53, 54
  virginiana, medium, broad, 37
Mahogany, mountain. *See Cercocarpus* spp.
Mahonia spp.
  aquifolium
    for city garden, 59
    for fall color, 51
    for attracting birds, 57
    attractive evergreen, 50
    for basic landscaping, 54
  bealei, for Japanese garden, 84
  drought tolerant, 91
  repens
    drought tolerant, 92
    slope stabilizer, 72
    for wet soil, 75
  showy fruit, 52
  for thorny barrier, 57
Maidenhair tree. *See Gingko biloba*
Malus spp.
  abuse tolerant, 48
  for attracting birds, 45
  baccata, medium height, broad, 37
  baccata 'Columnaris', small, narrow upright, 38
  for city garden, 46
  floribunda, 45
    small, broad, 37
    for fragrance, 45
    for patio garden, 43
  'Pink Spires', small, oval pyramidal, 38
  for shearing, 47
  showy, spring flowers, 41
  showy fruit, 41
  small, for shade, 42
  for wall planting, 44
  for winter silhouette, 40
Mandevilla spp.
  laxa, for fragrance, 68
  splendens, showy, spring-to-fall flowers, 65
Manzanita. *See Arctostaphylos* spp.
Maple. *See Acer* spp.
Marguerite, blue. *See Felicia amelloides*

Marguerite, golden. *See Anthemis tinctoria*
Marigold. *See Tagetes* spp.
Marjoram. *See Origanum* spp.
Marshmarigold. *See Caltha palustris*
Marsilea spp., for water garden, 81
Matthiola incana
  for cool summers, 30
  for fragrance, 28
  red-hued flowers, 13, 15
  spring flowers, 13, 18, 20
  vertical form, 24
  white-hued flowers, 20, 22
  winter flowers, 15, 19, 22
  yellow-hued flowers, 18, 19
Maytenus boaria, for patio garden, 43
Meadowrue, lavender mist. *See Thalictrum rochebrunianum*
Mealycup sage. *See Salvia farinacea*
Medium-height plants
  flowers, 23-24
  ground covers, 69
  shrubs, 49-50
  trees, 37-39, 42
Melaleuca spp.
  for bark interest, 39
  drought tolerant, 90
  quinquenervia, showy, summer-to-fall flowers, 41
Melia azedarach
  abuse tolerant, 48
  drought tolerant, 90
Melissa officinalis, for herb garden, 87
Menispermum canadense
  attractive foliage, 66
  for shady area, 68
Mentha spp.
  for herb garden, 86, 87, 88
  requienii
    for fragrance, 74
    for Japanese garden, 85
    low growing, 69
    for nooks and crannies, 74
Mertensia virginica
  blue-hued, spring-to-summer flowers, 16
  medium height, 23
  for shady area, 32
  for wet soil, 33
Mesquite. *See Prosopis* spp.
Metasequoia glyptostroboides
  pest free, 47
  for water garden, 82
  for winter silhouette, 40
Michelia figo, tall, 50
Mignonette. *See Reseda odorata*
Mimulus spp.
  × *hybridus*
    for cool summers, 30
    summer flowers, 18
    for wet soil, 33
    yellow-hued, summer flowers, 18
  for rock garden, 80
  for shady area, 32
Mint. *See Mentha* spp.
Mirabilis jalapa, 31
  drought tolerant, 89
  for fragrance, 28
  heat tolerant, 31
  rounded form, 25
Mirror plant. *See Coprosma repens*
Miscanthus sinensis, for water garden, 83
Mock orange. *See Philadelphus* spp.
Molina caerulea, for water garden, 83
Moluccella laevis
  for naturalizing, 33
  vertical form, 24
Momordica balsamina, for fast cover, 67
Monarda didyma, 33
  for cutting, 29
  heat tolerant, 31
  for herb garden, 87, 88
  medium height, 23

Monarda didyma (*continued*)
  for naturalizing, 33
  red-hued, summer flowers, 14
  for wet soil, 33
Mondograss. *See Ophiopogon japonicus*
Monkeyflower. *See Mimulus* spp.
Moonflower vine. *See Ipomoea alba*
Moorgrass. *See Molina caerulea*
Morning glory, dwarf. *See Convolvulus tricolor*
Morning glory vine. *See Ipomoea* spp.
Moss-pink. *See Phlox subulata*
Mountain ash. *See Sorbus* spp.
Muscari spp.
  armeniacum
    blue-hued, spring flowers, 16
    for rock garden, 80
    spring flowers, 16
  azureum, dwarf, 22
Myosotis sylvatica
  blue-hued, spring-to-fall flowers, 16, 17
  dwarf, 22
  for naturalizing, 33
  for shady area, 32
  for wet soil, 33
Myrica pensylvanica
  for city garden, 59
  easy maintenance, 58
  for herb garden, 87
  pest free, 60
  for seacoast, 61
  tall, 50
  for water garden, 82
  for wet soil, 61
  for winter interest, 52
Myriophyllum spp., for water garden, 81
Myrrhis odorata, for herb garden, 87
Myrtle. *See Myrtus communis*
Myrtus communis
  for attracting birds, 57
  attractive evergreen, 50
  drought tolerant, 91
  easy maintenance, 58
  pest free, 60
  for shearing, 60

N
Nandina domestica
  attractive evergreen, 50
  for basic landscaping, 54
  drought tolerant, 91
  easy maintenance, 58
  for fall color, 51
  'Harbour Dwarf'
    for fall color, 71
    for water garden, 82
    for Japanese garden, 84
    showy fruit, 52
Narcissus spp.
  bulbocodium
    dwarf, 22
    for rock garden, 80
  for fragrance, 28
  and hybrids
    for containers, 28
    for cutting, 29
    medium height, 23
    for naturalizing, 33
    spring flowers, 18, 20
    white-hued flowers, 20
    yellow-hued flowers, 18
Narrow-upright trees, 38-39
Nasturtium. *See Tropaeolum majus*
Natal-plum. *See Carissa*
Naturalizing, flowers for, 32-33
Nelumbo spp.
  nucifera, for Japanese garden, 85
  for water garden, 81
Nemesia strumosa
  for cool summers, 30
  low growing, 23
  yellow-hued, summer or winter flowers, 19

Nemophila menziesii
  blue-hued, spring flowers, 16
  for shady area, 32
Nepeta mussinii, for herb garden, 88
Nerium oleander
  for city garden, 59
  drought tolerant, 91
  fast growing, 56
  showy, spring-to-fall flowers, 53, 54
  tall, 50
  for training as tree, 60
Nicotiana alata
  for fragrance, 28
  medium height, 23
  red-hued flowers, 14
  for shady area, 32
  summer flowers, 14, 21
  white-hued flowers, 21
Nierembergia hippomanica
  blue-hued, summer flowers, 16
  low growing, 23
  for shady area, 32
  var. *violacea*, drought tolerant, 89
Nigella damascena
  for attracting birds, 30
  blue-hued, spring flowers, 16
  open form, 26
Nooks and crannies, ground covers for, 73–74
Nymphaea spp., *81*
  for Japanese garden, 85
  for water garden, 81
Nymphoides peltata, for water garden, 81
Nyssa sylvatica
  for city garden, 46
  for fall color, 40
  flood tolerant, 48
  large, for shade, 42
  pest free, 47
  for seacoast, 48
  for winter silhouette, 40

O
Oak. See *Quercus* spp.
Obedience. See *Physostegia virginiana*
Ocimum basilicum, for herb garden, 86, 88
Old-man's-beard. See *Chionanthus virginicus*
Olea europea
  drought tolerant, 90
  pest free, 47
  for shearing, 47
  small, broad, 37
Oleander. See *Nerium oleander*
Olive. See *Olea europea*
Onoclea sensibilis, for water garden, 83
Open form flowers, 25–26
Ophiopogon japonicus
  easy maintenance, 75
  for Japanese garden, 85
  medium height, 69
  for water garden, 83
Opuntia spp.
  drought tolerant, 91
  humifusa, for water garden, 83
Orange, Mexican. See *Choisya ternata*
Orange flowers, 17–19
Orange-red roses, 94
Orchid tree. See *Bauhinia* spp.
Oregano. See *Origanum* spp.
Oregon grape. See *Mahonia* spp.
Origanum spp., for herb garden, 86, 88
Orontium aquaticum, for water garden, 81
Osage orange. See *Maclura pomifera*
Osmanthus spp.
  attractive evergreen, 50
  drought tolerant, 91
  easy maintenance, 58
  fragrans
    for fragrance, 57
    for herb garden, 87
  heterophyllus, *50*
    'Gulftide', tall, 50

Osmanthus (continued)
  for thorny barrier, 57
  for screen, 56
  for training as tree, 60
Osmunda spp., for water garden, 83
Osteospermum fruticosum
  drought tolerant, 92
  showy, all-year flowers, 70, 71
Ostrya virginiana
  for city garden, 46
  medium height, for shade, 42
  for patio garden, 43
  pest free, 47
Oval to pyramidal trees, 37–38
Oxalis oregana, for shady area, 75
Oxydendrum arboreum, *44*
  for fall color, 40
  for fragrance, 45
  medium height, for shade, 42
  for patio garden, 43
  showy, summer flowers, 41
  showy fruit, 41
  for water garden, 82

P
Pachysandra terminalis, *4–5*
  for draping or trailing, 73
  easy maintenance, 75
  for fragrance, 74
  for Japanese garden, 85
  lawn alternative, 72
  medium height, 69
  for shady area, 75
Paeonia spp.
  hybrids, *13*
    attractive foliage, 26
    for cutting, 29
    for fragrance, 28
    for Japanese garden, 85
    red-hued flowers, 13
    rounded form, 25
    spring flowers, 13, 18, 20
    for water garden, 83
    white-hued flowers, 20
    yellow-hued flowers, 18
  suffruticosa, for shearing, 60
Pagoda tree, Japanese. See *Sophora japonica*
Painted-tongue. See *Salpiglossis sinuata*
Palm, Canary Island date. See *Phoenix canariensis*
Palm, fan. See *Washingtonia* spp.
Palm, Guadalupe fan. See *Brahea* spp.
Palm, Mediterranean fan. See *Chamaerops humilis*
Palm, Mexican blue. See *Brahea* spp.
Palm, queen. See *Arecastrum romanzoffianum*
Palm, windmill. See *Trachycarpus fortunei*
Palms, drought tolerant, 91
Paloverde. See *Cercidium* spp.
Paloverde, Mexican. See *Parkinsonia aculeata*
Pampas grass. See *Cortaderia selloana*
Pansy. See *Viola* × *wittrockiana*
Papaver spp.
  medium height, 23
  nudicaule, for cool summers, 30
  open form, 26
  red-hued flowers, 13, 14
  rhoeas, for naturalizing, 33
  spring-to-summer flowers, 13, 14, 18, 19, 20, 21
  white-hued flowers, 20, 21
  yellow-hued flowers, 18, 19
Papyrus. See *Cyperus* spp.
Parilla, yellow. See *Menispermum canadense*
Parkinsonia aculeata, drought tolerant, 90
Parsley. See *Petroselinum crispum*
Parthenocissus spp.
  quinquefolia

Parthenocissus (continued)
  for attracting birds, 68
  attractive foliage, 66
  for fall color, 66
  for shady area, 68
  slope stabilizer, 72
  tricuspidata
    for attracting birds, 68
    attractive foliage, 66
    for fall color, 66
    for Japanese garden, 85
    for shady area, 68
Passiflora spp.
  × *alatocaerulea*, for fragrance, 68
  showy, spring-to-summer flowers, 65
Patio-covering vines, 67
Patio trees, 43
Paulownia tomentosa
  fast growing, 43
  large, for shade, 42
Paxistima canbyi
  for rock garden, 79
  tall, 70
  for wet soil, 75
Pea, Atlantic. See *Clitoria ternatea*
Peach, flowering. See *Prunus* spp.
Pear. See *Pyrus* spp.
Peashrub, Siberian. See *Caragana arborescens*
Pecan. See *Carya illinoinensis*
Pelargonium spp.
  for herb garden, 87
  × *hortorum*, *14*
    attractive foliage, 26
    for containers, 28
    red-hued flowers, 13, 14, 15
    for rock garden, 80
    rounded form, 25
    spring-to-fall flowers, 13, 14, 15, 20, 21
    white-hued flowers, 20, 21
  peltatum
    draping or trailing, 27
    medium height, 69
Peltandra virginica, for water garden, 81
Pennisetum spp.
  for Japanese garden, 85
  for water garden, 83
Penstemon
  for cool summers, 30
  hartwegii, red-hued, spring-to-summer flowers, 13, 14
  heterophyllus purdyi
    blue-hued, spring-to-summer flowers, 16, 17
    drought tolerant, 89
    for rock garden, 80
Peony, herbaceous. See *Paeonia* hybrids
Peony, tree. See *Paeonia suffruticosa*
Peppermint, Nichol's willowleaf. See *Eucalyptus nicholii*
Peppermint tree. See *Agonis flexuosa*
Pepper tree. See *Schinus* spp.
Pepper vine. See *Ampelopsis arborea*
Periwinkle. See *Vinca* spp.
Periwinkle, Madagascar. See *Catharanthus roseus*
Persimmon. See *Diospyros* spp.
Pest-free shrubs, 60
Pest-free trees, 46–47
Petroselinum crispum, for herb garden, 86, 88
Petunia × *hybrida*
  blue-hued flowers, 17
  for containers, 28
  draping or trailing, 27
  for edging, 27
  heat tolerant, 31
  low growing, 23
  red-hued flowers, 13, 14, 15
  spring-to-fall flowers, 13, 14, 15, 17, 18, 19, 20, 21
  white-hued flowers, 20, 21
  yellow-hued flowers, 18, 19

Phalaris arundinacea var. *picta*
  drought tolerant, 92
  slope stabilizer, 72
Phaseolus coccineus, for fast cover, 67
Phellodendron amurense
  for city garden, 46
  large, broad, 37
  pest free, 47
  for winter silhouette, 40
Philadelphus spp.
  coronarius
    for city garden, 59
    drought tolerant, 91
    for fragrance, 57
    showy, spring flowers, 53
  fast growing, 56
Phlox spp.
  drummondii, *10–11*
    blue-hued flowers, 17
    for edging, 27
    red-hued flowers, 14
    summer flowers, 14, 17, 21
    white-hued flowers, 21
  subulata
    blue-hued flowers, 16, 17
    drought tolerant, 92
    dwarf, 22
    low growing, 69
    for naturalizing, 33
    red-hued flowers, 13, 14
    for rock garden, 80
    showy flowers, 70
    spring-to-summer flowers, 13, 14, 16, 17, 70
Phoenix canariensis, drought tolerant, 91
Photinia spp.
  attractive evergreen, 51
  × *fraseri*
    for all-year color, 51
    for basic landscaping, 54
    for screen, 56
    for shearing, 60
  serrulata, for training as tree, 60
Phyla nodiflora
  drought tolerant, 92
  lawn alternative, 72
  for rock garden, 80
  traffic tolerant, 73
Phyllostachys spp.
  for Japanese garden, 85
  for water garden, 82
Physostegia virginiana
  for cutting, 29
  red-hued flowers, 14
  summer flowers, 14, 21
  white-hued flowers, 21
Picea spp.
  abies, large, oval pyramidal, 38
  glauca
    'Conica', for rock garden, 79
    for seacoast, 48
    for wall planting, 44
  omorika, medium, oval pyramidal, 38
    for screen or buffer, 44
Pickerelrush. See *Pontederia cordata*
Pieris japonica, *8*
  for basic landscaping, 54
  for Japanese garden, 84
  for shady area, 59
  showy, spring flowers, 53
  tall, 50
  for water garden, 82
Pincushion-flower. See *Scabiosa caucasica*
Pincushion tree. See *Hakea laurina*
Pineapple guava. See *Feijoa sellowiana*
Pineapple sage. See *Salvia elegans*
Pine. See *Pinus* spp.
Pink. See *Dianthus* spp.
Pink flowers, 13–15
  roses, 93–94
Pink-pussytoes. See *Antennaria rosea*

Pinus spp.
  canariensis, for seacoast, 48
  densiflora, large, broad, 37
    'Umbraculifera', for rock garden, 79
  flexilis, large, oval pyramidal, 38
  mugo, small, oval pyramidal, 38
  mugo var. *mugo* 'Compacta'
    for Japanese garden, 84
    low growing, 49
    for rock garden, 79
  nigra
    for city garden, 46
    for seacoast, 48
  parviflora, for water garden, 81
  pinea
    drought tolerant, 91
    large, broad, 37
    for seacoast, 48
  for screen or buffer, 44
  strobus, for bark interest, 39
  strobus 'Fastigiata', large, narrow
    upright, 39
  strobus 'Nana'
    for rock garden, 79
    for water garden, 82
  sylvestris, for city garden, 46
  sylvestris 'Fastigiata', medium, narrow
    upright, 39
  thunbergiana
    for Japanese garden, 84
    for rock garden, 79
    for water garden, 81
Pistacia chinensis
  for city garden, 46
  drought tolerant, 90
  for fall color, 40
  large, for shade, 42
  for patio garden, 43
  pest free, 47
  for winter silhouette, 40
Pistia stratiotes, for water garden, 81
Pittosporum spp.
  attractive evergreen, 51
  for basic landscaping, 54
  crassifolium, for seacoast, 61
  easy maintenance, 58
  napaulense, for fragrance, 57
  phillyraeoides, drought tolerant, 91
  for screen, 56
  for shearing, 47
  tobira, *51*
    for city garden, 59
    for Japanese garden, 84
    for shearing, 60
    small, broad, 37
  tobira 'Variegata'
    for all-year color, 51
    medium height, 50
  tobira 'Wheeler's Dwarf', low
    growing, 49
  undulatum, for fragrance, 45
Platanus × *acerifolia*
  abuse tolerant, 48
  for bark interest, 39
  for city garden, 46
  flood tolerant, 48
  for seacoast, 48
  for shearing, 47
  for winter silhouette, 40
Platycodon grandiflorus
  blue-hued, summer flowers, 17
  heat tolerant, 31
  for Japanese garden, 85
  tall, 24
  var. *mariesii*
    medium height, 23
    for rock garden, 80
Plum. *See Prunus* spp.
Plumbago, blue. *See Ceratostigma*
  plumbaginoides
Plumbago auriculata, medium
  height, 50

Podocarpus macrophyllus
  drought tolerant, 90
  medium, narrow upright, 39
  for shearing, 47, 60
  var. *maki*
    drought tolerant, 91
    pest free, 60
  for wall planting, 44
Polygonatum commutatum
  attractive foliage, 26
  for shady area, 32
  for water garden, 83
Polygonum spp.
  aubertii
    for arbor or patio cover, 67
    drought tolerant, 92
    showy, spring-to-fall flowers, 65, 66
  capitatum, lawn alternative, 72
  cuspidatum var. *compactum*
    lawn alternative, 72
    slope stabilizer, 72
Polypodium virginianum, for Japanese
  garden, 85
Polystichum acrostichoides, for
  Japanese garden, 85
Pomegranate. *See Punica granatum*
Pond-side garden. *See* Water garden
Pontederia cordata, for water
  garden, 81
Poplar. *See Populus* spp.
Poppy. *See Papaver* spp.
Populus spp.
  abuse tolerant, 48
  for fall color, 40
  fast growing, 43
  flood tolerant, 48
  nigra 'Italica', *48*
    large, narrow upright, 39
    for seacoast, 48
  for screen or buffer, 44
  tremula 'Erecta', large, narrow
    upright, 39
  tremuloides, *40*
    for winter silhouette, 40
Portulaca grandiflora, *23*
  for attracting birds, 30
  draping or trailing, 27
  drought tolerant, 89
  dwarf, 22
  for edging, 27
  heat tolerant, 31
  red-hued, summer-to-fall flowers, 14, 15
Possumhaw. *See Ilex decidua*
Potato vine. *See Solanum jasminoides*
Potentilla spp.
  fruticosa
    for city garden, 59
    easy maintenance, 58
    for informal hedge, 56
    low growing, 49
    pest free, 60
    for shearing, 60
    showy, summer-to-fall flowers,
      53, 54
    for water garden, 82
    for wet soil, 61
  tabernaemontani
    easy maintenance, 75
    lawn alternative, 72
    low growing, 69
    for rock garden, 80
    showy, spring flowers, 70
Poterium sanguisorba, for herb
  garden, 86
Pot marigold. *See Calendula officinalis*
Pratia angulata, for rock garden, 80
Prickly pear cactus. *See Opuntia* spp.
Primrose. *See Primula* spp.
Primrose jasmine. *See Jasminum*
  mesnyi
Primrose tree. *See Lagunaria*
  patersonii

Primrose-willow. *See Ludwigia* spp.
Primula spp., *32*
  for cool summers, 30
  polyantha, low growing, 23
  for rock garden, 80
  for shady area, 32
  vulgaris
    blue-hued flowers, 16
    dwarf, 22
    red-hued flowers, 13, 15
    white-hued flowers, 20
    winter-to-spring flowers, 13, 15, 16,
      18, 20
    yellow-hued flowers, 18
  for water garden, 83
  for wet soil, 33
Privet. *See Ligustrum* spp.
Prosopis spp., drought tolerant, 90
Prunus spp., *41*
  for attracting birds, 45
  for bark interest, 39
  caroliniana, drought tolerant, 91
  cerasifera
    'Atropurpurea', drought tolerant,
      90, 91
    for Japanese garden, 84
    'Krauter Vesuvius', small, oval
      pyramidal, 38
    small, for shade, 42
  × *cistena*, for all-year color, 51
  for fragrance, 45
  laurocerasus
    for attracting birds, 57
    attractive evergreen, 51
    fast growing, 56
    for screen, 56
    tall, 35
  for lawns, 45
  lusitanica
    drought tolerant, 91
    for screen, 56
  for patio garden, 43
  for screen or buffer, 44
  serrulata, for Japanese garden, 84
  serrulata 'Amanogawa', small, narrow
    upright, 38
  showy, spring flowers, 41
  showy fruit, 41
  subhirtella 'Pendula', for water
    garden, 82
  subhirtella 'Shoegetsu', *4–5*
  tomentosa, showy fruit, 52
  for training as tree, 60
Pseudotsuga menziesii
  large, oval pyramidal, 38
  for shearing, 47
Pulmonaria saccharata
  attractive foliage, 26
  low growing, 23
  for shady area, 32
Punica granatum
  'Nana', drought tolerant, 91
  for shearing, 60
  showy fruit, 52
Purple flowers, 15–17
  roses, 94
Pussy willow, rosegold. *See Salix*
  gracilistyla
Pyracantha spp.
  for attracting birds, 57
  coccinea
    for city garden, 59
    drought tolerant, 91
    for thorny barrier, 57
  fast growing, 56
  fortuneana 'Cherri Berri', *52*
  koidzumii 'Santa Cruz', slope
    stabilizer, 72
  'Mohave', tall, 50
  showy fruit, 52
Pyrostegia venusta, showy, fall-to-
  winter flowers, 65, 66

Pyrus spp.
  calleryana
    'Bradford', medium, oval pyrami-
      dal, 38
    'Chanticleer', medium, narrow
      upright, 39
    for city garden, 46
    for patio garden, 43
  kawakamii
    for patio garden, 43
    showy, winter flowers, 42
    for wall planting, 44

Q
Queen-of-the-prairie. *See Filipendula*
  rubra
Queen's-wreath. *See Antigonon*
  leptopus
Quercus spp.
  agrifolia, drought tolerant, 90
  for attracting birds, 45
  for fall color, 40
  ilex, drought tolerant, 90
  palustris, large, oval pyramidal, for
    shade, 38, 42
  phellos
    flood tolerant, 48
    large, for shade, 42
  robur 'Fastigiata', large, narrow
    upright, 39
  rubra, large, broad, for shade, 37, 42
  subra, large, broad, 37
  virginiana, large, broad, 37
Quince, flowering. *See Chaenomeles*
  speciosa

R
Raphiolepis spp.
  for basic landscaping, 55
  drought tolerant, 91
  easy maintenance, 58
  indica, for seacoast, 61
    'Ballerina', low growing, 49
    for informal hedge, 56
    showy fruit, 52
Redbud. *See Cercis* spp.
Red flowers, 13–15
  roses, 93
Red-hot-poker. *See Kniphofia uvaria*
Redwood, coast. *See Sequoia*
  sempervirens
Reseda odorata
  for fragrance, 28
  open form, 26
Rhamnus spp.
  frangula 'Columnaris'
    for screen, 56
    small, narrow upright, 38
    pest free, 60
Rhododendron spp., *7, 59, 84*
  attractive evergreen, 51
  for basic landscaping, 55
  calendulaceum, for fall color, 51
  impeditum, for rock garden, 79
  keiskei, for rock garden, 79
  Knap Hill-Exbury hybrid azaleas, for
    Japanese garden, 84
  Kurume hybrid azaleas, for Japanese
    garden, 84
  P.J.M. hybrids, medium, 50
  for shady area, 32
  showy, spring flowers, 53
  viscosum, for wet soil, 61
  for water garden, 82
Rhoicissus capensis
  for arbor or patio cover, 67
  attractive foliage, 66
Rhus spp.
  aromatica, for attracting birds, 57
  aromatica 'Gro-low'
    for attracting birds, 74
    tall ground cover, 70

Rhus (continued)
for city garden, 59
copallina
fast growing, 56
showy fruit, 52
for winter interest, 52
for fall color, 51
lancea
abuse tolerant, 48
drought tolerant, 90
small, broad, 37
for screen, 56
typhina
drought tolerant, 91
showy fruit, 52
for winter interest, 52
Ribbongrass. *See Phalaris arundinacea*
var. *picta*
Ribes spp.
alpinum, for city garden, 59
speciosum, for thorny barrier, 57
Robinia pseudoacacia
abuse tolerant, 48
for city garden, 46
drought tolerant, 90
fast growing, 43
for fragrance, 45
'Idahoensis', showy, spring flowers, 41
Rockcress, wall. *See Arabis caucasica*
Rocket-larkspur. *See Consolida ambigua*
Rock gardens, *6*, 79–80
flowers for, 27, 80
ground covers for, 73
Rockrose. *See Cistus* spp.
Rodgersia aesculifolia, for water garden, 83
Rosa spp., 93–97
'Arizona', *94*
for attracting birds, 58
banksiae, drought tolerant, 92
for basic landscaping, 55
bicolor, 95
'Chivalry', *53*
for cutting, 96
disease tolerant, 97
easy to grow, 96–97
eglanteria, for herb garden, 88
for fragrance, 57, 95–96
for ground covers, 95
hardiest modern, 97
'Harison's Yellow', *95*
for hedges, *94*, 95
for herb garden, 87
hugonis, for winter interest, 52
hybrids
for arbor or patio cover, 67
for fragrance, 68
showy, spring-to-summer flowers, 65
hybrid teas, 93, *96*
lavender to purple, 94
low maintenance, 96–97
modern, hardiest, 97
multicolor, 95
'Nevada', *97*
orange-red, 94
pink, 93–94
red, 93
rugosa
for city garden, 59
for informal hedge, 56
for seacoast, 61
tall shrub, 50
for screens, 95
showy flowers, 53, 54
spinosissima
for attracting birds, 74
showy-flowered ground cover, 70
spring flowers, 70
spring-to-fall flowers, 53, 64
for thorny barrier, 57
virginiana
for seacoast, 61
for winter interest, 52
white to cream, 94

Rosa (continued)
wichuraiana
for city garden, 59
showy, summer flowers, 71
slope stabilizer, 72
Rose. *See Rosa* spp.
Rose, Japanese. *See Kerria japonica*
Rose campion. *See Lychnis coronaria*
Rosemary. *See Rosmarinus officinalis*
Rose-moss. *See Portulaca grandiflora*
Rose-of-Sharon. *See Hibiscus syriacus*
Rosmarinus officinalis, *88*
for herb garden, 86, 87, 88
'Prostratus'
for attracting birds, 74
for draping or trailing, 73
drought tolerant, 92
easy maintenance, 75
for herb garden, 88
showy, winter-to-spring flowers, 70, 71
slope stabilizer, 72
tall ground cover, 70
for seacoast, 61
Rounded form, flowers with, 25
Rudbeckia spp.
for attracting birds, 30
hirta
for cutting, 29
heat tolerant, 31
for naturalizing, 33
rounded form, 25
tall, 24
for water garden, 83
yellow-hued, summer-to-fall flowers, 19
Russian olive. *See Elaeagnus angustifolia*

S
Safflower. *See Carthamus tinctorius*
Sage. *See Salvia* spp.
Sagina subulata
for Japanese garden, 85
lawn alternative, 72
low growing, 69
for nooks and crannies, 74
for rock garden, 80
for shady area, 75
traffic tolerant, 73
Sagittaria latifolia, for water garden, 81
St. John's wort. *See Hypericum* spp.
Salal. *See Gaultheria shallon*
Salix spp., *43*
abuse tolerant, 48
alba var. *vitellina*
for bark interest, 39
for seacoast, 48
fast growing, 43
flood tolerant, 48
gracilistyla, for wet soil, 61
for winter silhouette, 40
Salpiglossis sinuata
for cool summers, 30
open form, 26
Saltbush. *See Atriplex* spp.
Salvia spp.
drought tolerant, 91
elegans, 88
farinacea
blue-hued, summer-to-fall flowers, 17
for containers, 28
for cutting, 29
heat tolerant, 31
for herb garden, 86, 87, 88
splendens
for containers, 28
red-hued, summer-to-fall flowers, 14, 15
× *superba*, attractive foliage, 26
vertical form, 24
for water garden, 83
Sand cherry, purpleleaf. *See Prunus* × *cistena*

Sandwort, Corsican. *See Arenaria balearica*
Santolina spp.
drought tolerant, 92
for herb garden, 88
Sanvitalia procumbens
draping or trailing, 27
drought tolerant, 89
dwarf, 22
heat tolerant, 31
yellow-hued, summer-to-fall flowers, 19
Sapium sebiferum
for fall color, 40
fast growing, 43
medium height, for shade, 42
Saponaria ocymoides
red-hued, spring flowers, 13
for rock garden, 80
Sapphireberry. *See Symplocos paniculata*
Sarcococca spp.
for fragrance, 57, 74
hookerana var. *humilis*, for Japanese garden, 85
ruscifolia, for informal hedge, 56
for shady area, 59, 75
Sasa veitchii, for Japanese garden, 85
Sassafras albidum, for fall color, 40
Satureja spp.
for herb garden, 86, 88
for rock garden, 80
Saururus cernuus, for water garden, 81
Savory, summer or winter. *See Satureja* spp.
Saxifraga spp., for rock garden, 80
Scabiosa spp.
for attracting birds, 30
caucasica
blue-hued, summer-to-fall flowers, 17
for cutting, 29
medium height, 23
open form, 26
heat tolerant, 31
Scarlet runner bean. *See Phaseolus coccineus*
Schinus spp.
drought tolerant, 90
showy fruit, 41
Schizanthus × *wisetonensis*
for cool summers, 30
rounded form, 25
Schizophragma hydrangeoides
for shady area, 68
showy, summer flowers, 65
Scilla siberica
blue-hued, spring flowers, 16
dwarf, 22
for rock garden, 80
for shady area, 32
Scirpus albescens, for water garden, 81
Scotch broom. *See Cytisus scoparius*
Screening
roses for, 95
shrubs for, 56
trees for, 44
Seacoast conditions
shrubs for, 61
trees for, 48
Sea-lavender. *See Limonium* spp.
Sea-pink. *See Armeria maritima*
Sedum spp.
acre, low growing, 69
attractive foliage, 26
drought tolerant, 92
easy maintenance, 75
for edging, 27
heat tolerant, 31
lawn alternative, 72
for nooks and crannies, 74
for rock garden, 80
showy, spring flowers, 70
spectabile
for attracting birds, 30
for containers, 28

Sedum (continued)
for cutting, 29
for dried arrangements, 29
medium height, 23
red-hued, summer-to-fall flowers, 14, 15
rounded form, 25
for water garden, 83
Sempervivum tectorum
for nooks and crannies, 74
for rock garden, 80
Senecio spp.
cineraria
attractive foliage, 26
for edging, 27
heat tolerant, 31
× *hybridus*
for shady area, 32
for wet soil, 33
Sequoia sempervirens, for screen or buffer, 44
Serbian spruce. *See Picea omorika*
Serviceberry. *See Amelanchier* spp.
Shadblow. *See Amelanchier canadensis*
Shade-giving trees, 42–43
Shady areas
flowers for, 31–32
ground covers for, 75
shrubs for, 59
trees for, 46
vines for, 68
Shearing
shrubs for, 60–61
trees for, 47
Shellflower. *See Pistia stratiotes*
Shepherdia argentea, drought tolerant, 92
Shibataea kumasaca, for Japanese garden, 85
Siebold viburnum. *See Viburnum sieboldii*
Silk-oak. *See Grevillea robusta*
Silk tree. *See Albizia julibrissin*
Silverbell. *See Halesia* spp.
Silverberry. *See Elaeagnus pungens*
Silvergrass, Japanese. *See Miscanthus sinensis*
Silver-lace vine. *See Polygonum aubertii*
Silver mound. *See Artemisia schmidtiana*
Slope stabilizers, 71–72
Small trees, 43
broad, 37
narrow upright, 38
oval pyramidal, 37–48
for shade, 42
Smilax lanceolata, attractive foliage, 66
Smoke tree. *See Cotinus coggygria*
Snakeroot. *See Asarum canadense*
Snapdragon. *See Antirrhinum majus*
Sneezeweed. *See Helenium autumnale*
Sneezewort. *See Achillea ptarmica*
Snowball, fragrant. *See Viburnum* × *carlcephalum*
Snowbell, Japanese. *See Styrax japonicus*
Snowberry. *See Symphoricarpos orbiculatus*
Snowdrop. *See Galanthus* spp.
Snowflake. *See Leucojum* spp.
Snow-in-summer. *See Cerastium tomentosum*
Snow-on-the-mountain. *See Euphorbia marginata*
Soapweed. *See Yucca glauca*
Soapwort, rock. *See Saponaria ocymoides*
Solanum jasminoides
drought tolerant, 92
showy, all-year flowers, 65, 66
Soleirolia soleirolii
for Japanese garden, 85

Soleirolia soleirolii (*continued*)
  low growing, 69
  for nooks and crannies, 74
  for shady area, 75
  traffic tolerant, 73
  for wet soil, 75
Solidago spp.
  hybrids
    for attracting birds, 30
    for dried arrangements, 29
    heat tolerant, 31
    for rock garden, 80
    yellow-hued, summer-to-fall
      flowers, 19
  odora, for herb garden, 87
Sollya heterophylla, tall, 70
Solomon's-seal, great. *See Polygonatum
  commutatum*
Sophora japonica
  broad, 37
  for city garden, 46
  drought tolerant, 90
  for fragrance, 45
  medium to large, 37, 42
  for patio garden, 43
  pest free, 47
  for shade, 42
  showy, summer flowers, 41
Sorbus spp.
  alnifolia, medium, oval pyramidal, 38
  for attracting birds, 45
  aucuparia
    'Fastigiata', small, narrow
      upright, 38
    medium height, for shade, 42
    showy, spring flowers, 41
  showy fruit, 41
Sorrel, redwood. *See Oxalis oregana*
Sourwood. *See Oxydendrum arboreum*
Southern yew. *See Podocarpus
  macrophyllus*
Speedwell. *See Veronica* hybrids
Spiderflower. *See Cleome hasslerana*
Spiderwort. *See Tradescantia* ×
  andersoniana
Spike gayfeather. *See Liatris spicata*
Spiraea spp.
  × *bumalda*
    for city garden, 59
    for fall color, 51
    for Japanese garden, 84
    low growing, 49
    for rock garden, 79
    showy, summer-to-fall flowers, 53, 54
  cantoniensis, for shearing, 60
  easy maintenance, 58
  fast growing, 56
  prunifolia, showy, spring flowers, 53
  thunbergii, for shearing, 60
  vanhouttei, for city garden, 59
Spring-flowering plants
  flowers
    blue hued, 15–16
    red hued, 13
    white hued, 19–20
    yellow hued, 17–18
  ground covers, 70
  shrubs, 52–53
  trees, 41
  vines, 65
Spruce. *See Picea* spp.
Spurge, cushion. *See Euphorbia
  epithymoides*
Spurge, Japanese. *See Pachysandra
  terminalis*
Squill, Siberian. *See Scilla siberica*
Stachys spp.
  byzantina
    attractive foliage, 26
    for dried arrangements, 29
    drought tolerant, 89
    for edging, 27
    heat tolerant, 31
    for herb garden, 88
    medium ground cover, 69

Stachys (*continued*)
  grandiflora, vertical form, 24
Starjasmine. *See Trachelospermum
  jasminoides*
Star magnolia. *See Magnolia stellata*
Statice. *See Limonium sinuatum*
Stepping-stones, ground covers for, 73
Stewartia spp.
  koreana
    for bark interest, 39
    for patio garden, 43
    small, oval pyramidal, 38
    for winter silhouette, 40
  pest free, 47
  pseudocamellia
    for bark interest, 39
    showy, summer flowers, 41
Stock. *See Matthiola incana*
Stokesia laevis
  blue-hued flowers, 17
  for cutting, 29
  heat tolerant, 31
  low growing, 23
  summer-to-fall flowers, 17, 21
  white-hued flowers, 21
Stonecress. *See Aubrieta deltoidea*
Stonecrop. *See Sedum* spp.
Strawberry, beach. *See Fragaria
  chiloensis*
Strawberry, mock. *See Duchesnea
  indica*
Strawberry tree. *See Arbutus unedo*
Strawflower. *See Helichrysum
  bracteatum*
Styrax japonicus
  for fragrance, 45
  medium height, for shade, 42
  for patio garden, 43
  showy, summer flowers, 41
  for water garden, 82
Sumac. *See Rhus* spp.
Summer-cypress. *See Kochia scoparia
  trichophylla* 'Childsii'
Summer-flowering plants
  flowers
    blue hued, 16–17
    heat tolerant, 31
    red hued, 13–14
    white hued, 20–21
    yellow hued, 18–19
  ground covers, 70–71
  shrubs, 53
  trees, 41
  vines, 65
Sunflower. *See Helianthus* spp.
Sunflower, Mexican. *See Tithonia
  rotundifolia*
Sunrose. *See Helianthemum
  nummularium*
Sweet alyssum. *See Lobularia
  maritima*
Sweetbox. *See Sarcococca* spp.
Sweetbrier rose. *See Rosa eglanteria*
Sweet cicely. *See Myrrhis odorata*
Sweet flag. *See Acorus* spp.
Sweet gum. *See Liquidambar
  styraciflua*
Sweet mock orange. *See Philadelphus
  coronarius*
Sweet olive. *See Osmanthus* spp.
Sweet pea. *See Lathyrus odoratus*
Sweet pepperbush. *See Clethra
  alnifolia*
Sweetshade. *See Hymenosporum
  flavum*
Sweet william. *See Dianthus barbatus*
Sweet woodruff. *See Galium odoratum*
Sydney golden wattle. *See Acacia
  longifolia*
Symphoricarpos orbiculatus,
  medium, 50
Symplocos paniculata, showy fruit, 52
Syringa spp.
  reticulata
    medium height, for shade, 42
    for patio garden, 43

Syringa (*continued*)
  for training as tree, 60
  vulgaris, *56*
    for basic landscaping, 55
    drought tolerant, 92
    for fragrance, 57
    for screen, 56
    showy, spring flowers, 53
    tall shrub, 50
Syzygium paniculatum, for
  shearing, 60

T
Tagetes spp., *9*, *25*
  for attracting birds, 30
  patula
    for containers, 28
    for cutting, 29
    for edging, 27
    low growing, 23
  patula 'Janie', dwarf, 22
  rounded form, 25
  yellow-hued, summer-to-fall flowers, 19
Tallhedge alder buckthorn. *See
  Rhamnus frangula* 'Columnaris'
Tallow tree, Chinese. *See Sapium
  sebiferum*
Tall plants
  flowers, 24
  ground covers, 69–70
  shrubs, 50
  trees
    broad, 37
    narrow upright, 39
    oval pyramidal, 38
    for shade, 42–43
Tamarix spp.
  drought tolerant, 92
  fast growing, 56
  hispida, for fall color, 51
  pest free, 60
  for seacoast, 61
Tanacetum vulgare, for herb garden, 88
Taro. *See Colocasia esculenta*
Tarragon. *See Artemisia* spp.
Taxodium distichum
  flood tolerant, 48
  large, oval pyramidal, 38
  pest free, 47
Taxus spp.
  attractive evergreen, 51
  baccata
    for city garden, 59
    'Repandens', for water garden, 82
    'Stricta', medium, narrow-upright
      tree, 39
  for basic landscaping, 55
  cuspidata, for city garden, 59
  cuspidata 'Nana'
    for informal hedge, 56
    medium-height shrub, 50
    for rock garden, 79
  × *media* 'Hicksii', small, narrow
    upright tree, 38
  for shady area, 46
  for shearing, 61
Tea olive, Gulftide. *See Osmanthus
  heterophyllus* 'Gulftide'
Tea tree. *See Leptospermum* spp.
Tecomaria capensis
  drought tolerant, 92
  showy, summer-to-fall flowers, 65, 66
Temporary plants. *See* Fast-growing
  plants
Terminology, 7
Ternstroemia gymnanthera, for shady
  area, 59
Teucrium chamaedrys
  drought tolerant, 92
  for herb garden, 88
  for rock garden, 79
  for shearing, 61
Thalia dealbata, for water garden, 81
Thalictrum rochebrunianum
  attractive foliage, 26

Thalictrum rochebrunianum
  (*continued*)
  blue-hued, summer flowers, 17
  for cool summers, 30
  open form, 26
  tall, 24
Theme gardens, 77–97
  dry climate, 89–92
  herb, 86–88
  Japanese, *76–77*, 84–85
  rock, 79–80
  roses, 93–97
  water, 81–83
Thermopsis caroliniana, tall, 24
Thorny shrubs, 56–57
Threadleaf tickseed. *See Coreopsis
  verticillata*
Thuja spp.
  attractive evergreen, 51
  easy maintenance, 58
  occidentalis, 58
    medium, oval pyramidal, 38
    for screen or buffer, 44
  occindentalis 'Fastigiata'
    medium, narrow upright, 39
  occidentalis 'Globosa'
    for Japanese garden, 84
    low growing, 49
    for shady area, 46
    for shearing, 47
Thunbergia spp.
  alata
    draping or trailing, 27
    for fast temporary cover, 67
    yellow-hued, summer flowers, 19
  grandiflora, for shady area, 68
Thyme. *See Thymus* spp.
Thymus spp.
  drought tolerant, 92
  for herb garden, 87, 88
  for nooks and crannies, 74
  praecox arcticus
    for herb garden, 88
    for Japanese garden, 85
    low-growing ground cover, 69
    traffic tolerant, 73
    for water garden, 83
  for rock garden, 80
  showy, summer flowers, 71
Tiarella cordifolia, for water
  garden, 83
Tickseed. *See Coreopsis* spp.
Tilia spp.
  americana 'Fastigiata', large, narrow
    upright, 39
  cordata
    for city garden, 46
    large, for shade, 43
Tipuana tipu, large, for shade, 43
Tithonia rotundifolia
  drought tolerant, 89
  heat tolerant, 31
  yellow-hued, summer flowers, 19
Toadflax. *See Linaria maroccana*
Tobacco, flowering. *See Nicotiana alata*
Tobira. *See Pittosporum* spp.
Torenia fournieri
  blue-hued, summer-to-fall flowers, 17
  for edging, 27
  for shady area, 32
  for wet soil, 33
Toyon. *See Heteromeles arbutifolia*
Trachelospermum jasminoides
  for draping or trailing, 73
  easy maintenance, 75
  for fragrance, 68, 74
  for herb garden, 88
  lawn alternative, 72
  for shady area, 68
  showy, summer flowers, 71
  tall ground cover, 70
Trachycarpus fortunei
  drought tolerant, 91
  large, narrow upright, 39

Trachymene coerulea
for cool summers, 30
open form, 26
Tradescantia × andersoniana, for water garden, 83
Traffic-tolerant plants, 72, 73
Trailing plants. *See* Draping or trailing plants
Tree mallow. *See Lavatera* hybrids
Tree-of-heaven. *See Ailanthus altissima*
Trillium spp.
erectum, for Japanese garden, 85
grandiflorum, low growing, 23
for shady area, 32
Trollius spp.
europaeus
for shady area, 32
yellow-hued, spring-to-summer flowers, 18, 19
medium height, 24
for wet soil, 33
Tropaeolum majus
for containers, 28
for cool summers, 30
draping or trailing, 27
for fast temporary cover, 67
for fragrance, 28
for herb garden, 86
for wet soil, 33
yellow-hued, spring-to-summer flowers, 18, 19
Tropical plants, *9*
Trumpetcreeper. *See Campsis radicans*
Trumpetvine, bloodred. *See Distictis buccinatoria*
Trumpetvine, blue. *See Thunbergia grandiflora*
Trumpetvine, golden. *See Allamanda cathartica*
Trumpetvine, lavender. *See Clytostoma callistegioides*
Tsuga canadensis
for Japanese garden, 84
large, oval pyramidal, 38
for screen or buffer, 44
for shady area, 46
for shearing, 47
for water garden, 82
Tulipa spp. and hybrids
blue-hued flowers, 16
for containers, 28
for cutting, 29
medium height, 24
red-hued flowers, 13
spring flowers, 13, 16, 18, 20
tarda
dwarf, 22
for rock garden, 80
white-hued flowers, 20
yellow-hued flowers, 18
Tulip tree. *See Liriodendron tulipifera*
Tupelo, black. *See Nyssa sylvatica*
Typha spp., for water garden, 81

U
Ulmus spp.
parvifolia
for bark interest, 39
for seacoast, 48
'Sapporo Autumn Gold'
for fall color, 40
medium height, for shade, 42
Umbrella tree, Texas. *See Melia azedarach*

V
Vaccinium spp.
for attracting birds, 58
corymbosum
for city garden, 59
for fall color, 51
showy fruit, 52

Vallisneria americana, for water garden, 81
Velvetgrass, Korean. *See Zoysia tenuifolia*
Verbena spp.
× *hybrida, 16*
blue-hued flowers, 17
draping or trailing, 27
heat tolerant, 31
low growing, 23
red-hued flowers, 14, 15
summer-to-fall flowers, 14, 15, 17, 19, 21
white-hued flowers, 21
yellow-hued flowers, 19
hybrids
for containers, 28
for edging, 27
peruviana
for draping or trailing, 73
drought tolerant, 92
dwarf, 22
for rock garden, 80
showy, spring flowers, 70
Veronica spp. or hybrids
blue-hued flowers, 17
red-hued flowers, 14
summer flowers, 14, 17, 21
vertical form, 24
for water garden, 83
white-hued flowers, 21
Vertical form, flowers with, 24
Viburnum spp.
for attracting birds, 58
for basic landscaping, 55
× *burkwoodii*
for fragrance, 57
for screen, 56
× *carlcephalum*
medium height, 50
showy, spring-to-summer flowers, 53
davidii
attractive foliage, 51
for Japanese garden, 84
low growing, 49
showy fruit, 52
dentatum, tall, 50
dilatatum, showy fruit, 52
lantana, small, oval pyramidal, 38
opulus
for city garden, 59
showy, spring flowers, 53
showy fruit, 52
for wet soil, 61
opulus 'Nanum'
for informal hedge, 56
low growing, 49
plicatum var. *tomentosum*, tall, 50
prunifolium
drought tolerant, 92
sieboldii, pest free, 60
tinus
for shearing, 61
showy, fall-to-spring flowers, 53, 54
showy fruit, 52
for training as tree, 60
trilobum
showy fruit, 52
for wet soil, 56
Vinca spp.
major, tall, 70
minor
for draping or trailing, 73
easy maintenance, 75
lawn alternative, 72
medium height, 69
for shady area, 75
traffic tolerant, 73
slope stabilizer, 72
Viola spp.
odorata
for fragrance, 74

Viola (continued)
for herb garden, 87, 88
for shady area, 75
for rock garden, 80
tricolor, trailing, 27
× *wittrockiana, 10–11, 18*
blue-hued flowers, 16, 17
for cool summers, 30
dwarf, 22
red-hued flowers, 13, 14, 15
for shady area, 32
for wet soil, 33
white-hued flowers, 20, 21, 22
winter-to-summer flowers, 13, 14, 15, 16, 17, 18, 19, 21, 22
yellow-hued flowers, 18, 19
Violet, sweet. *See Viola odorata*
Violet flowers, 15–17
Virginia creeper. *See Parthenocissus quinquefolia*
Vitex agnus-castus, small, for shade, 42
Vitis spp.
for arbor or patio cover, 67
for attracting birds, 68
attractive foliage, 66
drought tolerant, 92
for fall color, 66

W
Wakerobin, white. *See Trillium grandiflorum*
Wallflower. *See Cheiranthus cheiri*
Walls, plants for
flowers, 27
ground covers, 73
trees, 44
Wandflower. *See Galax urceolata*
Warminster broom. *See Cytisus × praecox*
Washingtonia spp., drought tolerant, 91
Washington thorn. *See Crataegus phaenopyrum*
Water chestnut, Chinese. *See Eleocharis dulcis*
Waterclover. *See Marsilea* spp.
Waterdragon. *See Saururus cernuus*
Water garden, *8*, 81–83
Waterhawthorn. *See Aponogeton distachyus*
Water hyacinth. *See Eichhornia crassipes*
Waterlily. *See Nymphaea* spp.
Water milfoil. *See Myriophyllum* spp.
Water pennywort. *See Hydrocotyle vulgaris*
Waterpoppy. *See Hydrocleys nymphoides*
Waterprimrose, creeping. *See Ludwigia* spp.
Waterweed. *See Elodea canadensis*
Wax begonia. *See Begonia × semperflorens-cultorum*
Wayfaring tree. *See Viburnum lantana*
Weigela florida
fast growing, 56
showy, spring flowers, 53
Wet soil, plants for
flowers, 33
ground covers, 75
shrubs, 61
trees, 48
White flowers, 19–22
roses, 94
Wild-olive. *See Halesia carolina*
Willow. *See Salix* spp.
Willow, Australian. *See Geijera parviflora*
Windflower, Greek. *See Anemone blanda*
Window boxes, flowers for, 27
Wintercreeper. *See Euonymus fortunei*
Winter-flowering plants
flowers
blue-hued, 17
red-hued, 15

Winter-flowering plants *(continued)*
white-hued, 22
yellow-hued, 19
ground covers, 71
shrubs, 54
trees, 42
vines, 66
Wintergreen, creeping. *See Gaultheria procumbens*
Winterhawthorn. *See Aponogeton distachyus*
Winter hazel, fragrant. *See Corylopsis glabrescens*
Winter silhouette
shrubs for, 51–52
trees for, 40
Wishbone-flower. *See Torenia fournieri*
Wisteria spp., 68
for arbor or patio cover, 67
drought tolerant, 92
floribunda, for Japanese garden, 85
for fragrance, 68
showy, spring flowers, 65
Witch hazel. *See Hamamelis* spp.

X
Xylosma congestum
attractive foliage, 51
drought tolerant, 92
easy maintenance, 58
pest free, 60
for shearing, 61
for training as tree, 60

Y
Yarrow. *See Achillea* spp.
Yellowflag. *See Iris pseudacorus*
Yellow flowers, 17–19
Yew. *See Podocarpus macrophyllus; Taxus* spp.
Yucca spp.
filamentosa
drought tolerant, 92
for water garden, 82
glauca, drought tolerant, 92

Z
Zantedeschia aethiopica
for wet soil, 33
white-hued, spring-to-summer flowers, 20, 21
Zelkova serrata
broad, 37
for city garden, 46
for fall color, 40
medium to large, 37, 42
pest free, 47
for shade, 42
for winter silhouette, 40
Zinnia, creeping. *See Sanvitalia procumbens*
Zinnia elegans, 9, 21
for attracting birds, 30
for containers, 28
for cutting, 29
heat tolerant, 31
red-hued flowers, 14, 15
rounded form, 25
summer-to-fall flowers, 14, 15, 19, 21
'Thumbelina', for edging, 27
white-hued flowers, 21
yellow-hued flowers, 19
Ziziphus jujuba, drought tolerant, 90
Zoysia tenuifolia
for Japanese garden, 85
lawn alternative, 72
low growing, 69